Learning Scenarios for Social and Cultural Change

ERZIEHUNGSKONZEPTIONEN UND PRAXIS

Herausgegeben von Gerd-Bodo von Carlsburg

BAND 82

PETER LANG
EDITION

Lara Rodríguez Sieweke (ed.)

Learning Scenarios for Social and Cultural Change

Bildung through Academic Teaching

Bibliographic Information published by the Deutsche Nationalbibliothek
The Deutsche Nationalbibliothek lists this publication in the Deutsche
Nationalbibliografie; detailed bibliographic data is available in the internet
at http://dnb.d-nb.de.
Library of Congress Cataloging-in-Publication Data
A CIP catalog record for this book has been applied for at the
Library of Congress
Cover image:
Detail of a mixed-media painting (untitled, 2015)
by Lara Rodríguez Sieweke.

This publication was supported by Linnaeus University, Sweden,
and the underlying conference "Education is Relation not Output?
Scenes of Knowledge and Knowledge Acquisition",
held in Linnaeus University on May 2016, was supported
by the Swedish Foundation for Humanities and Social Sciences.

ISSN 0723-7464
ISBN 978-3-631-72928-1 (Print)
E-ISBN 978-3-631-72929-8 (E-PDF)
E-ISBN 978-3-631-72930-4 (EPUB)
E-ISBN 978-3-631-72931-1 (MOBI)
DOI 10.3726/b11497

Contents

6   Contents

Anja Kraus and Lara Rodríguez Sieweke

Introduction: Learning Scenarios for Social and Cultural Change: *Bildung* through Academic Teaching

Research on the university within the humanities and cultural and educational sciences is relatively rare and has been mostly neglected in the general discourses on it (e.g., see Heinrich 1987, Hug 1996, Bourdieu 2002, and Derrida 2004). Among other disciplines, the arts have had representatives such as Beuys, Böll, Staeck and Eliasson, who have been involved in both the conceptualization and creation of universities. The latter takes up the importance of the experiment. In Eliasson's words, "by engaging in experimentation we can challenge the norms we live by.[1]" Eliasson, supported by the Berlin University of the Arts, founded the *Institut für Raumexperimente e.V.* (Institute for Spatial Experiments), a project which collaborated with numerous international universities and institutions, and aimed at investigating various "learning situations of uncertain certainty." Furthermore, the institute aimed to integrate a "multiplicity of voices" and to establish "a school of questions rather than of answers."

We depart from the fundamental idea of the university as being deeply connected to the ideal of *Bildung*, and to cultural (democratic) values. However, there are some unmistakable signs that contemporary humanists have not quite succeeded in explaining why *Bildung* and culture are decisive for the development of society. If the university should serve as an open space to develop democracy and to meet the huge social, cultural and ecological challenges of today, then one has to constantly and critically review the approaches to education from the different disciplines. Thus, the approaches exhibited in this anthology come from a wide range of knowledge forms constituting diverse knowledge formats.

The outstanding fields of challenge for academic education, or the selected "learning scenarios" that will be featured here are *globalization, interculturality, and interdependence; humanism and democracy; diversity and gender; visual culture and media;* and in relation to this, *artistic research.* These areas already imply certain perspectives on *Bildung* and cultural values. Our joint concern is to take

---

1   See the website of the *Institut für Raumexperimente* at http://raumexperimente.net/en/. Accessed on April 18, 2017.

into account the teaching initiatives that are directed to meeting the challenges arising in these fields. Therefore, we have encouraged proposals from the various fields of research – such as media education, art and aesthetic education, philosophy, ethnology, physical education, performance art and gender – that contribute to transforming the practical significance of their approaches into knowledge for university education. These can also be initiatives in the field of school education. By investigating different cultural archives and approaches to learning, multiple simultaneous and concurring claims of reality, experience, and meaning can be mapped in order to model university education on *Bildung*.

Many of the anthology's participants have shared their perspectives in the international conference "Education is Relation Not Output? Scenes of Knowledge and Knowledge Acquisition" held in May 2016 at Linnaeus University, Växjö, Sweden, and organized by Anja Kraus. Their proposals, while connected to their own areas of expertise, are in line with Eliasson: They pose questions rather than answers; they depart from situations of uncertainty; and they experiment.

The authors of this introduction, themselves coming from different fields, respectively pedagogy and philology, were struck, during the editing of this book, by how the representatives of the different disciplines seemed to share similar concerns, echoing the same references and often citing one another in their contributions. There is community in this diversity, and in fact, many of the authors are members of *Tacit Dimensions of Teaching and Learning*[2], a scientific network that endeavors to grasp the various and interrelated aspects of knowledge – including those that challenge articulation – and study their impact on pedagogy.

Artistic approaches set this anthology in motion, first with an intriguing voice from the contemporary art scene: Ellen Kobe recounts how her two roles as artist and curator influence each other in a symbiotic fashion, both hindering and enriching her artistic vocation. She presents some performances in which she "performs" her role as a curator, but describing artworks that are markedly absent. Through this recreation, she transforms what is familiar and monotonous, in this way calling attention to, among other things, the standardized operational processes of museums and how the verbal and non-verbal are used to communicate art.

Her art is further explored and interpreted by Lara Rodríguez Sieweke, who focuses on the educational potentials that Kobe's strategic use of "displacement" may bring about, particularly in her video artwork *FLORA PFLÜCKT WILDE BLUMEN* (2012), which engages in dialogue with Botticelli's world-renowned painting *Primavera*. The author especially observes how the aspects of space, time and gender are affected by this displacement of an artwork into a new context, and calls attention to how this raises multiple open-ended questions and interpretations, and encourages reflexive thought.

How to communicate the incommunicable? Working with *humanism and democracy* as a learning scenario, Peter Baumgartner and Isabell Grundschober are concerned with how informal learning or tacit knowledge can be communicated and validated. The authors endeavor to show how informal learning – the learning that happens in our daily life-experiences – is often overlooked and is justifiably in need of its own form of validation. Thus, the authors propose some ideas concerning the validation of tacit knowledge and introduce a model of validation used by the University of Chester.

The learning scenario of *globalization, interculturality and interdependence* has a strong presence in this anthology. The multidisciplinary team of authors (Katarina Elam, Marie-Louise Hansson Stenhammar, Tarja Karlsson Häikiö, Feiwel Kupferberg, Rasoul Nejadmehr, and Margareta Wallin Wictorin) behind "Educating Responsible Citizens. Intercultural Competence and Education" who start this section, express the necessity for a shift in perspectives and for surmounting Eurocentrism. What tools can be used to develop intercultural competence and to overcome the obstacles that stand in its way? The authors propose aesthetic education as being vital in promoting intercultural competence, highlighting the capacity of literature and particularly art, to aid in facilitating intercultural encounters and in developing empathy, which they describe as the core of intercultural competence.

Maria Peters and Christina Inthoff are also concerned with art education, their research project advocating the production of visual knowledge in order to encourage diverse educational perspectives, taking into account the increasingly complex cultural life of children. The portfolio they develop and exhibit in their article, KEPP (*Künstlerisch-experimentelles Prozessportfolio* or artistic-experimental process portfolio), focuses on process instead of result and incorporates various research fields, thus involving the students in an artistic research process that confronts them with a diversity of multidisciplinary strategies and approaches.

In Stela Maris Ferrarese Capettini's research, interculturality and diversity are the key issues dealt with as the author zeros in on the social space of the playground, in this case, the playgrounds of schools in Neuquén, Argentina. The questions she poses are: What type of games do 5- and 9-year old children play during their class breaks? Do the boys and girls play the same or different games? Do the children of Mapuche and Romany origins practice their traditional games, or do they play games that belong to the globalizing culture and are heavily influenced by the mass media?

Katja Böhme remarks on the growing interest on the topic of reflection in relation to pedagogical situations. With regard to this, she proposes art teacher education as a potentially fruitful research field, and focuses on experimental situations, which are often linked to insecurity and unpredictability. How could students reflect on these types of situations? Her article on the relevance of perception in the contexts of pedagogical reflection begins with a study involving photographs taken by a school pupil and a university student. The photographs, taken from these two perspectives, are then studied in terms of their potential for reflective processes.

Under the learning scenarios of *diversity and gender*, Anne-Marie Grundmeier and Maud Hietzge's contribution centers on the ever-fascinating figure of the mermaid; specifically, they study the practice of *mermaiding*, or wearing a costume mermaid's tail while swimming, and explore its potential for promoting child-centered learning and creativity, particularly within aesthetic education. Some of the questions that are posed are: How can the mermaid myths transform the child's daily reality? Can they be significant in terms of the self-representation of young girls? Can the mermaid figure help challenge societal norms on gender and diversity?

Also in this section, Hanne Seitz's article introduces the *Young Tenants* (*Junge Pächter*) project, which sought to give Berlin youngsters the opportunity to de-velop their creativity and participate in cultural life by providing the tenants with vacant spaces that they themselves were responsible for. The type of learning that takes place in this kind of self-organized and informal learning situation is investigated. The practice was regarded as *performative research* (Seitz), and the youngsters, who were considered as co-researchers, relied on both tacit and explicit knowledge to solve problems.

The final learning scenario delineated is *visual culture and media*. The questions surrounding this scenario are also substantial in this anthology. Michael Waltinger begins this section by calling attention to the fundamental role that media and cultural education have in promoting social cohesion in a world that is increas-ingly mediatized and globalized, and in developing cultural sensitivity and cultural relativism, which allow for an understanding of other cultures without asserting own standards. Among other issues, the author discusses the uneven flows of media images that often reflect the inequalities of the world; the reinforcement of stereotypes in dominant media; and the representations of Self and Other.

Aloisa Moser's main topic is also media education; however, her focus is on handling the quantity and quality of media with care, especially in its relation to child development. From a philosophical standpoint, Moser explores the development of the child in terms of language, learning to understand the world, and performing its first simple movements. Can less media be more? For the author, media – e.g. explications, tutorials, high chairs for toddlers – not only help but hamper development by discouraging the child from learning through her or his body and mind.

Tacit knowledge, in its relation to innovation and creativity, plays a significant role in Barbara Vollmer, Dietrich Dörner and Sibylle Rahm's article. Taking into account a world that is constantly changing in a myriad of ways, entailing, among other things, disorientation, the authors appeal for creativity as a problem-solving strategy for situations of uncertainty, especially centering on learning situations in the classroom. They attempt to examine group creativity: Their case study observes how 21 participants deal with simulations that invite creativity, and they are recorded as they create ideas together.

Finally, rounding off this section and the anthology, Anja Kraus' "Sensitive Threshold" addresses the necessity of body-based learning in education, considering art-based didactics to be paradigmatic in evoking corporeal reflexivity in youngsters. The author develops and displays a project that encourages self-responsibility, and the development of aesthetical and performative reflexivity in teens. The project space, called "Sensitive Threshold", invites pupils from a problematic area of Berlin to develop, together with the teacher, their own sound installation, reflecting on and choosing sounds that are present and significant in different aspects of their daily lives.

The main intention of this book is thus to model *Bildung* from the perspective of academic teaching and education. The general result of this undertaking is that *Bildung* is not mere scholarship, but is moreover a broad spectrum of approaches to knowledge. Diverse knowledge forms are what made science a relativized discipline (cp. Kuhn and Polanyi in Moleski 2008).[3] Knowledge forms constitute paradigms, that is, concepts or thought patterns which can include theories, research methods, postulates, and standards for what constitutes legitimate contributions to a societal field. The contributions in this anthology have brought to light that *Bildung* is reflected by practice, and this is connected to ethical considerations which, then, are among the most important factors in the conceptualization of *Bildung*.

Växjö, the 26th of May, 2017.

---

3   Moleski, Martin X. *Polanyi vs. Kuhn: Worldviews Apart.* The Polanyi Society. Missouri Western State University. Retrieved March 20, 2008.

Artistic Research – In Practice

·

Ellen Kobe

Mensch im Museum:
Description and Deliberation in Four Performances[1]

Abstract: The four performances described in my text belong to my MENSCH IM MU-
SEUM (PEOPLE IN MUSEUMS) series and reflect, among other things, how my role as
an artist inspires my role as an art curator and vice versa. I show how playing the part of
a curator in a performative space may aid in reflecting on the automatized processes of
museums and on the capacity of language to communicate art, even when the exhibition
walls are bare. I convey how it moreover brings together the established and planned space
with the space that welcomes improvisation and surprise. In relation to this, I describe
how, through performance, I am able to move my compendium of histories, places and
images into any location of my choosing.

As an artist who has worked also in art mediation, the museum with all its rituals
and rules interests me as an operating system. I intervene in its existing structures
and set spaces, draw on materials and artefacts, and suggest shifts in meaning,
however slight, in order to trigger shifts in perspective. The strategy of decontex-
tualisation – the contextual shift – likewise enables me to productively harness
the typical body language, posturing and jargon of museum practices as well as
the operational procedures of the institution itself.

When I enter a performative space, I negotiate at another level of self: I am
no longer only a private individual. I become the embodiment of my own invention: a character who gets me through a situation and enables me to carry it off.
Language's intrinsic potential for assertion engenders a giddy temptation to take
reality at face value ad absurdum, to dissolve the subject's grip on reality, and to
experience reality as a permeable web. In my performances, I leave certainties
behind. I can go to the brink of the crater, which is to say, to where the texture of
the fabric of fact is in flux. Speech, the performative act of speaking, is seized here
as an opportunity to take distance on reality, as an enquiry into the constitution of
the image. By making the factual absence of the image a prerequisite of my speaking of it, I give myself up to the crisis of its decomposition, to disillusionment,

---

1 Translated from the German by Jill Denton.

to liberation from the illusion of the image. It is an enquiry into and a step back from the space of fact: a chance to review the layers of familiarity in language.

How is a performance related to my work as an art mediator, and what distinguishes the one from the other? A hinge between the two is articulated by my serial work MENSCH IM MUSEUM. Contextual shifts accomplished in four performances variously challenge the perceived unity of word, image and space. By putting myself in "the mistaken context" I methodically disrupt this perceived unity and provoke "images in the mind's eye". I use the term "mistaken context" in my work to mean a gap in reality; a disruption; a void; the "mistake" born of despondency or failure; and the ruptures from which the unexpected and the uncanny ensue. It is the prerequisite of the productive moment. "This sort of replacement, suspension, and concentration happens universally, except for in dealings with art."[2]

The impulse for this serial work was the exhausting repetitiveness of the standardised guided tours of blockbuster exhibitions and the heavily frequented "tourist magnet" museums. Now, I wish to use alienation from my words spouting forth, thoughts that wander and subsequent slips of the tongue (so-called "mistakes") as tools of creative transformation. There is a possibility when working in several museums in parallel, for instance, that I might suddenly speak the wrong text for an image, or forget the name of an artist or an artwork, and then spontaneously juggle stock phrases from various contexts. This experience of things falling apart, of feeling disoriented, of having words on tap, and this oscillation between several settings, is now condensed in the performances.[3]

Given my dual role of artist and art mediator, and the temporal-economic constraints therein implicit, such transformation is of necessity minimalist. In short, I cannot pursue artistic activity while I am in the role of art mediator and must therefore make the latter profession a matter of my art. In an affirmative guise, I recreate the guided tour procedure, thereby altering certain details of the conditions configured in the museum by word, image and venue for a performance in an alternative art context.

---

2   Pazzini, 2000, 8.
3   "So if you want to do 'deconstruction' – you know, that thing Derrida did – then you must present something new, in your own language, in your own singular situation, with your own signature. You must invent the impossible and break with application in the technical, neutral sense of the term." Pazzini, 2000, 9.

Figure 1: MOMA GOES ON! Performance, Neue Nationalgalerie Berlin, 2004. Photo: Gerd Engelsmann.

MOMA GOES ON!

Performance I
The venue, the viewers and the guided tour procedure are authentic; only the paintings are missing.

Before the bare walls of the Neue Nationalgalerie Berlin, shortly after the end of an exhibition of work from the MOMA New York collection, I invite people to join me on a final guided tour. Having given almost three hundred guided tours during the exhibition's seven-month run, my words on each artwork are now automatic. Even for works that are no longer present, I find words. What images do they conjure for my public? A museum collection suggests permanence yet this performance in the Neue Nationalgalerie reveals the fleeting character of contemplation of art. It also challenges the idea that to interpret the modernist canon is solely an institutional prerogative. Who speaks, and what remains?

The "museum temple" was exhibited in the performance from an angle otherwise familiar alone to its employees: as an empty box with threadbare runners, redundant screws in bare walls and a frame of dust around each absent painting. The challenge now facing me was to make a work of art through my description of the missing artworks. Through the dint of repetition, gestures synchronised with text had become choreography. The switch from quantity to qualitative innovation inspired the profound satisfaction of eliciting something of my own from the overwound flywheel. In response to the art mediator's experience of exhaustion, vacuity and alienation, I the artist continued her task, but under altered circumstances. The artistic perspective enabled me to symbolically reconfigure the established terms and conditions by which art is received.

When an exhibition proves popular, the storm of visitors is strictly regimented: there are graded entrances, VIP tickets, or one can pay a little extra to assure fast-track entry. The museum by its very nature is a tool of differentiation, a bourgeois institution. It daily negotiates the parameters of sociocultural belonging. My first action was to invite everyone in on an equal footing, as VIPs. A journalist with the *Berliner Zeitung* took an interest in the performance and indeed reported on it the next day, with a front-page headline and article in the photo slot usually reserved for the latest major political event. So I kept the exhibition hype going a little while longer, with MOMA GOES ON!

In my working clothes and with the "Visitor Services" badge pinned to my black jacket, I greeted the group with the same words as always; except now, works of art were already packed and stacked on palettes in the foyer. At the latest, when the group entered the exhibition space, it became clear that I would be speaking in front of bare walls. Yet for points I had already made so many hundreds of times I performed the same gestures as always: a broad sweep of the arm, for example, to illustrate a visual composition. I myself was astounded by the precision with which I progressed through the museum, like a sleepwalker almost; and I arrived at the exit after exactly one hour. The guided tour had become a dance, choreographed to the beat of my words. Nowhere was this more striking than in face of the absence of Henri Matisse's "The Dance" (1910). Here, movement itself swelled with significance, becoming a new moving image in place of the imagined painting, which momentarily took a back seat to it.

I shift the focus from the image to language[4] and movement by quite literally and physically standing in for it. This, after all, is how I save my artist's skin. In financial terms, I have realised that this net value increased only after a circa ten-year latency, since I am now only charging thirty times my guided tour fee for a single performance. The difference in the degree of autonomy inherent to art respectively to art mediation hence appears to be primarily economic. For years, I have secured my existence as an artist by working as an art mediator, but in doing so, I have simultaneously hindered it. Art mediators-cum-artists are in my experience a contradiction in terms. I agree wholeheartedly with Karl-Josef Pazzini when he defines the relationship of art to its mediation: "Art education takes place in relation to art." Or when he argues that opportunity lies in "[e]stablishing art

---

4   "The sphere of meaning is situated not outside but inside language. Meaning is a sort of outcome or effect of semiotics and coincides with language. This is nowhere truer than in the visual arts" (Pazzini, 2000, 10).

education as an art in its own right."[5] That is a rightful and noble endeavour, one that Pazzini describes as "a difficult enterprise."[6]

My decision on whether I will give a guided tour of a museum or a performance rests on the size of the fee as well as on the social esteem that goes with it. To weigh the task of art education against that of making art has become obsolete. In light of the *educational turn*, which is to say, the trend among curators and artists to take up art education, my work is avant-garde: art and art education are therein mutually determined and fused. Pazzini formulated it thus: "An alternative to the Prussian-Protestant didactic has yet to be developed. It could begin in and with art. In any case, talk would then once again be of paintings. Simultaneously, contemporary art would come into play, since it meanwhile has little to do with representation."[7] It is a question, therefore, of a paradigm shift – from art as object to art as creative process.

Figure 2: GOYA TO GO! Performance, Galerie Nord, Kunstverein Tiergarten, Berlin, 2005. Photo: Coco Kühn.

GOYA TO GO!

Video screenshot: http://www.ellenkobe.de/seitentitel/

Performance II:
The viewers and the guided tour procedure are authentic, the paintings are missing, and one venue is asserted in another.

---

5   Pazzini, 2000, 1.
6   Ibid.
7   Ibid., 7.

The exhibition "Goya – Prophet of Modernism" is moved from the Alte Nationalgalerie Berlin to the Kunstverein Tiergarten contemporary art gallery. On a guided tour of bare walls, my words conjure the works of Goya. Connected by a headset system also used in the museum, I guide my group through the imaginary exhibition. Laying out the original labels for each painting on a ground plan of the museum sketched in chalk on the gallery floor suffices to evoke the fictitious show. The procedure is staged in its entirety, from standing in line to receiving a Goya sticker at the entrance, from buying a standard or VIP ticket at the counter to donning a headset. From the museum staff to the teeming public: everything is "real". Once again, only the paintings are missing. "Live Speakers" hand out flyers, the security guards warn against touching the artworks, and gratuities are handed over at the end of the guided tour. If required, a questionnaire regarding the tour's quality may be completed, and postcards in sealed envelopes are available for purchase in the museum shop.

The topic of absent paintings was pursued here too, but in this performance I focused more emphatically on the operational system, which is to say, the whole caboodle one goes through before actually getting to see whatever it is one has set out to see: from standing in line to buying a ticket to hooking up one's headset. "So, are you going to join me at the Kunstverein gallery?" I had asked the security guards and cashiers among my colleagues at the Alte Nationalgalerie. "We'll be giving our guided tour there too, but without any paintings." I had also pulled in the colleagues from Antenna Audio, who rent the museum an audio system so that we guides are audible only to the persons in our tour group, without drowning out everything else. It was an absurd situation: In the small rooms of the Kunstverein, I could easily have been heard without acoustic backup, yet everyone listened to me through headphones. In preparation for the tour, I had chalked a ground plan of the Alte Nationalgalerie on the floor, a freehand approximation of the shape of certain rooms and their proportions. I wanted to reduce the museum ground plan to a chalk outline on the street, akin to a "hopscotch" sketch by playing children, and in this way translate my group's progression, in my fictitious museum, from one room to another, from one square to the next. Like a runner, I now laid out, in the Kunstverein Tiergarten entrance, the five-metre-long banner flown from the roof of the Alte Nationalgalerie. Hence, the people entering the gallery walked across the words "Goya – Prophet of Modernism". On the pavement outside, although no crowds were to be expected, I placed signs announcing "A 4-hour wait from here on." To monitor the quality of the guided tour, two assistants from *Visitor Services* – "Live Speakers", as their orange T-shirts announced – handed out the Alte Nationalgalerie's original questionnaire, in which visitors could record their responses. The questionnaires ask whether the person guiding the tour has spoken loudly and clearly, shown a solid knowledge of the subject matter, and – in the eyes of the respondent – been "properly" dressed; and yet, the art mediator in question is not informed in advance of this enquiry. To subject guides to monitoring without their knowledge or consent is in my opinion discriminatory. My response was to integrate the questionnaire in my performance, in the best tradition of *appropriation art*.

Figure 3: JUBILÄUM! Performance on the 250th anniversary of the founding of the Leipzig Academy of Fine Arts (HGB, Hochschule für Grafik und Buchkunst) in the HGB gallery, 2014.

JUBILÄUM! (JUBILEE!)

Video screenshot: http://www.ellenkobe.de/jubilaeum/

Performance III:
The venue, the viewers, and the procedure of the opening address are authentic, the paintings are missing, the walls are bare and the catalogue is blank.

On the 250th anniversary of the founding of the Leipzig Academy of Fine Arts (HGB, Hochschule für Grafik und Buchkunst), I make an opening address for an "exposition imaginaire" hosted by the HGB gallery under the title JUBILÄUM! (JUBILEE!). I introduce my audience to the curatorial concept, thereby tracing connections between some of the works and the Academy's history. I thank those who have loaned works for their faith in the project, and the sponsors and patrons for their generous support. I further thank the university lecturers and the gallery staff for their excellent cooperation. Like those who speak before me, I too emphasise the significance of this anniversary and draw attention to the great humanist tradition of visual art and teaching, research and mediation. In conclusion, I hand a bouquet of flowers and an exhibition catalogue to a number of esteemed persons: the Governor of the Free State of Saxony, the Mayor of the City of Leipzig, the Chairman of the Board of the Sparkasse savings bank and the Vice Chancellor of the HGB.

Figure 4: The audience of JUBILÄUM!

Video screenshot: http://www.ellenkobe.de/jubilaeum/

I slipped into place among the prominent personages, playing my part of a curator opening an exhibition. The ceremony was in the HGB gallery, where I took a seat in the front row, elegantly dressed in black. All of a sudden, I found my hand was being repeatedly grasped and shaken. I realised that in taking a front-row seat I had joined the ranks of the local celebrities, at least in the eyes of the unsuspecting guests, who evidently took me for a politician or a cultural ambassador of some sort. This notion proved persistent: one can tell from the video recording that the penny took a while to drop. Sheer boredom predominated at first. After all, there is nothing so insufferable at a ceremony as having to sit through the fifth dismal speech in a row. When it came to my turn – it was announced I would make an opening address for the *JUBILÄUM!* exhibition – it was not immediately clear that I was performing. In the video, one can see the audience's gradual transition from dulled patience to amused attentiveness. When I was done the students howled with delight: I had addressed a topical, highly political issue. There had been no funding available and hence no possibility of staging an exhibition in order to mark this momentous anniversary. Yet here was I, giving thanks for the generous funding and interregional cooperation. I mentioned the fantastic international loans, thereby broadening horizons so as to at least invoke this remote possibility. In reality, their actual absence served only the better to highlight what we were missing. The images I described before those bare walls were all connected in some way with the institution's history. The intention was to have the public follow my address either by imagining the paintings described or being reminded by them of others. The description was sufficiently precise to gain a momentum all of its own, as I did too, in fact, for I found myself in this performance speaking of works I had never seen in real life. Initially, anonymously, I adapted my tone of voice and body language to the solemn occasion. Unsolicited, I made accomplices of the dignitaries. The prank reached its end only when I ceremoniously handed each of them a bouquet of flowers and an exhibition catalogue: a cloth-bound book with blank pages.

Figure 5: HERZLICH WILLKOMMEN! Performance at the opening of the "Berliner Liste" art fair at the Postbahnhof am Ostbahnhof, Berlin, 2014.

HERZLICH WILLKOMMEN! (WELCOME!)
Video screenshot: http://www.ellenkobe.de/herzlich-willkommen/

Performance IV:
The viewers and the guided tour procedure are authentic, one venue is asserted in another and descriptions of certain paintings are now projected on others.

At the opening of the "Berliner Liste" art fair, I propose a guided tour. However, I then effect a shift in context by reading aloud the text I wrote for my guided tour of the Sanssouci Palace in Potsdam: The splendour and wealth of images to be found in the Prussian summer palace are elaborated in the booths and corridors of the art fair architecture in the Postbahnhof. Welcome!

The palace guided tour procedure is staged in its entirety, from the queuing at the entrance to the purchase of a standard or VIP ticket at the counter, while the contemporary works of art are now overlaid with words and gestures that refer to the visually splendid Prussian monument. Thus, the spoken word and the objects it describes part company. By projecting a description of an absent image on the image before me, I negate the latter's existence. I also bring together two spaces as different as can be: the nuanced reference system of Sanssouci, where nothing is left to chance and context is everything, where architecture, interior décor, furnishings and works of art have fused over the centuries in an ever more refined

Gesamtkunstwerk originally inspired by the French court of the Sun King; and the *White Cubes* to which I apply this system of reference: booths bursting with images at the commercial art fair. The idea is to superimpose different spaces and use the original text of the palace guided tour as a basis for improvisation. For example, at the start of the video recording, a technician comes briefly into view. He apologises for the faulty microphone, telling me: "We'll just have to improvise now!" I deliberately kept this behind-the-scenes moment in the soundtrack, for it sums up the whole situation. There was much that could not be foreseen, however, such as the dog sprawled out in a booth, looking as if it were dead. I almost tripped over it. Instantly, I altered my text. Now I spoke of the greyhounds of Friedrich the Great, and their grave on the Palace's uppermost terrace in which he hoped to be buried alongside them. A few such happy accidents occurred and I accepted each of them as a gift to the situation. I had also done some planning for the tour of course, since I had asked some art dealers whether I might integrate their booth in my performance. But how perplexed they were, in the end, to see me arrive with a group and speak about other images than the ones they had on display – my strategy being to extricate various components from an exhibition situation then bring them together elsewhere, in a new constellation. This was accomplished in different ways in each of the four performances.

Art mediation becomes for me a matter of art, not the reverse. I take on the role of art mediator. As a member of a museum's service staff, my activity is narrow in scope and specific. As an artist, however, I am free: In performance, I step in and out of spaces and situations at will. Moreover, I carry within me an endless reservoir of images, venues and histories that I am able to transpose to any conceivable location. This is my treasure trove, the bonus in kind garnered in palaces, gardens and museums during my past work as an art mediator. When I edit video material after a performance, I am freer than ever, for I can then juggle multiple dimensions of time and space. For instance, I can show an image of a photographer taking photos of me during a performance as well as the outcome of their shoot. And then, it is as if an endless medial loop starts turning. It is important to me to expose the various ways perceptions are filtered. With a revolving door, one leaves a space by slipping quickly into a closed segment and is then compelled, since the door continues to turn, to see that same space from a new angle; and one therefore re-enters it as someone else. This, in art terms, is a potent opportunity. Viewers' past experience of seeing an image can blind them to its content. A connection to its reality must therefore be forged again with every new look.

The essence of the performances is to broaden the scope of language: to let a text write itself by tuning in to the inventiveness and free associations of the unconscious mind that can always be sensed in the wings, waiting for thought to give voice to it.

Bibliography

Pazzini, Karl-Josef: *Kunst existiert nicht, es sei denn als angewandte*; Hamburg 2000 [http://kunst.erzwiss.uni-hamburg.de/pdfs/kunst_existiert_nicht.pdf, last accessed 22.11.16]

List of Figures

Lara Rodríguez Sieweke

Displacement and Educational Potentials in Ellen Kobe's *FLORA PFLÜCKT WILDE BLUMEN*

Abstract: Artist Ellen Kobe's video artwork *FLORA PFLÜCKT WILDE BLUMEN* (2012) refers directly to Botticelli's *Primavera*, which in turn dialogues with Ovid's *Fasti*. While this will be looked at in this article, the focus will be on Kobe's use of *displacement*, an "aesthetic strategy of a move of significance"[1] in which an artwork is "displaced" into a new context. In Kobe's *FLORA*, displacement is especially significant in the aspects of time, space and gender. Due to these displacements, different possibilities emerge for the mythological spring goddess Flora and her surroundings, thus encouraging the viewer to engage in a reflexive and exploratory dialogue.

Keywords: Ellen Kobe's *FLORA PFLÜCKT WILDE BLUMEN*, Botticelli's *Primavera*, Ovid's *Fasti*, displacement, time, space, gender.

> *In nova fert animus mutates dicere formas / corpora*
> (Of bodies chang'd to various forms, I sing)
> --- Ovid, "Metamorphosis". Translation by John Dryden, Sir Samuel Garth, et al.

1. Introduction

The Artist and the Strategy of Displacement

Ellen Kobe (born 1968) is a Berlin-based artist whose artworks often involve performance and video in public spaces. According to her website, these works tend to explore history reception, contemporary art exhibitions that are held in historic sites, and gender identity questions. Her artistic method is *the principle of displacement*. Kobe writes, "By the principle of displacement in a performance situation, a certain aspect of the exhibition at hand can be decontextualized and by this, the unity of perception of words, images and spaces is questioned."[2]

---

1   See Christiane Brohl's *Displacement als kunstpädagogische Strategie* (Books on Demand, 2003) 7.

2   See: Kobe, Ellen. "PEOPLE IN MUSEUMS, MENSCH IM MUSEUM." https://lnu.se/contentassets/4e919269520e4e60a93db327dce6d5d7/kobe_-abstract.pdf. Last accessed on 15 May 2017.

Displacement, according to the Oxford Dictionaries, is in simple words, "the action of moving something from its place or position." This term has been used in various contexts: In postcolonial or migrant literature, it often refers to enforced, physical displacement that may lead to other displacements which may be emotional, psychological or cultural, to give some examples. Displacement is also a theme in contemporary, especially conceptual, art. "The Art of Displacement" (*The UN News* 2013) highlights, among others, the works *Fairytale* (2007) by Ai Weiwei, who coordinated and documented the displacement of 1001 Chinese citizens from China to Germany, and *Paradox of Praxis 1 (Sometimes Doing Something Leads to Nothing)* (1997) by Francis Alÿs, who Atlas-like pushed a large block of ice for seven hours through the streets of Mexico to make a statement about the futility of both manual labor and art.

Displacement activates the involvement of the spectator, who observes something familiar in an unfamiliar-to-it setting. Martin Seel, in *Aesthetics of Appearing* (originally published in 2000), speaks of a heightened attentiveness to what is "appearing" as defining the aesthetic experience. He therefore calls attention to the role of the spectator in art mediation, stating that "the perception of artworks necessarily incorporates interpretive and epistemic attentiveness" (16). Moreover, according to Seel, "[i]n the sensuous presence of an object, we become aware of a moment in our own presence" (33). In this way, the perceiver's dialogue with an artwork allows her or him to reflect on what keeps her or his attention on the work, and thus, on "what life possibility . . . is opened up by aesthetic behavior" (36). In like manner, Umberto Eco considers an artwork to be an "open product" or "work in movement" that is open to multiple possible interventions and interpretations. Eco, in *The Open Work* (originally published in 1962), asserts that "every reception of a work of art is both an *interpretation* and a *performance* of it, because in every reception the work takes on a fresh perspective for itself" (4).

Displacement has also been formulated as a didactic strategy for art education by pedagogue Christiane Brohl, who leans on Foucault's ideas on heterotopias and Robert Smithson's theory of non-sites. Brohl (trans. and qtd. by Anja Kraus 2014; 130) writes: "Displacement at first describes a spatial relocation of art situated in the institution of the museum and then moved to public spaces. Displacement signifies a change in the understanding of art . . . [It] is the special artistic work of the reading of a location by another location, the intuitive relating of materials, information and associations." Kraus, referring to Brohl's approach, states that "Fundamentally, the principle of displacement is based on the reciprocal interpretation of an art work and its situational context" (130). Relating this principle to learning, Kraus further writes: "By being relocated, the fact or 'thing' changes its meaning and significance.... Displacement can be described as explorative learning in the situational context of locations, things and discourses" (131).

Kobe uses displacement in various ways, a few of which will briefly be presented in this article. In *GOYA TO GO* (2005, part of her "PEOPLE IN MUSEUMS" series), she uses video, as it was initially used in the art world, to record her performance as a curator in a museum, an employment she currently holds. Instead of focusing on the paintings, attention is paid to the queuing of visitors, to the distribution of headsets, to the purchase of tickets, and to the visitors' interaction with the museum staff. In Kobe's performance, she enthusiastically describes masterpieces by Goya, which in fact are not present, as she gestures towards bare walls. In *RASTSTÄTTE* ("REST STOP", video, 2007), two horses are displaced into a park space in the center of Dresden. The artist takes into account the sensitive hearing of horses as she films their reactions to their new environment – a temporary, constructed nature in the middle of the city – where sounds of traffic abound.

Kobe's 2012 video artwork *FLORA PFLÜCKT WILDE BLUMEN* (or 'FLORA PICKS WILD FLOWERS'), which is this article's focal point, is a type of *tableau vivant* or living picture, which departs directly from Italian Renaissance master Sandro Botticelli's well-known painting *Primavera* (ca. 1482), which in turn draws from fragments of Ovid's 6-book poem *Fasti* (8 A.D.), whose texts appear in Kobe's video. The title explicitly references Flora, a Roman goddess associated with spring, flowers, youth and fertility.

The rediscovery of mythological themes and figures was a characteristic of Renaissance art. Art historian Richard Stemp in *The Secret Language of the Renaissance* (2006) comments on the dual purpose this could imply: The patrons could show off their knowledge while the artists could display their narrative and descriptive skills (152). *Primavera*, also known as *Allegory of Spring*, is certainly one of Botticelli's most widely-known works and is believed to have been commissioned by the influential Medici family for the wedding of one of its members. The painting is set in what appears to be an orange orchard, which is fruitful and flowerful. According to the most popular interpretations (also chosen by Stemp[3]) the mythological figures that grace this orchard / forest / garden are (from left to right) Mercury, The Three Graces, Venus and above her Cupid, Flora (or future Chloris), Chloris and Zephyrus. According to Stemp, the painting "can be read

---

3   See: Stemp, Richard. *The Secret Language of the Renaissance* (Duncan Baird Publishers, 2006) 156–157.

as a meditation on the nature of love and marriage" (156): The goddess of love, Venus, stands in the center of the scene while Cupid, her son and the god of desire, directs an arrow towards one of the three Graces, figures that represent beauty, grace and joy, among other qualities. In the rightmost part of the painting, the blowing, glowering wind god Zephyrus attempts to sweep the nymph Chloris into his arms. And between Venus and Chloris is Flora, Chloris' future self, now a goddess of spring and the wife of Zephyrus. On the leftmost side of the painting, messenger god Mercury appears to push away wispy clouds that may threaten the springtime scene.

Figure 1: Botticelli's Primavera.

Figure 2: Stills from Kobe's FLORA PFLÜCKT WILDE BLUMEN.

Primavera is featured at the very beginning of Kobe's 3-minute video, which begins with a still image of said painting. Then, a new "Flora" is superimposed over the painting's "Flora", as the painting dissolves to a "real" park, which the video description identifies as Gleisdreieck Park in Berlin. Flora, now an effeminate young man with long blond hair, smiles, and stretches and then leisurely yet deliberately casts seeds to the ground. The crown of flowers on his head dissipates any doubts about his identity; also, his sowing of seeds mirrors Botticelli's Flora's casting of flowers. The other characters that walk in and out of the frame, seemingly oblivious to Flora, are of immigrant background (also specified in the video description). They are: a group of young boys holding skateboards, a veiled woman, and a park ranger. They make no contact with each other or with the blond protagonist. Intertitles – fragments of Ovid's text narrating Zephyrus' rape of Flora, their subsequent marriage and her transformation into a spring goddess – are interspersed between the short scenes.

2. The Context of the Artwork: *FLORA PFLÜCKT WILDE BLUMEN* and the New Gleisdreieck Park

Metamorphosis has also been a major theme in the park's history: Gleisdreieck Park was formerly a railway junction (the name 'Gleisdreieck' in fact signifies 'triangle of rails') which then became a waste ground after the Second World War until "this unhoped-for refuge [was] reclaimed by flora and fauna ..." (*Visit Berlin*). After having been a central area of intersection and traffic and then becoming a wasteland, Gleisdreieck Park, which officially opened in 2011, was once again being turned into a point of meeting, envisioned to bring together people of different age groups and interests, and to connect the districts of Kreuzberg, Schöneberg and Mitte through its location. Another unique factor in the creation of this park is that the public was highly encouraged to participate in its construction. Several focus groups[4] were asked what they expected or desired from the new park, and what type of activities they wanted to engage in. Interestingly, the groups questioned were divided in a very particular way that focused on gender and ethnicity divisions such as: male and female youngsters with a "migration background", "German women", women with a "migration background", men with a "migration background", and senior citizens. It is clear that the intention of the park's new design was to be integrative and to be at the service of the current social reality, although strangely enough, "German men" (as opposed to "German women" and all that this broad term may connote) were not included in the focus groups. This, as well as the abovementioned transformation that Gleisdreieck experienced, and the consequent dialogue between past and present and natural and manmade, were a source of inspiration for the 23 artists commissioned for the open air exhibition "Gleisdreieck Berlin 2012 – Art in Public Space" (*Kunst im öffentlichen Raum*), which was organized by two Swiss curators, Francine Eggs and Andreas Bitschin. Kobe's work *FLORA PFLÜCKT WILDE BLUMEN* was part of this exhibition.

German newspaper *Der Tagesspiegel*'s review on the exhibition comments on the interplay between the visible and the hidden, noting that it was no simple task to find all the artworks, many of which blended into the park surroundings. Several of the artists were inspired by the traces of the old railway that were left over. For instance, in *Zwei Schienen* ('Two Rails'), Christine Berndt fastened copper foil to the rails, where she engraved fragments of literary works by Rose

---

4   See a report (2005) on these focus group surveys here: http://www.stadtentwicklung.berlin.de/aktuell/wettbewerbe/ergebnisse/2006/gleisdreieck/zebralog/site/pictures/Fokusgruppen_Gleisdreieck_Endbericht.pdf.

Auslaender and Hertha Müller. Many of these quotations recalled the period in which Jews were deported to concentration camps from this location; some of the words disappeared under the proliferating vegetation. Fabiana de Barros and Anna Schmid's installation *Kultur Kiosk/Letzte Tage!* (Cultural Kiosk/Last Days!) transformed a recognizable and commonplace part of city life into something that was at once old, and totally new: The kiosk became a red-orange cube-like structure that appeared half-sunken into the ground, as an old ruin half taken over by time. It was inside this small kiosk-ruin, which could accommodate around 5 to 10 people, that Kobe's film installation was played.

Kobe's artwork in this location encouraged a special dialogue between spaces: the park space, in which visitors were invited to walk through, observe, and listen to the newly-created park and the installations; the space inside the kiosk, which was part of the new park but where the sounds and light did not affect it; and the space in Kobe's video, where the park's atmosphere and sounds were in a way, relived. The interplay between past and present is succinctly expressed in the dialogue between Botticelli's painting and Kobe's video, and as we shall see, many current discussions come to light as a result of this exchange.

3. The Effects of Displacement in Terms of Space, Time and Gender

3.1 Space and Time

The desire to connect or disconnect an artwork to or from its traditional context – usually considered to be the museum – is not new. Marcel Duchamp, with "Fountain" (1917), famously transformed a urinal into a work of art by changing its context. Robert Smithson in "Some Void Thoughts on Museums" (1967) likens museums to tombs, claiming that "[t]he museum spreads itself everywhere and becomes an untitled collection of generalizations that immobilize the eye" (42). While many of Smithson's works are exhibited in museums, he was known for creating often temporary art in outdoor settings, where the artwork is subjected to change and decay. Similarly, in Brian O'Dougherty's *Inside the White Cube: The Ideology of the Gallery Space* (1986), art is seen as existing "in a kind of eternity of display. . . . This eternity gives the gallery a limbolike status; one has to have died to already be there" (15).

What happens to *Primavera*? In the first hand, Kobe plucks Flora from Botticelli's lush *Primavera* forest and sets her onto a flowering city park. With this action, she not only transforms the context within the artwork but without: The artwork is taken from the confines of the museum, and given a whole different form, for how shall *Primavera* survive in and harmonize with its new surroundings if not by taking a new shape?

Focusing on *Primavera* for a moment, Charles Burroughs (2012) studies it in relation to the *Fasti*, drawing special attention to the painter's construction of space and movement. According to him, "Botticelli uses space to represent time", depicting "a movement from early to late spring." Burroughs also points out how in the painting, only Venus and Flora look directly at the viewer. He particularly indicates the boldness that is expressed in Flora's figure: in her direct gaze, her chainmail-like sleeves, and in the way in which she appears to step almost onto the edge of the canvas, as if just about to step out of the painting. In relation to this, different variations of the contrapposto and S-curve stances in the figures help endow the painting with dynamism; however, as noted, the positioning of Flora's feet is special with regard to its closeness to the border. As Burroughs puts it, Botticelli's Flora "challenges the separation of pictorial space and the viewers' space." And as if in response to this 'nearly stepping out', Kobe, through her video, gives her Flora an invisible helping hand, pulling her into another time and space. Returning to how the painter uses space to represent time, similarly, Maggie Kilgour in her article "The Poetics of Time: *Fasti* in the Renaissance" (2014) speaks of the artist's attempt to capture "the movement of time in a medium that is primarily spatial" (226).

Botticelli's painting, whose most popular thematic interpretations, as mentioned above, are on love and marriage, masterfully encapsulates layers of movement, transition, and even violence. Levels of time coexist in one plane, and events that are just about to happen are combined with what has already passed and what might occur in the future: Again, observe how a blindfolded Cupid is poised to shoot a loving arrow at one of the Graces, menacing their hand-clasped harmony, or how Mercury attempts to prod away the clouds that are about to encroach on spring. Also, the wind god and messenger of spring Zephyrus is just about to blow his breezes; but more importantly, he is about to seize a startled and near-naked Chloris, whose mouth begins to sprout dark blossoms at his touch. Right beside Chloris is her future self, Flora, who has metamorphosed from rape victim to married woman and goddess. She casts blossoms to the ground, perhaps expecting them to fill the forest with new life, foreshadowing transformation. Her metamorphosis from nymph-maiden to goddess-wife is captured by the painter *in media res*. This undertone of violence coexists with an idyllic springtime space, framed by flowers and orange trees, and blessed by a gentle, Madonna-like Venus at the center of the composition. However, for Maggie Kilgour, Flora's narrative is the true heart of the painting, which "focuses on the moment of metamorphosis, when Chloris becomes Flora" (226).

Temporally, there have been several layers of transfer: from a mythological time to Ovid's description of its cycles and traditions, to Botticelli's reflection of the Renaissance's revival of mythology, and finally, to Kobe's transfer to a "modern" time, indicated by the clothes the characters are wearing and the sounds of cars in the background, which also suggest another space that may at any given time intrude on the deceptively peaceful park. As with *Primavera*, the soft, spring-like atmosphere appears to be a temporary façade. The presence of Kobe's Flora, this gentle young man with flowers in his hair, transforms this park into a heterotopy[5] or a space of otherness: Kobe's Flora, the long-haired and androgynous young man, transforms the park with his unexpected presence, even actively sowing seeds and in this action endeavoring to transform nature. The strangeness that is apparent in this young man and in the characters that do not react to each other is difficult to clearly make out.

In terms of composition, Botticelli's is controlled and his characters are carefully chosen and composed. Kobe's composition also appears to be attentively put together, even though an interview[6] with Kobe reveals that several characters in her video were random visitors in the park, free to step in and out of her frame, reflecting the park's integrative aims. This is no homogeneous space of gods and Graces. When one recalls the park survey's target groups and the absence of the "German man" (who one might assume to mean the increasingly notorious white, Western male) in them, it is interesting to find the white male in Kobe's video as being the one who sticks out, appears strange and is other. Or are they all other? Hans Ingvar Roth (1999) uses the park as a metaphor for a multicultural society, where people of different backgrounds visit regularly. Does Flora join the displaced or does she become the other; the traveler; the exiled or the self-exiled? To quote Trin T. Min-ha in "Other Than Myself / My Other Self" (1994), travelling can be described as "a process whereby the self loses its fixed boundaries – a disturbing yet potentially empowering practice of difference" (23). This can be related to the blurring of boundaries that occurs with displacement.

Christiane Brohl, in her 2003 book entitled *Displacement als kunstpädagogische Strategie* ("Displacement as a Strategy for Art Pedagogy") states that "[w]ith the allegorical employment of displacement, situations that are ambiguous and open are created by context artists. ... Their unclear situations provoke a dis-orientation (orientationlessness) on the recipients" (1; my trans.). She goes on to discuss these

---

5   Of Greek origin, the word heterotopy literally signifies "other place", deriving from *héteros* (other or different) and *tópos* (place).

6   The author interviewed Kobe via telephone on December 7, 2016.

"other places" or heterotopic spaces that are created by artists and that exist in their relation to "normal" spaces, transforming and questioning their order while deepening our awareness of the existing cultural and social structures (3). Similarly, Eva Sturm (2010), who specializes in art mediation, argues for "a differential art mediation . . . based on difference, on the heterogeneous, the non-final. . . ." Moreover, she states, "Perhaps, as with art, the point is to create spaces in which disagreement and disconnection can be cultivated, in which not everything is fixed and hierarchically ordered. Perhaps it is possible to create rooms in which nothing is as certain as it once seemed"[7] (my trans.). Kobe indeed creates an atmosphere or "other space" in which much is possible but nothing is certain. While Kobe's Flora appears to be gentle and carefree, he is also a figure that would normally not be expected in such a park: a young man with flowers round his head deliberately and gracefully casting seeds. He thus transforms the park into an "other space". Curiously, save for one instant with the veiled lady, he does not appear to see the people around him, and they do not appear to see him. It seems to be a space of non-encounters; non-action; perhaps of temporary truce; or of a time between transitions. Is it a haven away from the "real" world? Is it a kind of limbo where nothing ever happens, where no one ever speaks to or touches another? Or is it a provisional rest before something occurs, the infamous calm before the storm? Many more questions arise: Does the park guard embody a threat or a figure of protection? Having in mind Flora's backstory of rape, is this park one of possible choice encounters as opposed to forced encounters? Unlike *Primavera*, that had a visibly menacing Zephyrus, the threats in *FLORA PFLÜCKT WILDE BLUMEN* can only be guessed at. Kobe herself, in the film description, poses the question of whether this space is threatened or protected, or whether the characters will meet or stay separate.

A narrative, imaginary space can also be discussed, for instance, the gap of hidden actions between painting and video. What happens in between, unseen by the viewer? Is the artist a creator/goddess responsible for removing Flora from her previous situation and transferring her into a newly-fashioned world? In which of the worlds is Flora freer? Also, can Flora, a figure of metamorphosis, be seen as an artist or an artwork / subject of art? And to this, is Flora the agent or the object of transformation? His actions are slow and deliberate and as mentioned,

---

7   "Vermittlung – Performance – Widerstreit" by Carmen Mörsch and Eva Sturm, Art Education Research No. 2/2010, ZHdK Departement for Cultural Analysis, Institute for Art Education. Quoted in the website of the art association *Kunstverein Schichtwechsel*. Last access: 10 May 2017.

the sowing of seeds is a transformative act. In this way, he seems to be consciously attempting to renew the present reality.

A further topic of relevance is how space is perceived by the viewer, who perhaps has been perusing the many park installations on show, markedly different from the sculptures and fountains that are commonly associated with city parks. Then, the spectator takes a break from the "real" park to enter the small kiosk-ruin in which s/he no longer hears the park's sounds and is once more part of the park, in a different way, through Kobe's video. The "real" physical park is thus experienced in a new way.

Time is also strange and undefined. The movements are in slow motion: In the first scene, the young man, Flora, seems to awaken gently into the new world, perhaps escaping the nightmare of Zephyrus' dominance in his previous life. He moves gracefully, stretching and casting seeds. However, save for the first few seconds, his feet remained rooted to the ground, as if wanting to stay in place, fastened in this scene of tranquility. This could intimate on the viewer that the slow impression of unending spring is not quite real. At the same time, the positioning of his feet seems to mimic the traditional contrapposto posture, another wink at Botticelli.

Time in *FLORA* gives an impression of both timelessness and temporariness. The slowness of narration could also point to a time of mid-transformation, a time of gathering or recovering strength, of planting seeds. The viewer is always reminded, via the sounds of birds and traffic, of a life outside of the park's clasp; thus, as mentioned, this resting place is likely transitory, a standstill between sleep and waking that will inevitably once more be transformed.

The artist's choice of media is certainly worth noting. The *tableau vivant* form was also often based on paintings. The pictures on this *tableau vivant* are not still, but nevertheless, movement is scarce. Again, there is this in-between and uncertainty between fixedness and fluidity; moreover, we can observe the tension between the pastness that has been attributed to photography as opposed to the presence of cinema. "The implicit photographic past tense is revisited by the implicit cinematic present tense" is how Andrew Shail, who refers to Roland Barthes and André Bazin, summarizes it in his 2012 work *The Cinema and the Origins of Literary Modernism* (89). Returning to the topic of space, in the film studies classic *What Is Cinema?* (1967), Bazin distinguishes between painting and cinema. In his view, the painting, "by its surrounding frame ... is separated off not only from reality as such but, even more so, from the reality that is represented in it" (165). In contrast to this, he believes that "what the screen shows us seems to be part of something prolonged indefinitely into the universe. A frame is centripetal, the screen centrifugal" (166). Kobe, in her intertextual engagement with Botticelli's painting, proposes different characters and meanings, but will they be able to move beyond the pictures and out into the "real" world? The *tableau* fits very much with the atmosphere of awakening and awaiting. Interestingly, for Foucault, in his 1975 "Discipline and Punish: The Birth of Prison", *tableaux vivants* are media of transformation, transforming "the confused, useless or dangerous multitudes into ordered multiplicities" (141).

3.2 Gender

In terms of gender, Flora is androgynous[8] and is clothed in black jeans and a white shirt, and as noted, the crown of flowers on his hair makes his identity unmistakable, especially when seen in parallel to *Primavera*. Now free of gender confinements, he smiles mysteriously and gives an impression of serenity. How does making Flora a young white man change the story?

Changing Flora's sex and gender gives birth to several threads of thought. But first, who is Flora and what is associated with her figure? Stemp, in *The Secret Language of the Renaissance* (2006) connects Flora to Venus in *Primavera* in their representation of "the idea of fertility which is embodied by spring and expected in marriage" (156). Silvia Gherardi, in *Gender, Symbolism and Organizational Cultures* (1995) explores the symbolic order of gender, focusing on the relations between gender, power and culture. Within this topic, she outlines and compares the different female archetypes in Greek mythology: Persephone and Flora, goddesses of spring, are part of what Gherardi terms "vulnerable deities," who "express the need for affiliation. All … vulnerable goddesses were raped and dominated by male deities and suffered on account of the love relationship" (73). Persephone, whom Gherardi interprets to be the spring goddess in *Primavera*, is according to the author, a symbol for "the wait for something to happen, for someone to come and give shape to life" (81). Do these associations really change with Flora's gender, when we observe the vulnerable-looking young man in the video? Does the fact that he is now a man make him less vulnerable to destructive relationships? Does it give him a higher chance of being Zephyrus' equal? Is he now unencumbered by a history of domination and thus free from being defined by his relationships? Also, why are there no young women characters in the park (when compared to *Primavera*, which is dominated by beautiful, noble and well-known young women)?

---

8   In a survey conducted by the author in December 2016 in Sankt Sigfrids folkhögskola, a preparatory art school in Växjö, Sweden, 13 out of 21 students believed Flora to be a woman upon watching Kobe's video.

It is interesting that in this version of the narrative, it is the young white male who sticks out and is vulnerable. The fact that this young man is androgynous also contributes to the atmosphere of uncertainty. Feminists have previously seen androgyny as an ideal. Arleen B. Dallery in her article "The Politics of Writing: Écriture Féminine" (1989) refers to the "treasured ideal of androgyny [which is] itself based on fear of otherness" (65). Gherardi touches this topic too, stating: "Defining the female as passive, emotional, irrational and dependent is to deny that the male possesses these characteristics. . . . [T]he problem is how to avoid thought and language based on antithesis and dichotomy . . . on the univocality of the meaning of male or female" (71).

Additionally, another question that could be studied further is: What does it mean that the goddess of spring and renewal is a man, when we think in terms of fertility and motherhood? In *Gender: The Key Concepts* (2013), Mary Evans and Carolyn H. Williams speak of the NRTs, New Reproductive Technologies, and how "the feminist analysis of NRTs has confirmed the extent to which women who are unable to conceive . . . seek out NRTS in order to fulfill normative expectations about marriage, kinship, family, gender "and sex . . ." (161). Evans and Williams also quote anthropologist Marilyn Stathern, "who argued that technological assistance to conception would have a 'displacing effect' on normative kinship values . . ." (160).

Finally, Marvin Altner, who interviewed Kobe for *Gleisdreieck Berlin* (2012), the book on the exhibition, saw Kobe's Flora as a figure who can be seen in a way as echoing in a "subtly subversive" (66; my trans.) manner, the female protagonist in Pippilotti Rist's 1997 art video *Ever is Over All*: In a flowy blue dress and red shoes, she walks smilingly down the street, smashing car windows with a long-stemmed flower. At one point, she is followed by a friendly female cop.

4. Conclusion

The method of displacement and its relation to art mediation has been investigated in various ways (see for example the works of aforementioned authors like Brohl, Kraus and Sturm), helping to construct a framework for articles such as this one that study and interpret the employment of displacement in specific artworks.

This article has endeavored to explore the many threads of thought that Kobe's use of displacement has opened up, especially in the aspects of space, time and gender. A topic that could be investigated even further is that of metamorphosis, a theme which has given a remarkable cohesion to the relations between Ovid, Botticelli and Kobe, as well as to *FLORA PFLÜCKT WILDE BLUMEN*'s relationship to Gleisdreieck Park, itself in a process of metamorphosis. In the act of sowing seeds, in a way, Kobe's Flora is an agent of renewal, making way for new meanings to continue to transform the constantly changing scene.

Through displacement, Kobe in *FLORA PFLÜCKT WILDE BLUMEN* creates a situation that is ambivalent: a neither-here-nor-there space between spaces which is neither 'perfect' nature nor manmade structure, male nor female, human nor godlike, new nor old, nowhere nor somewhere, fixed nor free. The situation is disorienting, unfixed, and malleable to transformation.

Kraus (see her forthcoming article "Corporal Linkages Between Ethics and Aesthetics as a Task of Education") states that a central task of pedagogy is "the development of one's ethical sense for diverse approaches and structures of power, hindrances and counter-reactions in an actual context of practices, bodies and things" (8). For Kraus, artworks are a means to this task, as she discusses how "artworks may reveal hierarchical orders of the current images or constructs of a certain 'other'", leading to "new orders [that] might be proposed" (7). Furthermore, she states that "every artistic work is socially dimensioned and is a way of looking for orientation in existential regards. . . ." Thus, the common response of a spectator confronted with an artwork that is disorienting is to attempt to find her or his footing in the situation. This effect may create questions in the spectator, challenging her or his "orders" and perhaps also encouraging her or him to create new meanings, which may tend to be transformable rather than fixed. The spectator, this way, is steered by open-ended questions rather than by answers, thus creating a possibility for valuable and exploratory dialogue.

Works Cited

Alÿs, Francis. *Paradox of Praxis 1 (Sometimes Doing Something Leads to Nothing).* Performance, 1997, Mexico City.

Bazin, André. *What Is Cinema?,* translated by Hugh Gray, University of California Press, 1967. *QMplus.* Web. 22 May 2017.

Botticelli, Sandro. *Primavera.* Painting. Ca. 1482, Uffizi Gallery, Florence.

Brohl, Christiane. *Displacement als kunstpädagogische Strategie.* Books on Demand, 2003.

Burroughs, Charles. "Talking With Goddesses: Ovid's *Fasti* and Botticelli's *Primavera.*" *Word & Image,* Issue 1, 2012, pp. 71–83. Web. 2 May 2017.

Dallery, Arleen B. "The Politics of Writing: Écriture Féminine" *Gender/Body/Knowledge/Feminist Reconstructions of Being and Knowing,* edited by Alison M. Jaggar and Susan R. Bordo, Rutgers, 1989. *Google Book Search.* Web. 18 Oct. 2016.

"Displacement." Def.1. *oxforddictionaries.com*. Oxford Dictionaries. Web. 17 Oct. 2016.

Duchamp, Marcel. *Fountain*. Installation, 1917, New York.

Eco, Umberto. *The Open Work*, translated by Anna Cancogni, Harvard University Press, 1989. *Monoskop*. Web. 15 May 2017.

Eggs, Francine, et al. *Gleisdreieck Berlin – 2012: Kunst im öffentlichen Raum*, edited by Marvin Altner, Jovis, 2012.

"Eva Sturm, Carmen Mörsch | Vermittlung – Performance – Widerstand." *Kunstverein Schichtwechsel*, n.p., n.d. Web. 15 May 2017.

Evans, Mary and Carolyn H. Williams. *Gender: The Key Concepts*. Routledge, 2013.

Gherardi, Silvia. *Gender, Symbolism and Organizational Cultures*. Sage Publications Inc., 1995.

Foucault, Michel. *Discipline and Punish: The Birth of Prison*, translated by Alan Sheridan, Pantheon Books, 1977. *Google Books*. Web. 2 May 2017.

Foucault, Michel. *The Order of Things*, translated by Pantheon Books, Tavistock/ Pantheon, 1970.

Foucault, Michel. "Of Other Spaces" (1967), translated by Jay Miskowiec. *Diacritics* Vol. 16, No. 1, Spring 1986, pp. 22–27. *Jstor*. Web. 2 May 2017.

Kilgour, Maggie. "The Poetics of Time: The *Fasti* in the Renaissance." *A Handbook to the Reception of Ovid*, edited by John F. Miller and Carol E. Newlands, John Wiley and Sons, 2014. *Google Book Search*. Web. 17 Oct. 2016.

Kobe, Ellen. *FLORA PFLÜCKT WILDE BLUMEN*. Art video. 2012. http://www. ellenkobe.de/florapflueckt-wilde-blumen/ Web. Accessed 11 October 2016.

Kobe, Ellen. "PEOPLE IN MUSEUMS (MENSCH IM MUSEUM)." Education is Relation Not Output? Scenes of Knowledge and Knowledge Acquisition, International Conference, 16–19 May 2016, Linnaeus University, Växjö, Sweden. Lecture.

Kraus, Anja. "Materiality and Displacement." *Performativity, Materiality and Time*, edited by Mie Buhl et al., Waxmann, 2014.

Kraus Anja. "Corporal Linkages Between Ethics and Aesthetics as a Task of Education." *Culture, Biography & Lifelong Learning CBLL* (forthcoming).

Mahlke, Martina et al. "Bürgerumfrage zur Vorbereitung des landschaftsplanerischen Ideen- und Realisierungswettbewerbs für den Park am Gleisdreieck Berlin." *Berlin.de*, May 2005. Web. 25 May 2017.

O'Dougherty, Brian. *Inside the White Cube. The Ideology of the Gallery Space*. The Lapis Press, 1986. *ARC / Arts + Design. University of California, Berkeley*. Web. 20 May 2017.

Ovid. *Fasti*, translated by A.S. Kline. n.p. 2004. *Poetry in Translation*. Web. 17 Oct 2016.

Ovid. *Metamorphoses*, translated by Sir Samuel Garth, John Dryden et al., n.p., 1717. The *Internet Classics Archive*. Web. 17 Oct. 2016.

"Park at Gleisdreieck." *Visit Berlin*. n.p., n.d. Web. 2 May 2017.

Rist, Pippilotti. *Ever is Over All*. Art video. 1997, Museum of Modern Art, New York.

Roth, Hans Ingvar. *The Multicultural Park – A Study of Common Values at School and in Society*. Liber Distribution, 1999.

Seel, Martin. *Aesthetics of Appearing*, translated by John Farrell. Stanford University Press, 2005.

Shail, Andrew. *The Cinema and the Origins of Literary Modernism*. Routledge, 2012. *Google Books*. Web. 2 May 2017.

Smithson, Robert. "Some Void Thoughts on Museums." *Robert Smithson: The Collected Writings*, edited by Jack Flam, University of California Press, 1996.

Stemp, Richard. *The Secret Language of the Renaissance*. Duncan Baird Publishers, 2006.

The UN News. "The Art of Displacement." *Winsor and Newton*, 1 Nov. 2013. Web. 17 Oct. 2016.

Tomala, Jessica. "Achtung Kunst!" *Der Tagesspiegel* n.p., 21 July 2012. Web. 10 May 2017.

Trin T. Min-ha. "Other than Myself / My Other Self." *Travellers' Tales: Narratives of Home and Displacement*, edited by John Bird et al. Routledge, 1994.

Weiwei, Ai. *Fairytale*. Art as Field Study. *Documenta 12*, 2007, Kassel, Germany.

List of Figures

Humanism and Democracy
as Learning Scenarios

Peter Baumgartner & Isabell Grundschober

Is Tacit Knowledge Communicable?

Abstract: In this paper, we will present some ideas on how informal learning could be communicated. Within today's fast-changing society, most of our competences predominantly result from an on-going process of experiential learning at our workplace and in other day-to-day activities. So-called expert knowledge is not acquired or constructed in the short time span of our formal or non-formal learning career (school, studies) but during all our (life) activities in which we try to find solutions to challenges. Therefore, this kind of knowledge is not the outcome of arrangements that are particularly oriented to the intention of learning, but is a spin-off or side effect of intrinsically meaningful actions for all persons actively involved in these situations. This leads to the problem of learners being often unaware of the significance, depth or variety of their informal learning.

But how can we judge this kind of personal knowledge in a reproducible and comparable way? We need a theoretically sound procedure to validate informal learning. The validation of informal learning plays an important role when it comes to lifelong learning, as informal learning through people's professional, social and personal lives needs to be recognized. Successfully implemented validation procedures could act as the missing link between informal workplace learning and formal education and training. In this article, we propose the model of validation used at the University of Chester, considering it to be a useful approach to capture tacit knowledge through reflecting on practical learning experiences. As a concrete example, we have chosen the professional field of teaching, as this is where we are most experienced and thus more able to substantiate our theoretical claims.

1. Introduction

In this article, we apply our theoretical model on validation procedures for informal learning. As an example, we choose the teacher profession. Austrian teacher education for teachers in compulsory schools is facing great transformation at the moment. Legislation and curricula were changed and aligned with the Bologna process. The idea is that after doing their bachelor's degree, teachers start to work while doing their master's studies in the years that follow. Master programs should be designed for this target group, considering and recognizing prior informal learning at the workplace to ensure the quality of the studies.

For this purpose, validation procedures are highly important to identify, assess and recognise knowledge, skills and competences, which were already informally acquired. Successfully implemented validation procedures could act as the missing link between informal workplace learning and formal education and training. Progress has been made in implementing validation procedures, but at the moment, only few countries carry out comprehensive validations systems in all economic sectors (Cedefop, European Commission, and ICF 29). Especially informal learning with its tacit characteristics leads to methodological challenges in validation procedures (Cedefop 16). In this article, we approach potential obstacles to the validation of teachers' informal learning experiences and suggest possible solutions.

First, we outline some characteristics of informal learning. We hypothesise that the results of informal learning could be described by the Polanyian term of "tacit knowledge" and that it cannot be represented completely in a linguistic way. We show that the traditional lesson planning models that are used in teacher education nowadays face a similar linguistic problem.

Based on the these results, we will draw some conclusions on the design of a validation procedure for informal learning. As a continuing example, we use our own professional experience in teacher training to illustrate the significance and practical implementation of our considerations.

2. Making Tacit Knowledge Explicit

2.1 Language and the Concept of Tacit Knowledge

After looking deep into the different aspects of tacit knowledge, Michael Polanyi in his magnum opus *Personal Knowledge* (1958, reprinted in 1974 and 2013) summarises the essential characteristics with the following, currently celebrated words: "I shall reconsider human knowledge by starting from the fact that *we can know more than we can tell*" (*The Tacit Dimension*, 4, italics are in the original).

As an illustrative example, Polanyi mentioned the recognition of human faces, which is a skill everybody has without knowing explicitly how it works. We are able to describe the different traits of a face. However, this description is not unambiguous and does not account for many changing aspects like the perspective of our view, the facial expression (angry, laughing), or changing characteristics such as getting older or wearing a beard.

Face recognition is not only a paradigmatic example of the fact that we know more than we can tell. It also shows that we are principally able to communicate our knowledge. But to do so, language is not sufficient; therefore, we also need other forms of communication. The police uses a specific method to identify (and therefore recognise) faces by memory: The person who is invited to communicate his or her knowledge commands a repository of pictures of different parts of the face (forehead, eyebrows, eyes, nose, mouth, chin etc.), where each picture representing a part of the face is itself a collection of pictures with different characteristics of this particular face property (for example, a nose could be small, broad, long, snub etc.). In trying out how different pictures of the constituent parts of the face interact and affect each other, the witness is finally able to produce a face picture with a strong resemblance to the original. The usefulness of this technique is demonstrated by the software app "Flashface full" by Viktor Widiker (2012).

This example shows that we are able to communicate our knowledge but not with language alone; we also need other means. The philosopher Susanne Langer already pointed out that language has two important restrictions in relation to other symbol systems.

a) Discursiveness: Thoughts represented by verbal symbolism – as Langer calls language – have the restriction that only one idea after the other could be expressed in oral or written form.

> [A]ll language has a form which requires us to string out our ideas even though their objects rest one within the other; as pieces of clothing that are actually worn one over the other have to be strung side by side on the clothesline . . . only thoughts which can be arranged in this peculiar order can be spoken at all; any idea which does not lend itself to this "projection" is ineffable, incommunicable by means of words. *(Langer 65f.)*

Even if we could divide the face into different parts, it is not the property of these parts that determines the overall appearance of the face to us, but the relation of all the parts to each other. It is an interrelated network of relations that creates the essential characteristics of a face: A "broad" nose is only a relative feature of the face, determined by other parts of the face (e.g. the location and proximity of the eyes, the shape and size of the mouth, lips etc.). These relational attributes cannot be expressed linguistically, as speech knows only the sequential order of words.

b) Composable Semantic Units: Language is composed of semantic units (vocabulary), which are composed by certain rules (grammar) to construct new meanings. It is a general reference, which is constructed bit by bit and which needs to be situated in time and location by "non-verbal acts, like pointing, looking, or emphatic voice-inflections, to assign specific denotations to its terms" (Langer 78).

Another example of the limitation of verbal expression was the famous saying by Isadora Duncan (1877–1927) – a well-known dancer in her time – quoted by Gregory Bateson in order to underline the restricted functionality of language.

After a performance, Duncan was asked about the meaning of a specific dance, and what she wanted to say with it. She answered: "If I could tell you what it meant, there would be no point in dancing it" (Bateson 137 and again in p. 464).

Other symbolic systems like pictures have a multifaceted character which is not divisible and where the meaning is changed or destroyed whenever we try to decompose the wholeness or *gestalt* into different parts. These symbolic systems are total and direct references to the object they represent (Polanyi, *The Tacit Dimension*, 18).

When seeing a face, we are focusing on a comprehensive entity connecting unspecifiable particulars in a way that we cannot define. We are not focusing on certain particulars, but rather, on the whole appearance of the person's face (Polanyi, *The Tacit Dimension* 24). Therefore, it is instructive to understand that the example of face (re)composition is just an approximation in two ways: Firstly, it divides the complete experience of face recognition into the experience of playing with different parts of the face and secondly, it uses verbal symbolism as a communication resource either in the thought process of the person trying out different parts of the face or in telling a professional illustrator or – nowadays – a person trained in using the software that chooses and combines the different pictures representing the parts of the face. But even if this method works as a kind of useful approximation with workable results, there is still a big critique on this procedure not working in the way our mind does. We do not recognise a face by dividing it into different parts, playing around with the different shapes of these parts, and trying out different configurations.

A better example to capture the inherent properties of tacit knowledge may be pattern matching. We consider pattern matching to be a more effective way to understand how the mind recognises faces. Again, this procedure could easily be demonstrated by software applications: They calculate some characteristic features of faces and search through a database of already recognised and defined faces, namely persons' faces (Le). Drawing from the experiences of chess grandmasters, it is estimated that for all kinds of expert performance, an underlying database of pattern is necessary. It is estimated that such a repository consists of at least about 100,000 patterns. But instead of comparing and finding a match through a detached and separated similarity algorithm, as with the example of the software above, we follow the philosopher Dreyfus who argues that the human expert is driven by a compelling intuitive perspective, which means that (s)he is cognitively and emotionally immersed into the situation (Dreyfus 36). This immersion is also called "indwelling" by Polanyi, who understood this intuitive way of acting as a tacit component of knowledge. Thus, people use tacit knowledge in a natural, intuitive way, almost like an extension of their bodies. Through relying on their tacit knowledge, they can focus on a specific task (Polanyi, *The Tacit Dimension* 17). The skilled expert often does not know that he or she is carrying out complex actions (Dreyfus and Dreyfus, 13). Usually, a chess player rehearses the games of chess grandmasters to discover what the master had in mind. To understand the skilful performance, the player needs to mentally combine the movements that the grandmaster combined. Then, the player needs to combine them in a pattern similar to the master's pattern of movements (Polanyi, *The Tacit Dimension* 29f.).

2.2 Language and Informal Learning in the Teacher's Profession

Let us now examine the role of informal learning in teacher training education. We take the Austrian situation as an example because we know it best, but the situation is not very different in other countries. To help students attain their first knowledge on planning lessons, prospective teachers are often trained to design courses in terms of serial additions of various pedagogical components. A typical example is a form sheet for lesson planning, where students have to plan their lessons in a serial timeline, adding different educational components one after the other (Böhmann and Klaffke 21). The form itself communicates to the students what elements they have to observe and integrate in their planning. The header tells them to fill in the time, phase, teacher-student interaction, social form and media. There is a short column for notes, which does not fit into the other predefined slots. The form is based on a categorical system with abbreviations so that the narrow columns hold all the necessary information. So for instance, the different teaching phases are divided into getting started, introduction, presentation, teacher's lecture, discussion, working out, transfer, sum-up.

This model of lesson planning requires a linear sequence of decisions and one immediately feels the limitation of language in capturing the complexity of the teaching/learning situation: Students have to fill in the form one line after the other in a similar way to how one would hang clothes on the clothesline (Tsui 23). There is no interrelatedness between the different actions building up in the filled-out columns and lines. There is no transfer of meaning of an earlier action to a newer one: Each line stands for itself and has no interactions with previous or later actions or situations. The similarity of this approach with the example of face recognition is obvious. The elements of the lesson plan (time, phase, teacher-student interaction, social form and media) correspond to the particulars of the face (e.g. forehead, eyebrows, eyes, nose and mouth). However, while witnesses are able to communicate their tacit knowledge by compiling pictures of face parts, this is not the case in the teaching example. The teacher's form sheet is just a crude approximation to help teacher novices get their first experiences with lecture planning. Teachers with many years of teaching experiences do not use these kinds of tools to plan their lectures. Expert teachers cannot express their tacit knowledge of teaching with just the form sheet. The most important qualities of a good lesson could hardly ever be verbally expressed (Kohls and Köppe 196).

Why is this the case? What is the difference between the example of face recognition and the example of teacher training? We suspect that in the case of face recognition, the composable parts consist of pictures that are themselves an adequate form for direct and total referencing (at least of a part of the face), whereas filling out the form line by line only generally references the parts of the situation. To access and communicate the tacit knowledge of expert teachers, we would need a direct and total reference. Even if this reference would consist only of parts, we would still have to form them into a complete image. We believe that at the moment, we are lacking an adequate symbolic system that makes the expert knowledge of a teacher explicit and transmittable to teacher students, as the skill of the expert unfolds within the action (Quillien 162). Expert teachers are hardly able to distinctively explain their practice, but the complex ideas about their teaching are embedded in classroom routines (Tsui 37). Therefore, we have to settle on the direct observation of the real or (video-) recorded situation itself. But this is cumbersome and costly and it does not guarantee success, as the observed situation is very complex and includes attributes that are not essential and have to be interpreted. Even for this direct observation, we would have to develop a way to reduce complexity and to facilitate the process of interpretation.

Let us summarise what we have noted so far:

1. We know more than what we can express verbally.
2. This kind of knowledge is called tacit knowledge.
3. It seems that expert knowledge, which is shaped by lifelong experiences, that is, experiential learning, consists of a tacit dimension and at least partially consists of a huge repository of patterns.
4. To communicate tacit knowledge, we need a different kind of symbolism which is not sequentially ordered and (de)composable like language, but has a gestalt character.

3. The Validation of Tacit Knowledge

3.1 The Validation Procedure

Validation procedures are highly important to identify, assess and recognise the knowledge, skills and competences which were already informally acquired. For the purpose of this article, we shall understand validation as the confirmation, by a competent and legitimate body, that the learning outcomes acquired by an individual have been assessed with certain predefined criteria (Cedefop 16f.). Successfully implemented validation procedures could act as the missing link between informal workplace learning and formal education and training. Therefore, implementing validation procedures is a question of promoting lifelong learning, supporting individual employability, strengthening a country's competitiveness, and linking labour market demands with education and training (Bohlinger and Münchhausen 9f.).

In numerous countries around the world, ideas and challenges have appeared with regard to the development of strategies and systems to validate the learning acquired in different settings throughout one's lifespan. Most of the validation procedures focus on formal learning as the acknowledgment of certificates issued by state-recognised educational bodies. Another essential practical application is the translation or transfer of non-formal learning attested by educational organisations that are not part of the formal national educational system. There is not much experience yet with the validation procedure of informal learning.

To find solutions to overcome the obstacles of validation procedures, several EU-projects were conducted to develop and pilot validation procedures in Higher Education, e.g. the VALERU-Project (2013–2016) or more recently, the VINCE-project. Especially considering the refugee crisis and the need of supporting their inclusion in Europe, validation procedures gain further importance. Many refugees obtained an academic degree and/or have several years of professional experience, but are lacking documentation. The VINCE-project, which started in January 2017, is dedicated to developing and implementing validation procedures, which allow refugees to have their prior learning validated.

The main obstacle of validation procedures for informal learning is that they are strongly determined by the nature of tacit knowledge. Learning through experience primarily results in tacit knowledge, which could easily be adapted to different practical situations, but which is hard to communicate and therefore to validate (Schmidt-Hertha 233).

Therefore, validation procedures for informal learning require the special consideration of several aspects: On the one hand, many people do not remember when and what they have learned informally, as the essence of this type of learning goes without special attention and volition. Informal learning is learning without a special learning intention; it comes unplanned and accidently without formal educational arrangements. It is essentially driven by day-to-day (working) experiences and could also be called experiential learning. Dewey underlined that education needs to engage with and enlarge the experiences from informal learning (Dewey 12f.). On the other hand, informal learning is entangled with the subjective life experiences of the person, therefore bringing these experiences to light, where they may thus be validated with accountable objective criteria.

3.2 Validation in Teacher Education

Successfully implemented validation procedures could act as the missing link between workplace learning, and formal education and training systems, which could be especially beneficial for teacher training education, which traditionally has strong links with practice. Still, in the current evidence-based practice of teacher development programmes, less well-articulated forms of knowledge and learning are not as valued and theorized as explicit forms of knowledge (Markauskaite and Goodyear 238). Nevertheless, the teacher's working knowledge, or knowledge-in-action, is likely to be dynamic, experimental and deriving from different situations that are neither very coherent nor theory based. Pedagogical sense-making and the creation of meaning are important points in teaching (Markauskaite and Goodyear 241).

In the Austrian teacher training education, validation of prior (practical) learning is not recognized within its formal education system. One possible reason is that it is difficult to assess if somebody is a "good" teacher, or close to being a good teacher. What is good practice? And how can good practice be assessed? These are also questions which have recently been raised in Austrian teacher training education (Bundesministerium für Bildung und Frauen).

The Austrian teacher education for compulsory school teachers is facing major transformation at the moment. There were changes in legislation and curricula in accordance with the Bologna process, and the new education system entered into force in the winter semester of 2015/2016. The new system consists of a bachelor's degree with 240 ECTS and a master's degree with 60–90 ECTS, the latter being compulsory for teachers of general education subjects and optional for teachers in practical subjects of vocational education (§8 Abs. 2 HG). The idea is that after completing their bachelor's studies, teachers start to work at the same time as they do their master's in the following years. Master programs should be designed for this target group, considering and recognizing the prior informal learning at the workplace to ensure the quality of the master's studies. For this purpose, validation procedures are highly important to identify, assess and recognise the knowledge, skills and competences that were already informally acquired.

As we have shown, validating these informal learning experiences is challenging and there are manifold obstacles to overcome. Learning through experience primarily results in tacit knowledge, which could easily be adapted to different practical situations, but is difficult to communicate and therefore validate (Schmidt-Hertha 233). Furthermore, the learners themselves are often unaware of the significance, the depth or the variety of their informal learning (Smith and Clayton 448). Also, it is difficult to diagnose a teacher's skill: A teacher's performance could be assessed in a very cursory level, but due to the tacit nature of practical knowledge, it is hard to approach the teacher's real skill. Teaching routines and behaviours are just the tip of the iceberg, the visible part of a very complex process, as teaching is engaging "in a sophisticated and interlocking set of decisions …" (Jackson 24). Nevertheless, – as we already have said – the explicit linguistic expression of this informal knowledge has to be the basis for its recognition (Schmidt-Hertha 243).

The University of Chester gives an illustrative example of how tacit knowledge could be approached within a validation procedure in higher education. Danube University and the University of Chester closely cooperated in EU projects in terms of work-based learning and validation of non-formal and informal learning; therefore, we gained an insight into Chester's validation model. The validation procedure, which was elaborated at the University of Chester, applies very much to our theoretical considerations. The University of Chester offers Work Based and Integrative Studies (WBIS), which are tailored to the needs of the learners and their workplaces and contain a validated degree that enables learners to negotiate an award title. This way, adult learners obtain credit for previous non-formal and informal learning achievements. The validation model used in Chester is based on a developmental approach to awarding credit, and reflected practice plays an important role within the validation procedure. The Chester model of validation involves following steps (Talbot):

1. Information, advice and guidance: Prospective students come to the university and explain their plans for getting a degree in a certain field.
2. Identification: A Personal Academic Tutor (PAT) counsels them to remember and outline their experiences in order to identify necessary academic skills, which are codified and moulded into curricula, forming part of their desired degree.

3. Assessment: The applicant and the PAT, in a process of "negotiated learning", outline together the necessary competences and determine the gaps the student has to fill as well the tacit knowledge (s)he has to make visible in order to get assessed for validation purposes. An individual curriculum is designed to fit the needs of the applicant. It consists of visiting teaching modules to fill in the gaps and of designing work-based projects to demonstrate the tacit knowledge of the applicant. These projects draw heavily on the past or current experiences of the students and their academic discussion of these experiences with the use of contemporary scientific literature.
4. Validation: The student writes an essay about the project. But this is not just a report describing the work-based related situation and the actions by the student to master a certain challenge or to solve a problem; an essential part of the essay is the reflection of learning through the student's experiences in the light of scientific literature. Using sequential language, applicants try to outline their tacit knowledge by discussing their interventions under academic premises.
5. Certification: This essay can be validated and certificated like any other explicitly expressed knowledge.

We suggest a similar procedure for the validation of the tacit knowledge of experienced teachers, as this procedure seems adequate to approach the teachers' experiential, informal learning in the classroom. This idea was already described and used for many years in the continuing education and professional training of teachers as a kind of research method. Even if validating informal learning was not explicitly addressed, we interpret the research methodology in "Teachers Investigate Their Work: An Introduction to Action Research across the Professions" (Altrichter, Posch, and Somekh) as compatible with our own thinking.

Another approach which conforms with our considerations is linked with Actors-Network-Theory (Latour). This theoretical approach focuses not on the visible facts but on their dynamics in the hidden networks of inter-relationships. Instead of justifying and giving reason for groups, actions, objects and facts, Actors-Network-Theory follows actors in their environment to inspect their group building process, their interactions and interchanges. According to Bruno Latour, all matters of fact are the product of discussion processes about matters of concern where these facts were scrutinised and challenged. Not only are human actors agencies, but also objects, as they invite humans to certain actions and behaviour. For instance, a door handle "invites" humans to enter or leave the room. It is this hidden fluid dynamics that sociology uncovers and that cannot be interpreted as fixed and visible facts. In a manner similar to our difficulties in expressing tacit knowledge by linguistic means, Latour also struggles with words and their prefabricated static meaning. Most words in many languages designate already fixed objects and events as the result of a frozen dynamic. We are lacking words that refer to on-going processes, and that indicate processes of becoming.

It is therefore necessary – at least for the main languages of the Western hemisphere – to develop symbolic systems that are better able to capture dynamic situations as they are represented by the tacit knowledge that results from vibrant and energy-laden experiences. But in the meantime, our proposal to capture tacit knowledge by reflecting practical experiences and lessons could be used as a good approximation. The Chester model of validation, which follows a developmental approach and supports reflective practitioners, could act as a useful approximation to tacit patterns of teaching.

4. Summary and Conclusion

The main challenge of tacit knowledge is communicating it. Due to its intangible nature, as it is acquired unintentionally and used intuitively, people are not only often unaware of the full range of their skills and competences, but they also lack the means of communication to express all their tacitly acquired knowledge. We have shown, through the example of teacher education, that the current ways of approaching (tacit) teaching skills are inadequate. Form sheets for lesson planning, which force a linear sequence of decisions, could neither express own past experience nor the complex situations in the classroom. Verbal expressions are limited, as the skill of teaching unfolds within the action and a different symbolic system is necessary to, in some degree, communicate tacit knowledge.

The Chester model of validation follows a developmental approach, which is able to capture learning in a multifaceted way. It could act as a useful approximation to make explicit the tacit learning that derives from informal learning experiences. Nevertheless, a notational system, which expresses the wholeness or gestalt of educational settings, needs to be developed to further support the communication of practice from experts to novices in teacher education and to facilitate the validation of informal learning.

5. Bibliography

Altrichter, Herbert, Peter Posch, and Bridget Somekh. *Teachers Investigate Their Work: An Introduction to Action Research Across the Professions.* 2nd ed. Routledge, 2013.

Bateson, Gregory. *Steps to an Ecology of Mind: Collected Essays in Anthropology, Psychiatry, Evolution and Epistemology.* New edition. University of Chicago Press, 2000.

Bauer, Reinhard. "Didaktische Entwurfsmuster. Diskursanalytische Annäherung an den Muster-Ansatz von Christopher Alexander und Implikationen für die Unterrichtsgestaltung." Alpen-Adria Universität Klagenfurt, 2014. Web. 1 Feb. 2016.

Bohlinger, Sandra, and Gesa Münchhausen. "Recognition and Validation of Prior Learning." *Validierung von Lernergebnissen – Recognition and Validation of Prior Learning.* Ed. Sandra Bohlinger and Gesa Münchhausen. Bielefeld: Bertelsmann, 2011, pp. 7-26.

Böhmann, Marc, and Thomas Klaffke. "Die Neuen kommen! Gut starten in Schule und Kollegium. Supplement zum Friedrich Jahresheft." *Friedrich Jahresheft.* Seelze: Friedrich Verlag, 2010.

Bundesgesetz Über die Organisation der Pädagogischen Hochschulen und ihre Studien (Hochschulgesetz 2005 – HG). N.p. Web. 5 Feb. 2016.

Bundesministerium für Bildung und Frauen. "Bundesministerium für Bildung und Frauen Warum brauchen wir eine neue LehrerInnenausbildung?" *PädagogInnenbildung Neu.* N.p., 26 May 2014. Web. 1 Feb. 2016.

Cedefop. *European Guidelines for Validating Non-Formal and Informal Learning.* Luxembourg: Office for Official Publications of the European Communities, 2015. Web. 1 Feb. 2016. Cedefop Reference Series 104.

Cedefop. *European Guidelines for Validating Non-Formal and Informal Learning.* Luxembourg: Office for Official Publications of the European Communities, 2015. Web. 1 Feb. 2016. Cedefop Reference Series 104.

Cedefop, European Commission, and ICF. *European Inventory on Validation of Non-Formal and Informal Learning – 2016 Update. Synthesis Report.* Luxembourg: Publications Office, 2017.

Dewey, John. *Experience and Education. The 60th Anniversary Edition.* West Lafayette, Indiana: Kappa Delta Pi, 1998.

Dreyfus, Hubert L. *On the Internet.* Milton Park, Abingdon, Oxon; New York, NY: Routledge, 2009.

Dreyfus, Stuart E., and Hubert L. Dreyfus. *A Five-Stage Model of the Mental Activities Involved in Directed Skill Acquisition.* Berkeley: Operations Research Center, University of California, 1980. *Google Scholar.* Web. 1 Feb. 2016.

Jackson, Robyn Renee. *Never Underestimate Your Teachers. Instructional Leadership for Excellence in Every Classroom.* ASCD, 2013.

Kohls, Christian, and Christian Köppe. "Evaluating the Applicability of Alexander's Fundamental Properties to Non-Architecture Domains." *PURPLSOC: Pursuit of Pattern Languages for Societal Change/PURPLSOC: The Workshop 2014 Pursuit of Pattern Languages for Societal Change.* Ed. Peter Baumgartner and Richard Sickinger. Krems: Department for Interactive Media and Educational Technologies, Danube University Krems, 2015, pp. 188–210.

Langer, Susanne K. *Philosophy in a New Key: Study in the Symbolism of Reason, Rite and Art*. 3rd ed. Harvard University Press, 1957.

Latour, Bruno. *Reassembling the Social: An Introduction to Actor-Network-Theory*. New Ed. Oxford University Press, 2007.

Le, Duc. "Face Detection and Recognition on the App Store." *App Store*. N.p., 9 Nov. 2015. Web. 1 Feb. 2016.

Markauskaite, Lina, and Peter Goodyear. "Tapping into the Mental Resources of Teachers' Working Knowledge: Insights into the Generative Power of Intuitive Pedagogy." *Learning, Culture and Social Interaction* 3.4 (2014): (2014), pp. 237–251. *CrossRef*. Web.

Polanyi, Michael. *Personal Knowledge: Towards a Post-Critical Philosophy*. Corr. Ed. University of Chicago Pr., 1974.

–. *The Tacit Dimension*. Reissue. University of Chicago Press, 2009.

–. *The Tacit Dimension*. Garden City, New York: Doubleday & Company, Inc., 1966. Web. 26 Jan. 2016.

Quillien, Jenny. *Delight's Muse. On Christopher Alexander's The Nature of Order*. Iowa: Culicidae Architectural Press, 2008.

Schmidt-Hertha, Bernhard. "Formales, non-formales und informelles Lernen." *Validierung von Lernergebnissen – Recognition and Validation of Prior Learning*. Ed. Sandra Bohlinger and Gesa Münchhausen. Bielefeld: Bertelsmann, 2011, pp. 233–251.

Smith, Larry, and Berwyn Clayton. "Student Insights and Perspectives on the Validation of Learning Outcomes." *Validierung von Lernergebnissen – Recognition and Validation of Prior Learning*. Ed. Sandra Bohlinger and Gesa Münchhausen. Bielefeld: Bertelsmann, 2011, pp. 445–460.

Talbot, Jon. "A Case Study in the Development of a Work-Based Learning and the Possibility of Transfer to Continental European Universities. The WBIS Program at the University of Chester, England." *Prior Learning Assessment Inside Out* 2.2 (2014): n.p. Web. 1 Feb. 2016.

Tsui, Amy B. M. *Understanding Expertise in Teaching. Case Studies of ESL Teachers*. Cambridge: Cambridge University Press, 2003. *books.google.at*. Web. 1 Feb. 2016. Cambridge Applied Linguistics.

Widiker, Viktor. "FlashFace Full on the App Store." *App Store*. N.p., 11 Feb. 2012. Web. 1 Feb. 2016.

Globalization, Interculturality and
Interdependence as Learning Scenarios

Katarina Elam, Marie-Louise Hansson Stenhammar,
Tarja Karlsson Häikiö, Feiwel Kupferberg, Rasoul Nejadmehr,
and Margareta Wallin Wictorin

Educating Responsible Citizens. Intercultural Competence and Aesthetic Education

Abstract: What is aesthetic education good for in pedagogical regards and how can it be compared with the competencies that intercultural education aims at? Our main argument in the article is that the core of intercultural competencies consists of a number of overlapping modes of knowledge, skills and capabilities such as active empathy, critical approach to hidden colonial and racial heritages, dialogic relationships with the world and the other, as well as openness to experiences that are radically different from one's own. We regard these skills, competencies and knowledge as main elements of "educating responsible citizens." This article is a joint product of researchers working within different disciplines and with different knowledge interests. They share an interest in the question of if and how aesthetic education can lead to the particular intercultural competence of educating responsible citizens.

Keywords: Intercultural competence, aesthetic education, empathy, responsible citizens

Introduction: Arguments for the Arts as Tools in Intercultural Education

In Sweden, intercultural education was first mentioned in a public inquiry in 1983 (SOU1983, 57), which stated: "Intercultural education includes all children and all adults in the school – also outside the school" (43). In another public inquiry, intercultural pedagogy was considered a "natural foundation of all education", and here it was recommended that an intercultural perspective should permeate teacher education (SOU1998:99 17–18). Most recently, intercultural pedagogy has been discussed in an anthology by Goldstein-Kyaga, Borgström and Hübinette (2012) where they characterize a vision of education as something "double"; partly as a profession, i.e. teaching, and partly as a discipline in the humanities and social sciences "specializing in cultural processes and human cultural conditions" (9). The authors suggest that the pedagogical aim is to study how different cultural phenomena can be seen as conditions for learning, socialization and development. Cultural differences can in this way be integrated into the educational settings and thus contribute to learning without falling into considerations based purely on ethnicity. However, intercultural education is on the one hand a matter of perspective rather than of profession; it is not sufficient to equip teachers with some professional skills to deal with pupils with non-European backgrounds. Rather, we need to shift perspective and see education in such a way that overcomes Eurocentrism and embraces European and non-European knowledge perspectives on an equal basis. On the other hand, there is a modern or cognitivist perspective, which tends to reduce knowledge to science, and education to a scientific discipline. Through this mechanism, intercultural education remains an integral part of the current educational paradigm (Nejadmehr, 2012). As such, it disseminates Eurocentrism and contributes to the persistence of racism and colonialism, as these oppressive phenomena are part and parcel Westerns heritages (Bernasconi and Lott, 2000; Gray, 2007; McCarthy, 2009; Mack, 2010). An education attuned to the multicultural environments of today's schools revisits its basic principles. This means a revision of the relationships between science and education, since science itself emerged and developed in tandem with Europe's colonial expansion and slavery (Nejadmehr, forthcoming). An increasing diversification challenges a conception of a society that is culturally homogeneous and thus, questions about interculturalism, human rights and citizenship become ever more urgent (Nejadmehr, 2012). Communication through media other than verbal language is common in all cultures. Making pictures, dancing, singing etc. are part of several situations in everyday life, such as special occasions, and especially, various ceremonies and rituals. It involves forms of communication that in various ways complete verbal language and increase the possibility of human interaction in a wide sense. To reduce aesthetic modes of communication into something that is only about expression means that only one side of a complex interaction is illuminated. Communication with pictures has been in existence for far longer than the use of writing. And although no images are perceived equally and in a natural way by everyone everywhere, images and other aesthetic modes of expression overcome barriers for communication that verbal language sometimes represents. Therefore, the concept of arts used as tools in education is presented by the authors as a means to create intercultural competence. This contribution focuses on developing this hypothesis.

The Problem

Lahdenperä and Sandström (2011) write about the ethnocentric view on school that is characterized by the history and ideologies of every country. Values and ideals for teaching and the prevailing view of knowledge have their origin in this ethnocentric view. Lahdenperä and Sandström argue that the Swedish school can

Our approach to intercultural education is participatory and practice-oriented, and it considers this kind of education as an empowering one. We ask the question of how the common efforts of the different educational stakeholders and actors can make such an education possible. We also recognize that there are real obstacles in the way of intercultural education such as implicit and explicit biases, structural racism and xenophobia. These obstacles are of different kinds and at different levels and demand different levels of engagement. However, they demand practical steps to identify tools to overcome them and make an intercultural education possible. Starting from a problem-solving state of mind, we carefully identify obstacles and analyze problems. Our efforts are then aimed at finding the proper tools to remove obstacles in the way of solving the problems. Practically, such a process can go through different stages. Here, we focus on three interconnected main steps:

1) Tool-Designing Step

Following critical analyses of the problem at hand, this step is a constructive one, where tools are carefully designed. These tools can be conceptual, curricular, political, cultural, psychosocial, social, economic or a combination of a number of them. In a diagnostic analysis, the contemporary educational paradigm is problematized. Such a problematization aims at transforming the current educational paradigm in order to make it intercultural. Generally, during the last century, many subaltern knowledge perspectives like those of women, indigenous people, former colonies and the working class made enormous attempts to make their voices heard in education. Migration and digital communication have brought different cultures and peoples together in an increasingly globalized world. The narrow-mindedness of hegemonic knowledge and educational perspectives, racism and discriminatory power structures has also been revealed. Moreover, it has been demonstrated that the arts can in some cases prove to be a powerful tool for intercultural education. The hegemonic role of scientific knowledge has thus been questioned. In the next section, we will try to illustrate how the arts can be applied as useable tools through which the obstacles in the way of intercultural education can be removed.

The Arts as Tools for Intercultural Education

As one of the most important tools for the possibility of intercultural education, the arts can contribute to a general atmosphere of dialogue among different knowledge perspectives. By facilitating communication across cultures, the arts can encourage and enhance interculturality in education as well as in society in a sustainable way. Such a social climate facilitates interculturality and makes it easier to overcome prejudices like racism, discrimination and xenophobia. Different literary and artistic expressions can combat implicit and explicit discriminatory prejudices and norms of daily life such as cultural stereotypes that function as impediments in the way of intercultural education. They may also have a positive influence on shaping self-confidence in marginalized people through facilitating intercultural encounters.

Intercultural encounters can take place in the world of everyday life and in the world of art and literature. Among the unique qualities of the arts is the ability to create time-spaces for critical thinking and reflection. Providing a critical distance as well as spaces for reflection, artistic and literary encounters can facilitate intercultural interchanges that face-to-face dialogues cannot. Artistic expressions can put into play the intercultural dialogues and encounters, the contextual and the transcendental; they are on the one hand cultural products and as such dependent on the specific contexts in which they are produced. On the other hand, they can easily go beyond their contexts of production into a context of dissemination and communication that is borderless; they can reach beyond cultural confines and connect people with different cultural backgrounds who might otherwise not participate in a dialogue with each other.

It should also be mentioned that works of art are ambivalent. They can contribute to creative meetings between people and to learning from each other, but they can also contribute to stereotyping and conflicts. We can thus design and communicate artistic expressions in such a way that they can work as tools to overcome the obstacles that stand in the way of intercultural education. One way to remove these obstacles is to go beyond the dominant Western canon and its normative aesthetic, and prepare the ground for different traditions to attain and express their own voices on their own conditions. Properly understood, art and art expressions may contribute to intercultural education by:

- re-structuring knowledge/power relations in order for education to be a way to empower marginalized groups and to make social mobility through education possible for any and all;
- re-thinking "the others", their communities and their knowledge perspectives and educational needs;
- re-thinking their empowerment and participatory roles in society as well as in educational policy making;
- understanding knowledge and education as dynamic, fluid, alive, transformative and as never fully finished;

- understanding the importance of being open to the unknown and not-yet-known;
- shedding light on invisible prejudices and presumptions and helping teachers, students and people in general to suspend them and to listen to each other in nuanced ways;
- understanding cultures and identities as fluid, open, mobile and multiple.

Through these processes, the arts can encourage aesthetic learning processes, offer spaces for voice-attaining or many-voicedness (Skidmore 2012) and bring forward stories that otherwise might remain unheard. It is our hypothesis that aesthetic education, precisely because aesthetic knowledge to a large degree defines itself as a constant dialogue between Self and Other (Cooley 1964), is well adapted to this particular learning goal (intercultural competence). But aesthetic knowledge (through education), as we know from history and contemporary societies, can easily be misused both for commercial and political purposes (Sturken and Cartwright 2001). Hence, we also need to remain critical to aesthetic knowledge and its potentials, which is why intercultural competence through aesthetic education is not merely a cultural but also a moral issue. This calls for a more precise definition of aesthetic experience, dialogic imagination and empathy as tools in intercultural education.

Empathy through Art: A Tool for Intercultural Education

Art has the ability to create empathy and enable participants to shift perspective and see the world from the perspective of the Other, a basic precondition for intercultural education. Although we think that different kinds of aesthetic experience may challenge stereotypes and attitudes, it has to be clear that this cannot be a simple process. The concept of empathy appears rather frequently in intercultural contexts. Still, there is not just one definition of empathy circulating, and there are different opinions about whether or not it is fruitful to use the concept at all when considering art reception. The kind of mental operation we mostly think of as crucial for empathy is to "put oneself in another's shoes". This phrase is used, for instance, when parents and teachers admonish children when they tease or bully each other. But although this is part of the development of empathy, it cannot be enough in order to experience the emotion, especially not in relation to a fictional character. Svenaeus (2011) states that empathy is grounded in the embodied feeling of pain, which is reflecting the pain of a living person in front of me. And I am not feeling this pain after *thinking* that this person is suffering. Conversely, it precedes mere intellectual understanding of the other's situation. More is needed for a full-blown feeling of empathy. Yet, it is enough for us to understand that reading a novel will not be a sufficient context for empathy, at least defined in this way.

Boler (1997) discusses empathy in connection to comic books and states the risk of simplification as a significant problem. Her critique of what she calls "passive empathy" is that this will allow people to identify with a character in an undisturbed and easy way. This can be a mode of reading, she says, that may permit people to abdicate responsibility. Although Boler admits that while literature may promote an emotional reaction and even an identification with the character, it will likely not motivate consequent reflection or action. Responsibility, thus, seems to be a critical issue when discussing empathy. The question is if responsibility of this kind can be extended to embrace categories other than human beings. Researcher R.D. Bradshaw (2016) documented an interesting research project which aimed to foster empathy in students by integrating visual art in the classroom. The students developed a kind of ecological literacy through a combination of art creation and interpretation (addressing environmental issues), discussion, and writing. When for instance discussing images of animals, the students realized that they themselves were actors in the food chain. They also experienced that they could give voice to the voiceless. In this way, the project exhibits a different and very creative manner of challenging students to think from perspectives different to their own. The overall learning goal of schools should hence be to foster precisely this type of open, active, and responsible type of empathy.

Aesthetic Learning Processes as a Tool for Intercultural Learning

The concept of aesthetic learning processes was introduced in Denmark in the 1990s (Lindström 2009) and established in Sweden through reports arguing for an integration of visual arts and other aesthetic activities such as dance, film, drama, etc. in the Swedish school curriculum. Swedish research (Amhag et al 2013; Häikiö 2007; Lindstrand and Selander 2008) in the field has been characterized by attempts to define aesthetic learning and a fairly comprehensive set of concepts have been developed (Hansson Stenhammar 2015). This new focus on aesthetic learning is part of a broader international reorientation of research focus from the practical aesthetic activities to strategies of thinking (Eisner 2002; Hetland andWinner 2007). This shift means an emphasis on thinking strategies that can be developed precisely through aesthetic learning processes aiming at increasing the capacity for a dialogical imagination.

The thinking strategies are expressed through action and a dialogue that is focused on creative thinking, innovation and reflection (Cox 2007). The main motivation of this research is to demonstrate the arts' value in relation to innovation

(Hansson Stenhammar 2015). The international research field on aesthetic learning processes can be divided into four major research themes: a) the place of art in education, b) critique of how Western colonial and imperialist perspectives have been applied to non-Western cultures, and how this has affected non-Western education, c) how far arts education has been adapted to the utilitarian educational philosophies, and d) gender perspectives on how normative power structures affect educational programs (Cox 2007). Generally, learning and knowledge have a strong relationship to each other. It is difficult to speak of learning without touching knowledge as an effect of learning. The educational scientific discussion often focuses, from a hierarchical perspective, on this relationship between learning and knowledge: *process* and *product*. Learning involves many different complicated and complex processes. The complexity of aesthetic learning processes is made visible, *inter alia*, by the abundant conceptual apparatus that also describe this particular form of learning (Lindström, 2009). In relation to an intercultural perspective on learning, it is important to discuss and highlight the character of the aesthetic learning process as described by Hetland and Winner (2007) in which the formation of thinking is central. Based on this definition, we cannot connect the aesthetic learning processes solely to the aesthetic subjects. In order to promote intercultural learning, it is important that it is also understood as a general didactic method that has its roots in an artistic creative process. Intercultural learning cannot be limited only to certain classes or linked to certain subjects in the same way that aesthetic learning processes cannot be connected solely to the aesthetic field. Seen from a transformative learning perspective, aesthetic education becomes interesting, because such education in itself aims at broadening our imagination, enabling us to see the world as a constant dialogue between the Self and the Other. This aspect of aesthetic learning has been emphasized by Bakhtin as dialogic imagination (Bakhtin 1980; Holquist 1992). Bakhtin's concerns have played a large role in re-defining what goes on in the classroom (Dysthe 1995; 2003), and they have also changed how aesthetic subjects are viewed. Both these developments have made aesthetic learning processes more relevant for intercultural education. The creation of meaning is a fundamental factor in all human relationships where communication occurs, and requires mutual responsibility for understanding to be possible. There must be a willingness to take in the values and feelings of others, but also a willingness to listen (Bakhtin, 1981, 1993). The aesthetic learning process enables such a development through its investigative nature where dialogism, re-examination and transformation are the central bases for learning. These processes are also about being able to see outside oneself, and critically examine and reflect on culture in the sense of multiplicity of perspectives and voices. Each voice has its own words, but they interact with others (Bakhtin, 1981). This also applies to contemporary art as an object and as a tool for learning where the work itself can be understood as a double-voiced art (Evans, 2009).

2) How to Overcome Obstacles Standing in the Way of Intercultural Education?

In the previous section, we showed how different tools for making intercultural education possible can be designed. In this section, we focus on how these tools can be used practically. In this step, the tools are to be connected to obstacles that stand in the way of intercultural education. By designing tools, identifying obstacles and connecting them to each other, our efforts are aimed at using tools effectually and removing obstacles. Implicit biases, for instance, are such an obstacle. The tool that we have designed to remove this obstacle is transformative learning. By connecting transformative learning to implicit biases, we reveal them and can accordingly remove them from the path of intercultural education. The following section takes on this challenge.

Transformative Learning and Paradigm Shifts

To become interculturally competent, we need to counteract our implicit and explicit prejudices that impede intercultural education. As suggested above, the pedagogical aim of educating responsible citizens is a very complex one that is constantly open to new understandings. One of the issues that need to be dealt with is the hidden relation of power both in the classroom and in the national curriculum.

Current attempts to define intercultural competence seem to fit the idea that the overall aim or learning goal of intercultural education should be an education that encourages an active, open and responsible pedagogy that also includes the development of empathy as part of understanding others. This calls for different types of educational practices, among which the concept of transformative learning is suggested. The concept was developed by Mezirow (2000), who defined the standpoint from critical theory and developmental psychology as a continuation of Bruner's theories (5). Mezirow states that transformative learning "refers to the process by which we transform our taken-for-granted frames of reference (meaning perspectives, habits of mind, mind-sets) to make them more inclusive, discriminating, open, emotionally capable of change, and reflective so that they may generate beliefs and opinions that will prove more true or justified to guide action" (2000, 7–8). He explains that transformative learning has to do with the insight that is gained from experiencing other perspectives, and that can guide further actions based on "participation in constructive discourse" where the experience of others has an impact (2000, 7–8).

Mezirow's definition of transformative learning has aspired other scholars to re-define what the concept stands for in a renewed context, for instance, in relation to visual art education. For example, Cronqvist (2015) argues that transformative learning is about how to transform the common assumptions and frames of reference of knowledge and learning into part of the artistic development of visual art educational students. Karlsson Häikiö (2017) describes how transformative learning can be used as a pedagogical tool in creative activities in preschool and how it can be part of a constant changing of reference frames in the development of the professional skills of teachers in their everyday work with visual and digital tools. Wallin Wictorin (2014, 2015) has shown how transformative learning contributes to increased intercultural awareness, focusing on how comics can be used as an educational medium for children and youngsters to recognize both similarities and differences between different cultures and to learn about other ways of living.

A widened perception of the visual is a substantial part of a larger change of perspectives from a modern to a postmodern society in our Western cultural sphere. The visual field includes both learning (education) as visual art, and art as part of the expanded concept of visual culture (Mirzoeff, 1998). A visually oriented pedagogical practice embraces a widened concept of visual culture and definitions of the visual world, ways of seeing, visual positioning etc., and can be used in acquiring knowledge with new methods, because visual methods are today commonly used within different research fields (Berger, 1972; Illeris, 2009; Pink, 2009; Rose, 2012). The issues that are today central to visual art education related to art-based practice, are inspired by different philosophical and theoretical perspectives, such as critical and poststructuralist approaches, as well as ethical and political ideals that relate to, for instance feminism, ecology, intercultural pedagogics, sustainability and post-colonialism.

The interpretation process that takes place in every meeting between the Self and the Other is intensified in the classroom. The interaction between teacher and student is traditionally characterized by the pragmatic purpose of transferring a common cultural heritage, which combines human knowledge about the world and the nature of aesthetic or cultural values, as well as basic norms and values for human interaction. Paradigm shifts and new philosophical approaches to education have presented more non-hierarchical views on learning concerning views of acquiring visual knowledge that are in their turn part of a major change in qualitative scientific production in general, which also applies to changes in views on visual knowledge production. A traditional school context is guided by certain beliefs that frame and restrict freedom of thought through 'truth regimes', where meanings are prescribed, limiting opportunities for knowledge acquisition outside the norm (Atkinson, 2015, 49; Deleuze 2004). Atkinson (2015) has – besides seeing art as an empowering force in education – set different teaching positions against each other: an educational context where everything is already known (pedagogics of the known) and where knowledge is based on substances that are predetermined, controlled and measurable; an educational position where the learning process is dependent on dialogue and open processes in the educational situation; and an explorative approach to knowledge acquisition based on that which is not yet known (pedagogics of the not-known). Through more dialogic teaching positions, a non-hierarchical learning situation is created, leading to new structures of learning and teaching and knowledge production.

Multimodality, Intermediality and Mediated Languages

A common denominator for aesthetic learning processes is that they are characterized as reflective, exploratory, and creative, including both logical and intuitive thinking as well as the aesthetic activity itself, where the creative process is a central feature. Previous studies in education show that art is mainly discussed and legitimized on the basis of its existential value and its possible transfer effects, and that art can foster academic achievement in subjects other than the aesthetic (Winner et al. 2013). This is also noticeable in the various discourses that legitimize aesthetic learning in the Swedish municipal school and in teacher training (Saar, 2005; Lindgren 2006; Ericsson and Lindgren 2013). But this is now changing, as aesthetic learning processes are endowed with new meaning in school and teacher education, as the discourse *aesthetic activity as communicative competence* (Ericsson and Lindgren 2013) can be understood as an overall construction of legitimacy for aesthetic learning in school and teacher education. Within this discourse, the focus on artisanal skills in different aesthetic forms of expression has shifted to a focus on art's communicative elements. Here, multimodal mediation is central and visual competence is legitimized in relation to the needs defined by a media technological society (Ericsson and Lindgren 2013, 17). Attempts to characterize the aesthetic subjects and aesthetic learning processes are vast. Research has shown that the communicative competence which here is seen as synonymous with aesthetic learning cannot be automatically linked to reflexive and problematizing learning processes but more to aims related to aesthetics and creativity by using various expressions in order to achieve visual or auditory effects (Winner et al. 2013). Among the concepts that have emerged to frame and clarify what a dialogic imagination would mean in practice, are the concepts multimodality or multiliteracies (Cope and Kalantzis 2015). The former concept, which has been most used (Kress et al. 2001; Kress and van Leeuwen 2006), can be seen as an attempt to overcome the "textbound" limitations of English language studies. This led to an increasing interest in "the role of image, gesture, gaze and posture – in other words, multimodality" (Jewitt, 2011, 1) or the different representations of communication. By using various media in the production of stories and narrative practices with words and pictures, various horizons of understanding could be created that are related to a more diverse and complex understanding of our world (Wallin Wictorin 2015).

Kupferberg (2014) states that the increasing 'medialization' in society cannot be separated from the tools that the different media are bound to from a material perspective; thus, all tools for communication can be seen as cultural and mediating tools that are in an interdependent relationship to each other. Kress and van Leeuwen's (2001) definition of multimodality is when a mixture of character systems and different representation systems, such as visual and written language, among others, are used together. In multimodality or intermodality, a starting point is the assumption that different communicative forms co-exist simultaneously. Multimodality is defined as a simultaneous communication between different semiotic resources (Selander and Kress 2010; Kress 2009/2011) or when different communicative forms or sign systems, as for instance, words and images or sound and light, interact in an expression or create significance and meaning. From a cultural semiotic perspective, modalities are meaning-creating resources that are constituted culturally (Kress, 2009/2011 pp. 54–57). Marner and Örtegren (2013) are critical of this concept of multimodality and want instead to describe a phenomenon where "different media types such as writing, image, sound are present in one and the same text", intermodality here referring to the relationship between different *"modes"* (qtd. in Stam 2015, 32).

In a multimodal understanding of language, aesthetic forms of expression as mediating communicative forms of learning (Amhag et.al. 2013) can also be regarded as language (Hansson Stenhammar, 2015). In the inclusion of various mediations, as well as in the understanding of language, thinking may also be included in the sense that people's thinking takes on creative expression in modes such as facial expressions, body gesticulation, and besides the use of the spoken and written word, the act of listening (Bakhtin 1981), as well as aesthetic semiotics (Hansson Stenhammar 2015). In this sense, we also can speak of thinking as action, based on Vygotsky's (1978, 1934/2007) theories about the relationship between thinking and language. In this regard, knowledge of intercultural communication becomes a central aspect of the teacher's action competence of intercultural didactics and intercultural awareness.

3) Intercultural Education as Empowerment

In the first section, we designed and introduced some tools for the removal of obstacles in the way of intercultural education discussed in the second step. Aesthetic learning and transformative learning were among them. These tools were connected to obstacles like implicit biases. As a result of the preceding two steps, the third step becomes an enabling one, where the educated become interculturally competent. They not only act ethically in their relationships with each other (taking into consideration their knowledge perspectives and educational needs), but are also skilled enough to design and use tools that remove the obstacles that stand in the way of intercultural patterns of action. A proper way to grasp the complicated intercultural competencies is to, following Wittgenstein (1958), see it through the notion of family resemblance. Intercultural competencies then become a group of skills and competencies related to each other through overlapping similarities, instead of sharing an eternal essence to be discovered and applied to any context. There are characteristics that can be added or deleted depending on the context of application. Among these characteristics are: mutual empathy, openness to others, and recognition of uniqueness in other people.

At this level, marginalized social groups like ethnic minorities attain their own voice and we use the enabling conditions of intercultural dialogue, for instance, as part of classroom practice. To have a *voice* is to have self-confidence, self-esteem and the capacity to freely develop and express one's interest in the public and educational settings. The public sphere as a space of togetherness is a space signified by power relations, where different voices can compete at making valid their perspectives, knowledge and interests (Schmidt, 2011). Voice-attaining activities are acts of empowerment that enable people to participate in social and educational processes. Such a condition is polyphonic and a proper context for intercultural education. By attaining their own voice and making it heard in public settings, marginalized groups are empowered. They become interculturally skilled and competent in ways that can work together. Intercultural competence can be both the starting point and the end-results of intercultural education. Roughly speaking, intercultural communication can be described as something that is required when significant cultural differences generate different interpretations and expectations of how we should communicate with each other. Furthermore, empathy is mentioned as an essential quality, along with intercultural experience and the ability to listen to others. Other researchers (Bleszynska 2008) also consider the conscious work on the attitudes of openness and respect to be the most important task in order to develop intercultural competence and understanding. Perry and Southwell (2011) list three areas which they consider to be particularly in need of further studies: The first is to obtain a richer understanding of the different ways that intercultural competence can be developed. The second highlights the need for more empirical studies where possibilities for different methods to develop intercultural skills can be assessed. The third, finally, states the need for more studies examining how intercultural competence can be developed among different categories of people; from school children to college students and adults.

Conclusions

The main learning goal of intercultural education or the core of intercultural competence can be described as a widened form of empathy which is active rather than passive and open for other perspectives. In this article, we argued that in order to accomplish this goal we need to rethink both what we mean with learning in general and the role of aesthetic learning. On a general level, we would like to appeal for a change in focus from traditional learning and its accompanying paradigms to transformative learning, since the latter both sheds light on and tries to get rid of the implicit biases that may block intercultural education. We have also looked into the concept of the dialogic imagination and how this has changed the role of aesthetic education in the classroom. We have pointed out the potentials of aesthetic learning processes for intercultural purposes. Additionally, we have raised the issue of multimodality as a practical pedagogical tool for educating responsible citizens. We propose the employment of multimodality to stimulate dialogical aesthetic learning processes where different aesthetic languages, traditions and media may learn from each other; also, it may offer spaces for voice-attaining and for bringing forward stories that might otherwise remain unheard. We consider that atmospheres of polyphony can stimulate conversations across cultures and knowledge perspectives, and function as a transformative educational force.

Literature

Amhag, Lisbeth, et al., editors. *Medierat lärande och pedagogisk mångfald* [Mediated learning and pedagogical diversity]. Studentlitteratur, 2013.

Atkinson, Dennis. "The Adventure of Pedagogy, Learning and the Not-Known." *Subjectivity*, Vol. 8.1, 2015, pp. 43–56.

Bakhtin, Mikhail. *The Dialogic Imagination: Four Essays.* University of Texas, 1981.

Bakhtin, Mikhail. *Toward a Philosophy of the Act*, edited by Vadim Liapunov, and Michael Holmquist, 1993. University of Minnesota Press, 1999.

Becker, Howard S. *Outsiders. Studies in the Sociology of Deviance*. The Free Press, 1966.

Berger, John. *Ways of Seeing*. Penguin Books, 1972.

Bernasconi, Robert and Tommy Lee Lott, editors. *The Idea of Race*. Hackett Publishing Company, 2000.

Bleszynska, Krystyna M. "Constructing Intercultural Education." *Intercultural Education* 19(6), 2008, pp. 537–545.

Bradshaw, R. Darden. "Art Integration Fosters Empathy in the Middle School Classroom." *The Clearing House: A Journal of Educational Strategies, Issues and Ideas* 89: 4–5, 2016, 109–117.

Boler, Megan. "The Risk of Empathy: Interrogating Multiculturalism's Gaze." *Cultural Studies* 11:2, 1997, pp. 253–273.

Cooley, Charles Horton. *Human Nature and the Social Order*. Schocken, 1964.

Cope, Bill and Mary Kalantzis. "The Things You Do to Know: An Introduction to the Pedagogy of Multiliteracies." *A Pedagogy of Multiliteracies: Learning by Design*, Palgrave, 2015, pp. 1–36.

Cox, Gordon. "Some Crossing Points in Curriculum History, History of Education and Arts Education." *The International Handbook of Research on Arts Education*, edited by Liora Bresler, Springer, 2007, pp. 1–6.

Cronqvist, Eva. *Spelet kan börja: Om vad en bildlärarutbildning på samtidskonstens grund kan erbjuda av transformativt lärande* [The Play can Begin; On What Contemporary Art Can offer of Transformative Learning to Visual Art Teacher Education]. Licentiate thesis. Linnéuniversitetet, 2015.

Currie, Janice and Janice Newson. *Universities and Globalization: Critical Perspectives*. Sage Publications, 1998.

Delors, Jacques et al. *Learning: The Treasure Within*. Report to UNESCO of The International Commission on Education for the Twenty-first Century. Unesco Publishings, 1996.

Dysthe, Olga. *Det flerstämmiga klassrummet* [The Polyphonic Classroom]. Studentlitteratur, 1995.

Dysthe, Olga, editor. *Dialog, samspel, lärande* [Dialogue, interaction, learning]. Studentlitteratur, 2003.

Elam, Katarina. *Emotions as a Mode of Understanding: An Essay in Philosophical Aesthetics*. Diss. Disciplinary Domain of Humanities and Social Sciences, Faculty of Arts, Uppsala University, 2001.

Eisner, Elliot W. *Art and the Creation of Mind*. Yale University Press, 2002.

Evans, David. *Appropriation: Document of Contemporary Art*. Whitechapel Gallery and The Mitt Press, 2009.

Goldstein-Kyaga, Katrin, et al., editors. *Den interkulturella blicken i pedagogik. Inte bara goda föresatser* [Intercultural Gaze in Education; Not Just Good Intentions]. Södertörns högskola, 2012.

Gray, John. *Black Mass; Apocalyptic Religion and the Death of Utopia*. Farrar, Straus and Giroux, 2007.

Habermas, Jürgen. *Technik und Wissenschaft als Ideologie*. Suhrkamp, 1968.

Hansson Stenhammar, Marie-Louise. *En avestetiserad skol- och lärandekultur – en studie om lärprocessers estetiska dimensioner* [A De-aesthetized School and Learning Culture – a Study on the Aesthetic Dimensions of Learning Processes]. Diss. Centrum för utbildningsvetenskap och lärarforskning. Art Monitor, Göteborgs universitet, 2015.

Hetland, Lois, et al. *Studio Thinking; The Real Benefits of Visual Arts Education*. Teachers College, Columbia University, 2007.

Holquist, Michael. *Dialogism. Bakhtin and His World*. Routledge, 2002.

Häikiö, Tarja. *Barns estetiska lärprocesser; Atelierista i förskola och skola* [Children's Aesthetical Learning Processes; Atelierista in Preschool and School]. Diss. Acta Universitatis Gothoburgensis, Göteborgs universitet, 2007.

Illeris, Helene. "Ungdomar och estetiska upplevelser – Att lära med samtida konst." *Estetiska lärprocesser – upplevelser, praktiker och kunskapsformer* [Aesthetic Learning Processes – Experiences, Practices and Forms of Knowledge], edited by Fredrik Lindstrand and Staffan Selander, Studentlitteratur, 2009.

Karlsson Häikiö, Tarja. "Dokumentation, transformation och intra-modala materialiseringar." *Posthumanistisk pedagogik; Teori, undervisning och forskningspraktik* [Post Humanistic Education; Theory, Teaching and Research Practice], edited by Bosse Bergstedt, Gleerups, 2017.

Kress, Gunther. "What is Mode?" *The Routledge Handbook of Multimodal Analysis*, edited by Carey Jewitt. Routledge, 2009, 2011.

Kress, Gunther, et al. *Multimodal Teaching and Learning. The Rhetorics of the Science Classroom*. Continuum, 2001.

Kress, Gunther and Theo van Leeuwen. *Multimodal Discourse*. Hodder, 2001.

Kress, Gunther and Theo van Leeuwen. *Reading Images; The Grammar of Visual Design*. Routledge, 2006.

Kupferberg, Feiwel. "Medierat lärande och pedagogisk teori." *Medierat lärande och pedagogisk mångfald* [Mediated learning and pedagogical diversity], edited by Lisbeth Amhag et al., Studentlitteratur, 2013.

Lahdenperä, Pirjo and Margareta Sandström. "Klassrummets mångfald som didaktisk utmaning." *Allmändidaktik – vetenskap för lärare* [General Didactics – Research for Teachers], edited by Sven-Erik Hansén and Liselott Forsman, Studentlitteratur, 2011, pp. 91–114.

Lindgren, Monica. *Att skapa ordning för det estetiska i skolan; Diskursiva positioneringar i samtal med lärare och skolledare* [Bringing Order for Aesthetics in School. Discursive Positions in Talks with Teachers and School leaders]. Diss. Göteborgs universitet: Art Monitor, 2006.

Lindgren, Monica and Claes Ericsson. "Diskursiva legitimeringar av estetisk verksamhet i lärarutbildningen." [Discursive legitimations of artistic activities in teacher training] *Educare*, 1, 2013, pp. 7–40.

Lindstrand, Fredrik and Staffan Selander, editors. *Estetiska lärprocesser: upplevelser, praktiker och kunskapsformer.* [Aesthetic Learning Processes: Experiences, Practices and forms of Knowledge]. Studentlitteratur, 2009.

Lindström, Lars. "Konsten som kunskapsväg." *Konstens metod som kunskapsväg* [Artistic Methods as Ways to Knowledge], edited by Maria Marklund and Rabert Berg, Lärarhögskolan, 1994.

Lindström, Lars. *Nordic Visual Arts Education In Transition.* Stockholm: Vetenskapsrådet, 2009.

Mack, Michael. *Spinoza and the Specter of Modernity; The Hidden Enlightenment of Diversity from Spinoza to Freud.* Continuum, 2010.

Marner, Anders and Hans Örtegren. "Four Approaches to Implementing Digital Media in Art Education." *Educational Inquiry*, vol. 4, no. 4, 2013, pp. 1–18.

McCarthy, Thomas. *Race, Empire and the Idea of Human Development.* Cambridge University Press, 2009.

Mezirow, Jack. "Transformative Learning: Theory to Practice." *Transformative Learning in Action: Insights from Practice. New Directions for Adult and Continuing Education*, no. 74, edited by Patricia Cranston. Jossey-Bass, 1997, pp. 5–12.

Mezirow, Jack. "Learning to Think Like an Adult: Core Concepts of Transformation Theory." *Learning as Transformation – Critical Perspective on a Theory in Progress*, edited by Jack Mezirow and Associates. Jossey-Bass, 2000, pp. 3–33.

Mirzoeff, Nicholas. "What Is Visual Culture?" *The Visual Culture Reader*, edited by Nicholas Mirzoeff, Routledge, 1998, p. 3–13.

Nejadmehr, Rasoul. "Multicultural Education in Sweden." *Encyclopedia of Diversity in Education*, edited by James A. Banks. Sage Publications, 2012.

Nejadmehr, Rasoul. "The Problem of Scientific Education: A Genealogical Critique of Western Hegemony in Education." *Confero: Essays on Education, Philosophy and Politics*. Forthcoming.

Nussbaum, Martha. "Compassion: The Basic Social Emotion." *Social Philosophy and Policy,* 13 (1), 1996, p. 27.

Perry, Laura B. and Leonie Southwell. "Developing Intercultural Understanding and Skills: Models and Approaches." *Intercultural Education,* 22:6, 2011, pp. 453–466.

Pink, Sarah. *Doing Visual Ethnography.* Sage, 2013.

Rose, Gillian. *Visual Methodologies: An Introduction to Researching with Visual Materials.* Sage Publications, 2012.

Saar, Tomas. *Konstens metoder och skolans träningslogik* [Artistic Methods and the Training Logic in School]. Karlstads universitet, Institutionen för utbildningsvetenskap, 2005.

Searle, John. *The Construction of Social Reality.* Penguin Books, 1996.

Simmel, Georg. *The Sociology of Georg Simmel.* Translated, edited and introduced by Kurt H. Wolff, The Free Press, 1964.

Skidmore, David. "The Polyphonic Classroom: Are We All Special Educators?" *Bildning för alla! En pedagogisk utmaning,* edited by Thomas Barow and Daniel Östlund, Kristianstad University Press, 2012, pp. 35–44.

Schmidt, Sandra. "Theorizing Space; Students' Navigation of Space Outside the Classroom." *Journal of Curriculum Theorizing,* Volume 27, Number 1, 2011.

SOU1983:57. *Olika ursprung – Gemenskap i Sverige; Utbildning för språklig och kulturell mångfald.* Swedish Government Official Reports, Ministry of Education and Research: Stockholm.

SOU1998:99. *Acceptera! Betänkande från den nationella samordningskommittén för Europaåret mot rasism.* Stockholm: Norstedts förlag.

Stier, Jonas and Margareta Sandström. *Interkulturellt samspel i skolan.* Studentlitteratur, 2009.

Stam, Maria. *Medier, Lärande och det mediespecifika: En undersökning om den rörliga bildens plats och betydelse i ett ämnesövergripande projekt* [Media, learning, and the specific in media: A Study on the Place and Importance of Moving Images in an Interdisciplinary Project]. Licentiate thesis, Institutionen för Estetiska ämnen, Umeå universitet, 2016.

Sturken, Maria and Lisa Cartwright. *Practices of Looking; An Introduction to Visual Culture.* Oxford University Press, 2001.

Sveneaus, Fredrik. "Autonomi och empati; Två missbrukade och missförstådda ideal." *Praktisk kunskap i äldreomsorg* [Practical Knowledge in Elderly Care], edited by Lotte Alsterdal, Södertörns högskola, 2011.

Vella, John A. *Aristotle. A Guide for the Perplexed.* Continuum, 2008.

Vygotsky, Lev Semyonovich. *Mind in Society: The Development of Higher Psychological Processes*. Harvard University Press, 1978.

Vygotsky, Lev Semyonovich. *Tänkande och språk* [Thought and Language]. Daidalos förlag, 1934/2007.

Wallin Wictorin, Margareta. "Comics in Postcolonial Senegal – Suggesting and Contesting National Identity." *Comics and Power: Representing and Questioning Culture, Subjects and Communities*, edited by Erin La Cour, et al., Cambridge Scholar Publishing, 2015.

Wallin Wictorin, Margareta. "Tecknad pedagogik. Tecknade serier som medium för lärande i Senegal." [Cartoon Education. Comics as a Medium for Learning in Senegal] *Blickar – kulturvetenskapliga perspektiv på utbildning*, edited by Niklas Ammert, et al. Linnaeus University Press, 2014, pp. 149–161.

Winner, Ellen, et al. *Art for Art's Sake? The Impact of Arts Education*. Educational Research and Innovation, OECD Publishing, 2013.

Maria Peters and Christina Inthoff

Performance, Competence and Diversity: Visual Knowledge Productions in Art Education (Perspectives from the Research Project Creative Unit FaBiT)

Abstract: This article is about the visual expression and reflection skills that can be found in pupils' artistic and research-based learning processes. A multidimensional culture and social status based society (see Nohl 2014: 48) places high demands on the perception, expression and reflection skills of its members. To anchor diversity as a perspective within education, our research project explores learning arrangements aimed at initiating artistic-research learning processes at the university. Promoting the student's visual knowledge production is necessary to encourage reflection on the multifaceted approaches that can be used to examine individual and collaborative perspectives. We developed a portfolio that is called the *artistic experimental process portfolio* (in German, Künstlerisch-experimentelles Prozessportfolio or KEPP for short), which integrates several discourses and research fields (educational science, creativity research, aesthetics, art education, media studies). It deals with changing perspectives, and in this process, the students detect their personal interests and questions and get impulses for further reflection.

Introduction

The cultural life of children and adolescents has become increasingly diverse and complex. Particularly in view of the immigration of refugees, the cultural prerequisites that bring learners into the classroom are extremely diverse. The demand for differentiation in learning groups is increasing, which means that children and young people are able contribute their skills as cultural experts to the classroom and there further develop them. A multidimensional culture and social status based society (see Nohl 48) places high demands on the perception, expression and reflection skills of its members. In this context, the teaching of art at school has a key function. Like no other discipline, art focuses on building content and methodological skills in heterogeneous learning groups, allowing for a critical and creative approach to the way images are produced, received and reflected on.

To anchor diversity as a perspective within education, our research project on art education explores learning arrangements aimed at initiating artistic research learning processes.[1]

Using the representation of an understanding of diversity in the classroom as an opportunity in art lessons, the following paper addresses the discourse on competence orientation, which takes on these new challenges. At the same time, the concepts of competence and performance are examined in more detail and in their significance for educational processes. Finally, the design and reflection concept of the *artistic-experimental process portfolio* (in German: "Künstlerisch-experimentelles Prozessportfolio", the short form is KEPP) is presented and described concerning its effectiveness as a diversity-sensitive and competence-oriented art lesson.

Diversity as a Resource

Diversity is seen in terms of the different external and internal characteristics that make people distinguishable from one other. In particular, cultural differences exist, not only on the level of nationality, ethnic culture, religion, language, gender and age, but also in the conflict-rich, multidimensional area of "various interrelated factors such as wealth levels, educational backgrounds, environmental orientations, etc.", which is a guiding principle concerning all people with or without a migration background (Lutz-Sterzenbach et al. "Remix der Bildkultur" 16).

For R.R. Thomas (a pioneer of Diversity Management), the concept of diversity is an understanding of diversity in which people's individual and social characteristics become significant, not only in their differences, but also in their similarities (Thomas 5). This approach helps to recognize cultural diversity without simultaneously carrying out cultural separation: "The call to consider all individual differences as well as all existing commonalities . . . draws attention to differences without imposing specific characteristics or behaviors on individuals"

---

1   The research project is called "Fachbezogene Bildungsprozesse in Transformation (Fa-BiT)" [Subject-specific learning processes in transformation]. The interdisciplinary research group is based in the University of Bremen and was founded in the context of the Excellency Initiative University of Bremen (duration 2014–2017). We are six colleagues from the subject-specific educational disciplines (Fachdidaktiken) of the arts, English, French, maths, music and Spanish working together to find answers to the questions: What types of teaching processes are necessary in heterogeneous learner groups and how can they be implemented? How does educational change happen and how can we make it happen?

(Spelsberg 32). With this concept of diversity in heterogeneous learning groups, individual skills as resources and potentials can be discovered, used and further developed.[2]

Diversity is beneficial in three respects for the design of teaching and learning arrangements in art education: 1. It is the starting point and *Leitmotiv* (see Spelsberg 24) and shows itself in the attitude of not considering the increasing heterogeneity in learning groups to be negative and burdensome but instead addressing it in a valued and differentiated way. 2. A consideration of diversity enriches the methodical design of teaching and learning processes. Teaching designs are developed which enhance multi-perspective visibility. 3. Skills relating to being aware of and dealing with diversity can be seen as the goal of the lesson. It is necessary to enable the pupils to take part in cultural participation. They should be strengthening their ability to recognize contradictions and differences in processes of negotiation, in order to design their own cultural biography (see Keuchel 53). For this, it is important that the pupils exercise their abilities in critical reflection and the ability to deal with ambiguities (see Trunk 222).

For a couple of years, the conditions for diversity-based processes in the art education discourse have been linked to a search for suitable concepts of intercultural and transcultural practices in art education (see Lutz-Sterzenbach et al. "Nürnberg-Paper 2013"). In a diversity-oriented art lesson, "a possible space for the development of transcultural processes" (Eremjan 21) is opened up; children and young people can discover and negotiate "individual and common orientation and value systems" in an exploration of pictorial contexts (Eremjan 139). As the diversity of the learners is used as a resource through specific instructional arrangements, a "diversity competency", can form as an "indispensable component" in the thinking and actions of learners and teachers (Spelsberg 247).

Competencies and Performance

Competencies are deliberate dispositions of action that can only be achieved through performance and in their application, thus becoming visible and communicable. Competencies are the basis of our actions, and on the other hand, basic skills and strengths can develop through action. Such a conception of competency places emphasis on the performance of learning: "One cannot simply assume that we have certain competencies or have them at one's command. Competencies

---

2   It is not possible to address the critically assessable strategic use of human diversity in economic enterprises, with an economic objective as "diversity management" (see Spelsberg 25).

approach us, we experience them in a performative encounter of reflection, emotionality [inner participation], expressive capabilities, visible outer processes and materiality" (Kraus 154).

The emphasis on performance in the discourse on competencies that is expressed here is interpreted in the most frequently cited competency definition of F.E. Weinert, although it is not explicitly executed by him. Weinert sees competencies as cognitive performance dispositions, to which volitional, motivational, and social abilities and willingness are linked in order to be able to use "problem solutions in variable situations successfully and responsibly" (27). In such an understanding of goal-oriented problem management, artistic-aesthetic processes, for example, with their largely indeterminable dynamics of the search for meaning, tend to quickly be regarded as 'ineffective'.

From the perspective of the performative on the development of competencies in art lessons, there is also a focus on the reflection on the pedagogical staging of performative action in its "creative and reality-generating moments" (Wulf and Zirfas 299). For these moments, not only cognitive but also "physical, social, situational and staged processes" (ibid.) are constitutive. Such a relation suggests the admission of a fundamental indeterminateness of competency acquisition. Instead of mediating problem-solving competencies, the focus is rather on staging situations in which the self-evident can be questioned, and routinely organized forms of learning can be put to the test (see Otto 201). In such a process of problematisation, skills and abilities related to dealing with ambivalences, moments of indeterminacy and the lack of clear meaning could be developed and practised (see Inthoff 58).

Competency orientation that focuses on the performance of learning could be productive for teaching art. The definition of Eckhard Klieme et al. that competencies should be seen as, in principle, "context-specific, learnable and mediated performance dispositions" (Klieme and Leutner 880) frees art from the traditional myth of the 'natural' endowment of artistic genius and the notion of an inherited and stable single intelligence concept. With the orientation on competencies, genuinely subjective events and the reference to action in the production, reception and reflection of pictorial works can be considered more intensively. Competencies emphasize the development of individual strengths and not the identification of deficits in norm-oriented comparative situations (see Aden and Peters).

Art education is countered by the fact that competencies are concerned with "meeting requirements in specific situations" (Klieme and Leutner 879), i.e. being bound to concrete contexts and content. The teaching of art has always been a subject in which learning is linked to the idea of practical courses of action in the context of life-related requirements (see Aden and Peters). A further aspect of competency orientation can be applied to the artistic disciplines: Competencies describe aspects of specific actions and reflexive abilities that learners must have acquired in a long-term process of practising through a variety of ways. The content and processes are "systematically networked, constantly applied and kept active" (Klieme et al. 28–29). In this way, competency formulations leave room for individual, varied learning and detours and thus promote the development of subjective perspectives, questions and opinions.

There are therefore good arguments in the teaching of learning for advocating a competency orientation that focuses on learning processes. Nonetheless, the competency debate has for several decades split the discipline into different camps. There are many national and international efforts to formulate image competencies (see Seydel; Blohm; Wagner; Kirchner; Bering and Niehoff; Peez). For some, the concept of competency is a key word for more pupil-oriented education. They believe that differentiated and transparently formulated knowledge, abilities and skills can lead to a wide range of possibilities for feedback and early diagnosis to provide individual support for pupils. For the others, it is a provocation. They regard it as a "small-scale competence orientation" (Maset and Hallmann), which is ultimately fixed for performance control, and misses what distinguishes art and education. They fear that the impersonal power of the factual, the standards, and the norm dominates subject-oriented reflection processes, phantasy activity, and criticism. For them, education is becoming a quantifiable commodity that equates to the stagnation of potential self-development in educational processes (see Aden and Peters).

Some teachers solve this problem by analyzing the difficult-to-measure aspects, e.g. feeling, sense, judgment and creativity as "aesthetic surplus" (Grünewald and Sowa 302), which is effective but cannot be clearly defined. However, in order to meet the requirement of competency orientation, they instead formulate verifiable and assessable "basic competences" (ibid.). As with practical skills, methodological knowledge and art-historical knowledge about the images and image varieties need to be taught in art education. This reduction of the concept of competency implies that there is a risk that only the supposedly measurable basic competencies can be applied in the art lesson and that they are specifically described and solicited in core curricula. Further teaching concepts, e.g. the initiation of experimental, artistic-researching processes of design and reflection in which the artistic expression of the individual is developed in the sense of aesthetic education, are claimed to be in the process of being increasingly pushed out of the art lesson. Before the heterogeneous discourse in art education, an interesting question arose on how the individuality, incalculability and complexity of art in the individual shaping and reflection process of the pupils in combination with an orientation towards competencies and core curricula can be made productive (see Seydel 6; Peters and Inthoff).

KEPP as a Resonance Space for Experience and Exchange

One of the main ideas of art education is that it should be activity-oriented. However, pupils and teachers are often fixed on the artistic product being created, and not on the actual process of production (see Kirschenmann 241). The students may have difficulties in documenting, reflecting on and presenting their own formation of ideas and their learning processes. Promoting visual knowledge production may be necessary to encourage reflection on the multifaceted individual and shared perspectives. It may therefore be important to develop new methods for process visualisation and process reflection in art teaching that are suited to the pupils' biographical and culturally diverse learning conditions.

In the following, the artistic-experimental process portfolio (KEPP) is described as an instrument and a learning subject in the field of competence and performance. KEPP follows a didactic concept that is part of the dissertation project of Christina Inthoff.[3]

The research project KEPP refers to a tradition within visual knowledge production and endeavors to offer aesthetic research focusing on experiences of daily life, arts and scientific approaches (see Kämpf-Jansen 84; Lindström 57). Current visualisation conceptions like concept maps, which visualize mental concepts (see Zumbansen 4) offer direction but still lack artistic alignment; orientation could encourage discourse on *Artistic Research* (see Dombois).

With the KEPP, the discourse of portfolio work is considered to be expanded by means of art didactic considerations. The word portfolio has its origin in disciplines like art or architecture. The first syllable "port" has the Latin derivation "portare" which means "to carry something"; the second, "foglio", means "leaf". It is not surprising that there are multiple portfolio assessments known. Thomas Häcker, who is critically and constructively involved in the current portfolio discussion in Germany, sees self-reflection (Häcker (b) 177) as an elementary educational task and a key element in portfolio work.

---

3   The dissertation project by Christina Inthoff is part of the interdisciplinary research group in the Creative Unit: "Subject-Specific Learning Processes in Transformation (FaBiT)" at the University of Bremen, supervised by Prof. Dr. Maria Peters.

The four letters of the KEPP refer to defining reference fields of the KEPP concept. The term *artistic* allows references to art; for example, to the theme of the artist's book, as well as references to artistic strategies and forms, and to the context of artistic research. *Experimental* describes the exploratory access and handling of the KEPP as an envisioned opportunity space and suggests an open and research-oriented teaching. The object KEPP cannot be equated with a 'beautiful book', because it also deliberately allows inadequate, sometimes silly or seemingly failed contents and actions. In the art lessons, the students are involved in an artistic research process. They are confronted with different strategies and themes that not only artists work with. The themes are from very different disciplines, for example society, ecology or politics. The strategies – such as observing, collecting and arranging – are known from science or daily life. Artistic research differs from research in science or daily life, as its aim is not to find a specific answer or solution to a problem. Artistic research as a learning process in art lessons tries to achieve the goal of **finding problems and connecting them with oneself in an artistic way.** The competence of "Seeing defects, seeing the odd, the unusual . . ." (Torrance 16) is called **problem sensitivity**. It is described in Torrance's theory of creativity. Problem sensitivity in the context of education can be described as a higher perception of the environment, the ability of self-reflection and multidimensional thinking. In art lessons, this may include the need for visualization and collaborative acting. In a game between truth and fiction, and meaning and non-meaning, it can be seen that there is no contradiction between a productive indeterminacy in the aesthetic experience process and the formation of problematisation competence.

The focus on process requires tasks that do not require a specific result. Instead, pupils draw attention to the course of artistic-creative actions and promote reflection on the documentation and transformation of decisions and experiences. The term *portfolio* frames the references of artistic and experimental processes, and links these with specific practices of collaboration and reflection in art lessons (see Peters and Inthoff 113). In this way, the KEPP could be considered as being a further development of previous documentary practices used in art teaching, e.g. sketchbooks, pictorial diaries or workshop books (see Burkhardt 7).

The KEPP is an object of the lesson. It aims at being integrated into the lessons at different levels (object levels, pupil level, meta-level) and at different times (pre-actional, actional, post-actional). The KEPP conception, in particular, its recursiveness in the repetitive execution of individual phases (see Csikszentmihalyi 121), is linked to the creative process. In the sense of "experience-accompanying records" (Sabisch 5), perception and action are not simply documented, but constituted as experience only in the process of sign-based reflection and communication. Reflective entries in the sense of "world-wide practices" (Badura and Hedinger 31) can promote and support the perceptions, expressions and reflections of pupils (see Inthoff and Peters 61). Any entry can already be interpreted as a response to an existing resonance and at the same time be regarded as a further product to be processed in the artistic research process.

In the conception of teaching with the KEPP, the features of performativity and interactivity, among others, are thought to help to perceive, communicate, evaluate and critically investigate thought processes. In addition to individual production and reflection, collaborative processes developed through the cooperation of pupils must be considered. Thus, an intersubjective exchange, the problematisation and joint negotiation of meaning in the socio-cultural fabric are considered to be productive in the KEPP (see Stein 70).

Works Cited

Aden, Maike, and Peters, Maria. "Chancen und Risiken einer kompetenzorientierten Kunstpädagogik." *Zeitschrift Kunst Medien Bildung (zkmb)*, 2012, www.zkmb.de/index.php?id=78- . Accessed 6 December 2015.

Badura, Jens, and Hedinger, Johannes . "Sinn und Sinnlichkeit." *What's Next? Kunst nach der Krise; ein Reader*, edited by Johannes Hedinger and Torsten Meyer, Kadmos, 2013, pp. 31–35.

Bering, Kunibert, and Niehoff, Rolf. *Bildkompetenz. Eine kunstdidaktische Perspektive*. Athena-Verlag, 2013.

Blohm, Manfred. "Bildkompetenzen und Kunstunterricht. Überlegungen zu Fragen von Bildungsstandards und Bildkompetenzen." *BDK-Mitteilungen*, no. 4, 2009, pp. 2–5.

Burkhardt, Sara. "Portfolios im Kunstunterricht. Arbeitsprozesse dokumentieren und reflektieren." *Kunst+Unterricht*, no. 379/380, 2014, pp. 4–13.

Csikszentmihalyi, Mihaly. *Kreativität. Wie Sie das Unmögliche schaffen und Ihre Grenzen überwinden*. Klett-Cotta, 2007.

Dombois, Florian. "Kunst als Forschung. Ein Versuch, sich selbst eine Anleitung zu entwerfen." *Hochschule der Künste Bern HKB*, 2006, pp. 21–29.

Eremjan, Inga. *Transkulturelle Kunstvermittlung. Zum Bildungsgehalt ästhetisch-künstlerischer Praxen*. Transkript, 2016.

Grünewald, Dietrich, and Sowa, Hubert. "Künstlerische Basiskompetenzen und ästhetisches Surplus. Zum Problem der Standardisierung von künstlerisch-ästhetischer Bildung." *Kunstpädagogik im Projekt der allgemeinen Bildung*, edited by Johannes Kirschenmann, et al., kopaed, 2006, pp. 286–313.

Häcker, Thomas (a). *Portfolio: ein Entwicklungsinstrument für selbstbestimmtes Lernen. Eine explorative Studie zur Arbeit mit Portfolios in der Sekundarstufe I.* Schneider Verlag Hohengehren, 2007.

Häcker, Thomas (b). "Portfolio revisited. Über Grenzen und Möglichkeiten eines viel versprechenden Konzepts." *Kontrolle und Selbstkontrolle. Zur Ambivalenz von E-Portfolios in Bildungsprozesse,* edited by Torsten Meyer et al., VS Verlag für Sozialwissenschaften, 2011, pp. 161–183.

Inthoff, Christina. "Reflexive Aufzeichnungspraxen im künstlerisch-experimentellen Prozessportfolio – KEPP. Kunstpädagogische Perspektiven auf eine Lernkultur der Diversität." *Making Change Happen. Wandel im Fachunterricht analysieren und gestalten,* edited by Sabine Doff, and Regine Komoss, Springer Verlag, pp. 57–62.

Inthoff, Christina, and Peters, Maria. "Impulse zur Aufzeichnung und Reflexion. Das künstlerisch-experimentelle Prozessportfolio (KEPP)." *Kunst+Unterricht,* no. 379/380, 2014, pp. 60–64.

Kämpf-Jansen, Helga. *Ästhetische Forschung. Wege durch Alltag, Kunst und Wissenschaft; zu einem innovativen Konzept ästhetischer Bildung.* Salon Verlag, 2000.

Keuchel, Susanne. "Diversität, Globalisierung und Individualisierung. Zur möglichen Notwendigkeit einer Neuorientierung in der Kulturpädagogik." *Diversität in der Kulturellen Bildung,* edited by Susanne Keuchel and Viola Kelb, Transkript Verlag, 2015, pp. 37–57.

Kirchner, Constanze. *Kunstunterricht. Kompetent im Unterricht der Grundschule.* Schneider Verlag Hohengehren, 2012.

Kirschenmann, Johannes. "Reden über Kunst. Bildungstheoretische Begründungen und kunstpädagogische Positionen." *Reden über Kunst, Fachdidaktisches Forschungssymposium in Literatur, Kunst und Musik,* edited by Johannes Kirschenmann, et al., Spinner, kopaed Verlag, 2011, pp. 225–244.

Klieme, Eckhard et al. *Zur Entwicklung nationaler Bildungsstandards.* Bildungsforschung, 1, 2007/2009.

Klieme, Eckhard, and Leutner, Detlev. "Kompetenzmodelle zur Erfassung individueller Lernergebnisse und zur Bilanzierung von Bildungsprozessen. Beschreibung eines neu eingerichteten Schwerpunktprogramms der DFG." *Zeitschrift für Pädagogik,* vol. 52, no. 6, 2006, pp. 876–903.

Kraus, Anja. "Zur Beziehung von Kompetenz und Performanz. Eine Herausforderung für die Schulentwicklung." *Kunstpädagogik im Kontext von Ganztagsbildung und Sozialraumorientierung. Zu einer strukturellen Partizipation in der kunstpädagogischen Praxis,* edited by Ulrike Stutz, kopaed Verlag, 2012, pp. 146–158.

Lindström, Lars. "Creativity: What Is It? Can You Assess It? Can It Be Taught?" *International Journal of Art & Design Education*, vol. 25, no. 1, 2006, pp. 53–66. <http://onlinelibrary.wiley.com/doi/10.1111/j.1476-8070.2006.00468.x/abstract>. Accessed 2 November 2015.

Lutz-Sterzenbach, Barbara, et al. (a) "Nürnberg-Paper 2013: Interkultur – Globalität – Diversity. Leitlinien und Handlungsempfehlungen für eine transkulturelle Kunstpädagogik". 2013. <http://www.fk16.tu-dortmund.de/kunst/cms/assets/files/SOMMER_2-0-1-3/Nuernberg-Paper%202013%20neu_02.pdf>. Accessed 4 February 2016.

Lutz-Sterzenbach, Barbara, et al. (b) "Remix der Bildkultur – Remix der Lebenswelten. Baustellen für eine transkulturelle Kunstpädagogik." *Bildwelten remixed. Transkultur, Globalität, Diversity in kunstpädagogischen Felder*, edited by Barbara Lutz-Sterzenbach, et al., Transkript Verlag, 2013, pp. 3–23.

Maset, Pierangelo, and Hallmann, Kerstin. "Formate der Kunstvermittlung." 2016 <http://kunst.erzwiss.uni-hamburg.de/ful-home/blog/?paged=2>, Accessed 25 November 2016.

Nohl, Arnd-Michael. "Bildung, Kultur und die Mehrdimensionalität kollektiver Zugehörigkeiten." *Bildwelten remixed. Transkultur, Globalität, Diversity in kunstpädagogischen Feldern*, edited by Barbara Lutz-Sterzenbach, et al., Transkript Verlag, 2013, pp. 37–52.

Otto, Gunter. "Ästhetik als Performance – Unterricht als Performance?" *Schreiben auf Wasser. Performative Verfahren in Kunst, Wissenschaft und Bildung*, edited by Hanne Seitz, Klartext, 1999, pp. 197–202.

Peters, Maria and Inthoff, Christina. "Kompetenzorientierung im Kunstunterricht." *Die Entwicklung kompetenzorientierten Unterrichts in Zusammenarbeit von Forschung und Schulpraxis. Komdif und der Hamburger Schulversuch alles»könner*, edited by Ute Harms, et al., Waxmann, 2016, pp. 101–125.

Peez, Georg. *Art Education in Germany*. Waxmann, 2015.

Sabisch, Andrea. "Aufzeichnung und ästhetische Erfahrung." Edited by Karl-Josef Pazzini et al., Hamburg, 2009. <http://hup.sub.uni-hamburg.de/volltexte/2009/90/pdf/HamburgUP_KPP20_Sabisch.pdf>. Accessed 29 December 2015.

Seydel, Fritz. "Kompetenzfach Kunst: Zu einem Reizwort im aktuellen kunstpädagogischen Diskurs." *BDK-Mitteilungen*, no. 2, 2007, pp. 6–10.

Spelsberg, Karoline. *Diversität als Leitmotiv. Handlungsempfehlungen für eine diversitäts- und kompetenzorientierte Didaktik. [Eine explorative Studie im Kontext einer Kunst- und Musikhochschule]*, Münster, 2013.

Stein, Morris J. "Kreativität und Kultur [1953]." *Kreativitätsforschung*, edited by Gisela Ulmann, Kiepenheuer & Witsch, 1973, pp. 65–75.

Torrance, E. Paul. *Guiding Creativite Talent*. Prentice Hall, 1962.

Thomas, R. R. *Redefining Diversity*. American Management Association, 1996.

Trunk, Wiebke. "Räume für transkulturelle Diversität und Dissens in der Kunstvermittlung." *revisit. Kunstpädagogische Handlungsfelder teilhaben, kooperieren, transformieren*, edited by Andreas Brenne, et al., kopaed, 2012, pp. 213–224.

Wagner, Ernst. "Aufgaben, Bildungsstandards, Kompetenzen. Versuch einer Klärung der Begriffsvielfalt." *Kunst+Unterricht, no.* 341, 2010, pp. 4–13.

Weinert, Franz E. *Leistungsmessungen in Schulen*. Beltz Verlag, 2001.

Wulf, Christoph, and Zirfas, Jörg. "Bildung als performativer Prozess – ein neuer Fokus erziehungswissenschaftlicher Forschung." *Bildung über die Lebenszeit*, edited by Reinhard Fatke, and Hans Merkens, Verlag für Sozialwissenschaften, 2006, pp. 291–301.

Zumbansen, Lars. "Strukturbilder. Erkenntnismittel im Kunstunterricht." *Kunst+Unterricht, no.* 376, 2013, pp. 4–11.

Stela Maris Ferrarese Capettini[1]

Cultural, Ethnic and Gender Diversity in the School Playground[2]

Abstract: In the primary school, the playground is a social space in which different ethnic[3], national[4] and gender identities converge. Reality is not static but dynamic, developing with the interaction of the participants, who in this investigation are girls and boys of different cultural backgrounds in the context of school breaks. According to Hegel (1966), the entirety of that which is observed is the truth constituted by each unity. In our investigation, that entirety is constituted by the unities of game, culture and gender, in the social context of class breaks. These unities assist in answering our questions. School is created by society, which also gives the space for playing games a social connotation that accordingly reflects societal behaviors. Class breaks are a part of relational life, where each participant brings the reality that she or he experiences outside the school playgrounds; therefore, when doing our research, we also take into account the social problems that exist beyond this space. We have focused on the games played by girls and boys aged 5 and 9 years old, also observing their interaction with each other and comparing their relationships to each other in kindergarten with their relationships to each other in primary school. The settings for this research are several public primary schools in Neuquén, Argentina. We have analyzed the reasons that create differences in human relations and the influence that an archaic occidental structure, which tends to establish cultural and gender prejudices, can have on differentiated evolution. This influence has also been observed in the construction of human relations in the school patio, where obsolete urban norms are still followed.

Multi-Ethnicity and Society

Argentina is a modern state that encompasses a multiplicity of ethnic identities (original and migrant towns) thus forming a multi-ethnic and multicultural society. This society is divided by social classes according to economical income. This gives rise to the emergence of two identities: the national identity and the

---

1 Ph.D. Candidate in Human and Social Sciences. Founder of *Allel Kuzen, Museo del Juguete Étnico* (Museum of Ethnic Toys) in Neuquen, Argentina. Website: www.museo deljugueteetnico.com.
2 Translated from the Spanish by Lara Rodríguez Sieweke.
3 Mapuche, Tehuelche, Aimara, Romany, etc.
4 Argentinian, Chilean, Bolivian, Paraguayan, Dominican, Venezuelan.

social class identity. However, ethnicity gives way to an ethnic identity, which runs alongside the previously mentioned ones. For Nair (2006), identity

> is precisely the nucleus of all culturalism, we know little that is certain about how individual as well as collective identities function. It is enough to say that it corresponds to something very deep, whose ability to function is more or less similar to religious faith, that is, something that has to do with the sacred, with authenticity, with the essential. But in any case, it would be an error to underestimate the extraordinary power of mobilization and of emotion, contained in identitarianism. The power of identity is unlimited. . . . Well do those who fight for national or cultural recognition know this; well do those who watch their identity being denied by a collective experience this. . . . It also has multiple dynamics. Often it acts as a differentialist negation, an ontological separation of the other from myself, in society, in humanity. Reduction and separation, which generate what Freud calls "the narcissism of small differences", in the end, lead to a hierarchizing of possessions, of culture, of human beings.

> es precisamente el núcleo de todo culturalismo, sabemos poco, a ciencia cierta, acerca de cómo funciona la identidad tanto individual como colectiva. Basta con decir que corresponde a algo muy profundo, cuyo funcionamiento es más o menos parecido a la creencia religiosa, es decir, algo que tiene que ver con lo sagrado, con la autenticidad, con lo esencial. Pero, en todo caso, sería un error subestimar el extraordinario poder de movilización, de emoción, contenido en el identitarismo. El poder de la identidad es ilimitado. . . . Bien lo saben los pueblos que luchan para su reconocimiento nacional o cultural; bien lo experimentan los que se ven negados a su identidad dentro de una colectividad dada. . . . también tiene dinámicas múltiples. A menudo, actúa como una negación diferencialista, una separación ontológica del otro en mí, en la sociedad, en la humanidad. Reducción y separación que genera lo que Freud llama "el narcisismo de las pequeñas diferencias" y que, al fin y al cabo, desemboca en una jerarquización entre las pertenencias, la cultura, los seres humanos. (21–22)[5]

The Game and Its Historical Background

The human being has been creating games since primordial times. In the multicultural society, the act of playing keeps being practiced, even though perhaps not all games are in force, especially the games that represent the identities of all the ethnic identities present in a society. It is possible that some games have dominated or absorbed other games.

Children play and create games utilizing elements from their immediate surroundings. "Each culture is molded from the ground in which it grows and from the products with which it interacts; that is to say, the environment" ("Cada cultura está moldeada por el suelo en que crece y por los productos de éste con que se

---

5   The translations of all the quotations have been made by Lara Rodríguez Sieweke.

desenvuelve; es decir, por el medio ambiente"; Thompson, Eric qtd. in Roldan, Julio; 11). Currently, in the cities, we find objects that are external to one's own ethnic culture in the form of toys that are imposed by the market. Through this medium, a way of life emerges which is different to the life lived in rural areas, where these objects are not yet present in the majority of places.

In some societies with religious tradition, in certain moments of their development, girls and boys along with women were mere spectators of the action that had been forbidden to them as a game-rite or practiced sport, but that at the same time formed part of the communicational action in which the player achieved a state of ecstasy so as to generate a communication with the gods, with the Great Beyond, in order to reorganize the everyday world which had been disordered due to man's disobedience to the gods.

The children in the contemporary world of games live in a historical period that is different to the one just described. The change in sociocultural conditions has established that the religious should be unified in one sole God who is distributed into the different current religious beliefs. New ludic roles were established for women of different ages, as well as for male children, who enjoy a positive change upon entering the male ludic world. This world is one that has been forbidden to girls in their sociocultural role, and that dilutes the game as a mythical-ritual communicational element, which is replaced by other quotidian rites in occidental adult life. However, there are also societies that have persisted in maintaining their ludic tradition.

Since primordial times, in the majority of societies, games have been divided into gender, the man being the one who plays throughout all of his life and the woman being the one who is isolated from the game from an early age due to archaic social structures that exclude her from this activity. These structures are determined by biological reasons (menstruation) and social reasons (to behave like a lady, not to dirty herself, to pay attention to hygiene, etc.) while the opposite is allowed for males. According to Lorena Angulo Aranciba (3):

> Man and woman are differentially socialized. Activities, functions, behaviors, feelings, attitudes and even values that are not only different but in many cases, opposite, are expected from both sexes. The internalization of those models (with a basis on reward – punishment) achieves the aim of social control over the masculine self and his activities. Men and women who have been socialized discriminatorily in all the systems that they participate in since their birth, generate completely stereotypical masculine and feminine identities, which allow for an ideological reproduction of those models of "being" and "acting", making invisible (even for the protagonists) the inequities, discriminations and exclusions.

Hombre y mujer son socializados diferencialmente. Se espera de ambas actividades, funciones, comportamientos, sentimientos, actitudes y aún valores no sólo diferentes sino, en muchos casos, opuestos. La internalización de esos modelos (con base en premio – castigo) logra el objetivo de control social sobre el ser y quehacer masculino. Hombres y mujeres socializados discriminatoriamente en todos los sistemas en los cuales participan desde su nacimiento, generan identidades masculinas y femeninas incompletas y estereotipadas, las cuales permiten la reproducción ideológica de los modelos de "ser" y "actuar", haciendo invisible (aún para los propios o propias protagonistas) las inequidades, discriminaciones y exclusiones.

Furthermore, Angulo Aranciba adds:

Progressively, the masculine roles acquired such power that they relegated, up until today, all the activities of women to the background, and in fact, to a subordinate level. Subordination supposes obedience, submission, acceptance, loss of identity and of decision as a person. Acceptance of authority, the rules and the sanctions, were deserved by the woman for being a woman.

Progresivamente los roles masculinos fueron adquiriendo un poder tal que relegó, hasta nuestros días, toda la actividad de la mujer a un segundo plano, y de hecho a un plano subordinado. Subordinación que suponía obediencia, sumisión, aceptación, pérdida de identidad y de decisión como persona. Aceptación de la autoridad, las reglas y las sanciones a que se merecía la mujer por ser tal.

These aspects, which have been perpetuated in education throughout different historical periods, even prevailing today, impede the personal development of women, thus depriving the world of half of human experience.

Games, Culture and Identity

Men and women play games using elements found in their surroundings as well as elements found in the sociocultural group that constructs their identity. Currently, in the multicultural society, different foreign objects such as commercialized toys, influence the construction of an own cultural identity.

In the particular case of ethnically differentiated children who live in the urban centers of Argentina and coincide in public primary schools that belong to the national educative system, games are an important part of life. Among these games, we can find those that come from an own ancestral tradition, as well as those of occidental origin, whose creation is often induced by television and other electronic media such as computers and cellphones. Both sexes realize some games separately and some games together. Claude Zaidman (qtd. by Julia Delalande, 57), in his investigation about coeducation in the primary school, brings up the sexual

---

differences found in games by presenting the point of view of a teacher who uses the terms 'less' and 'small' to describe the game-playing of girls.

We are discussing the maintenance or loss of an own culture; the assumption or rejection of the foreign, as with Bonfil's (44) theory of cultural control; and the maintenance or modification of social structures. In Argentinian schools, physical education classes are no longer coeducational from the ages of 8 or 9. In this way, a classification and separation in the classroom in terms of sex is initiated, indicating, with no scientific proof that supports such segregation, a difference in "strength", "interests", "potential for initiation in sports", etc. This segregation is not the result of the capriciousness of physical education teachers; rather, it is the result of androcentric, ancestral human relational structures.

To Analyze with a Focus on Gender

To speak of gender is to analyze the sexual division in human activities. This division is more of a sociocultural construction than a biological one. It is important, according to Natalie Zemon Davis (1975) as quoted in Joan W. Scott, to observe the roles of men and women throughout the different periods: "It seems to me that we should be interested in the history of both men and women. . . . Our goal is to discover the range in sex roles and in sexual symbolism in different societies and periods, to find out what meaning they had and how they functioned to maintain the social order or to promote its change" (1054).

Sexual identity starts to develop at birth, basing itself on the primary relation the girl or boy has with her or his family, and on the set of codes that form an individual's symbolic imagination. Each person forms an image of her or his self, and of what it means to be a woman or a man. In this same process, the families assign roles with regard to family and labor. It is "normal" to observe that a girl, from early childhood, is delegated tasks that have to do with collaborating with her mother. On the other hand, the boy is usually assigned errands that have to do with cleaning the car, cutting the grass, etc. A change of roles is often socially frowned upon. Girls and boys learn these roles and these imposed and heavily charged concepts of masculinity and femininity, and this leads to the castration of certain roles. Thus it would be difficult, in childhood, for a woman to develop knowledge related to automobile care and for a man to develop culinary skills or other skills seen as feminine. A transgression of these typical duties would lead to teasing and stereotyped expressions, to the boy being called a "little woman" and the girl a "tomboy", terms that are still heard in determined social and family environments.

Something similar can be observed in the practice of certain games, some of which are set up to be practiced exclusively by boys (for example, balls) or girls (jumping rope).

The ways that children are raised differ in each culture and it is thus no simple task to establish universal norms for upbringing and learning. Although we are all born with the same biological structures, it is culture that determines the patterns of culture and conduct.

The Romany girls in the observed setting are considered – even currently, by many family groups – to be an important element of procreation; thus, these girls traditionally only attend primary school to learn to read and write, often abandoning school in the fifth grade. The Mapuche girls, on the other hand, complete all the grades in primary school, many of them going on to complete high school and university studies.

The Argentinian School System and the Relation between Ethnically Differentiated Children

School is a social institution that has been created partly by society, to fulfill a role that society itself has predetermined. Revising one's own experience, perhaps one can observe the non-existence of heterogeneity, the preponderance of homogenization, and the punishment that is meted out to 'the different' (a term we use in relation to the girls and boys who did not fulfill all those scholarly norms of behavior as well as the preference or non-preference that is given to children based on their economic backgrounds or facial features).

This is a relational space that combines cultural elements, each person's own house norms, and the pre-established rules, all of which are validated by said institution. The classroom tasks and activities are not always appreciated by all the students. The ages dealt with in our study, 5 and 9 years old, are periods of high ludic interest, especially at age 5. Due to this, the school environment – whether it is kindergarten or primary school – should consider the practice of playing in relation to school work, especially regarding the 5-year-old children who currently learn to read and write in order to enter primary school at age 6. This tends to cause serious emotional problems due to the inhibition of spontaneous playing and the decrease of time allotted to this activity, which is highly important for this age. We do not question the topic of literacy, as it is not in our area of investigation. We only analyze the human practice of playing, in both sexes, at specific ages, during the class recess or break.

Games, Gender, and School Breaks

The school break space is not a socially neutral environment, as girls and boys are generally not together. The geographical division that develops in this space is divided by sexes, especially if there are spaces allotted to several football fields to be used from grades 1 to 7. This space thus opposes the classroom space, which is a socially and spatially neutral environment in which both sexes interact and where the student body is divided into mixed groups.

The abovementioned sociocultural construction of the role of a girl, through historical processes in our societies, extends itself to the area of school breaks and the domain of games. The curricula of subjects like physical education (in coeducational schools) have always and solely been constructed from a masculine perspective instead of from a perspective that takes into account both sexes. This construction is still in force today.

The current times are defined by a marked human hedonism, which could indicate that the ludic and relational aspects of communication that afford pleasure to the human being, such as games, sports activities, living together, etc. would have the possibility to strongly develop from a perspective of gender equality. However, this is not what occurs when we observe the day-to-day development of social life. On the contrary, it seems as if life would orient itself via channels that attempt to depersonalize and alienate the human connection, instead increasingly encouraging this connection to participate in the consumerist functions and artificial dimensions that are typical for this contradictory type of society.

The Presence of Archaic Misogynist Structures in the Games Realized in the School Breaks

According to Mónica García Frinchaboy, the discrimination of girls in the school environment has a sexist character that is reflected by society's leaders (37). Furthermore, she adds that sexism can be found in schools when they manifest their interiorizing of girls, given that

> didactic subjects that resort to polarized and hierarchized sexual stereotypes, offering identifying models, when the curriculum, in an androcentric way, situates the male human as the only valid observer of reality; when some students are treated managerially taking into account stereotyped conceptions of the feminine and the masculine; ... when male students are thought of as active, intelligent, concrete, restless, while the girls are thought of as tidy, perseverant, obedient and studious, a stereotyped conception of what men and women in schools are like is not only *shown* but is *surely* in consequence acted upon.

materiales didácticos recurren a estereotipos sexuales polarizados y jerarquizados, ofreciendo modelos identificatorios, cuando el currículum, *androcéntricamente,* coloca al ser humano varón como único observador válido de la realidad; cuando alumnas y alumnos son tratados de gerencialmente sobre la base de concepciones estereotipadas de lo femenino y lo masculino . . . cuando se piensa que los alumnos son activos, inteligentes, concretos, inquietos, mientras que las alumnas son prolijas, perseverantes, obedientes y estudiosas, no sólo se *muestra* una concepción estereotipada de cómo son varones y mujeres en la escuela, sino que *seguramente* se actúa en consecuencia. (37)

A Study on Cultural, Ethnic and Gender Diversity in a School Playground

The subjects of this investigation are 5- and 9-year-old girls and boys who are of Mapuche, Romany and Occidental descent, encompassing this way the European and Oriental lineages that will be discussed in this study. These children, who go to schools in different neighborhoods of the city of Neuquén, Argentina, have been observed in terms of their mutual interaction in the school space that is denominated as a recess or class break space. In a multi-ethnic and multicultural society that has conservative organizational structures that help maintain social prejudices on skin color, ethnicity and gender, thoughts are ritualized according to modern structures of competition, consumerism, hedonism and marked individualism.

The public primary schools that constitute this study are: a) Escuela Primaria Común (Common Primary School) Nº 67 of the Mariano Moreno neighborhood during the afternoon shift: The Romany population of this school is 54% and the Argentinian Occidental population is represented by 46%. b) Escuela Primaria 118 of the neighborhood Villa Farrel during the afternoon shift: This school has a 15 % representation of Romany folk, the rest of the children being of Occidental Argentinian descent. c) Escuela Primaria Común Nº 56 of the Belgrano neighborhood, observed during the morning and afternoon periods, has a 12% Romany population and the rest, as with the other schools, Occidental Argentinian. d) Escuela Primaria Común Nº 312, 311 y 347 from the neighborhoods Toma Esfuerzo and Gran Neuquén Norte, afternoon shift: Here, the Mapuche population is 23%, the rest being of Occidental backgrounds.[6] e) Escuela Primaria Común Nº 125 of the neigborhood Área Centro has an Occidental Argentinian population.

In this study, we have used the concepts of ethnic identity for the groups, each group possessing defined and differentiated patterns of ethnic culture. Therefore, we can point to the concept of "being Mapuche" (Ferrarese *El juego como el proceso de*

---

6   That is to say, descendants of Europeans (even third or fourth generation descendants) who have an Argentinian nationality.

elaboración de identidad 10–11) when taking into account a subject whose mother and/or father are of Mapuche origin. Said parents either possess one or two Mapuche last names or have a Spanish last name acquired in some cases during the "conquest of the desert". They either live in the rural area or live in towns or cities in the province, identifying themselves as being Mapuche based on their physical features and sociocultural characteristics (in some cases). There are cases in which this identification is made with a good level of self-esteem; however, other times this identity is denied. We can also relate this to the concept of "being Romany".

The characteristics of 5-year-old girls and boys[7] are marked in general by periods of brief attention. A process of socialization that runs parallel to the practice of games gives rise to a difficulty in sharing toys and games with other children. It is possible that a child's toy is confiscated due to a child's not wanting to share it; however, this is not indicative of a selfish child but rather of an age-related period of the child's development. They enjoy looking at picture books, and like being able to create stories. They have high energy levels and develop activity in the major muscle groups. The fine motor skills begin to develop. They usually are curious and they like to explore the physical world; at the same time, in this progress towards separation and independence, they need strong emotional support from their families. Their curiosity is insatiable as is their desire to discover things. They are generally always active but they are easily exhausted and irritated during periods of repose. They enjoy conversing and collaborating in the house and in the living room, and even though they do not like losing, they are able to participate in social games. They enjoy running but they also enjoy activities such as drawing and painting.

Girls and boys aged 9 are in the stage of forming groups of friends. They acquire a moral conscience and a scale of values that should serve as a guide of conduct. They develop a sort of personal independence, being capable of taking initiative, planning and acting without continual parental supervision. They acquire physical abilities that allow them to practice shared games. Society requires them to develop the role that is expected of them according to their sex. There are some cases in which physical education classes separate girls and boys in the class, implying that girls do not have the same capacity for development that boys have.

These general identifications in both of the discussed ages have cultural particularities depending on the different ethnic groups the subjects belong to. These

---

7   This observation is drawn from over 30 years of day-to-day work with school-aged children, following studies realized on how to teach while bearing in mind the childlike characteristics found in the different ages. I consider that these tables are only informatively useful because each human being is unique and therefore, in the act of teaching, one should take this uniqueness into consideration.

particularities tend to become more blurred in life lived in big cities as opposed to in rural communities.

In the schools that have been studied, the school breaks are immersed in the current times: 9-year-old girls and boys use mobile phones as toys (to play the games that they are equipped with) or as media to play music in. They are often used during class breaks, despite being forbidden in the classroom.

The girls do not play sports during the breaks in the observed schools, while the boys generally play football. One reason for this could be the lack of material for sports, and in the case of the boys, they often bring materials from their homes. Toys such as the jumping rope or the bands used for French skipping are usually borrowed by the physical education teachers or in some cases are brought from home by one of the female pupils. We have not found differentiated ethnic games of Romany and/or Mapuche origin during the school breaks. Romany and Mapuche children play the same games that the other children play.

The Romany girls do not use their traditional attire in school due to the prohibitions effectuated by the institutions, but they do wear them outside the school setting. In the case of the Mapuche girls, they use "foreign" clothing due to the centuries of cultural imposition and domination. In the case of the boys from both these ethnical groups, the differences in attire are less clear in their childhood.

In the beginner's level, the game playing habits of the 5 year olds are different because the game is a part of the day-to-day activities of this age group. Similarly, girls and boys enter this level with social patterns of ethnic, cultural and class-related discrimination that are inculcated by their families. Therefore, it is possible to observe that the choice of games can depend on ethnicity or socioeconomic class.

Works Cited

Altuve, Eloy. *Juego, historia, deporte y sociedad en América Latina*. Universidad de Zulia, 1997.

Angulo, Leonor "Discriminación y educación sexista dentro de la educación formal." *Actas V Congreso Argentino-Chileno de Estudios Históricos e Integración Regional*. Universidad Nacional de San Juan, 2003, pp. 34–40.

Bally, Gustav. *El juego como expresión de libertad*. Fondo de Cultura Económica.

Bennett, Neville, et al. *Teaching Through Play*. Buckingham Open University. 1997.

Brooker, Liz. "La primera infancia." *Perspectiva Nº 6*. The Open University, 2010, pp. 2–4.

Bonfil Batalla, Guillermo. "La teoría del Control Cultural en el estudio de los procesos étnicos." *Revista Papeles de la Casa Chata, Año 2 Nº3*, 1988, pp. 23–43.

Delalande, Julia. *La cour de récréation. Pour une anthropologie de l'enfance.* Presses Universitaires de Rennes, 2001.

Deleón Meléndez, Ofelia. "Mujer indígena y cultura popular tradicional protagonista en la conservación y transmisión (un planteamiento teórico y una propuesta de investigación desde una perspectiva de género)." *Tradiciones de Guatemala Nº 49.* Centros de estudios Folklóricos de la Universidad de Guatemala, 1998, pp. 1–15.

García Frinchaboy. "Iguales oportunidades." *Revista Monitor año 2 número 3,* Ministerio de Educación de la Nación, 2001, pp. 4–6.

Ferrarese Cappettini, Stela Maris. *El juego como el proceso de elaboración de la identidad: El caso de los niños Mapuches de la ciudad de Neuquén.* MA thesis, Universidad de La Frontera, 2000.

Ferrarese Cappettini, Stela Maris. *El juego de niñas y niños en las escuelas como dispositivo en el proceso de elaboración de la identidad étnico-cultural y de género.* Museo del Juguete Étnico, forthcoming.

Nair, Sami. *Diálogo de culturas e identidades.* Complutense, 2006.

Nedich, Jorge. *El pueblo rebelde. Crónica de la historia gitana.* Vergara, 2010.

Roldán, J.: *Estudio de los juegos de pelota del área de Dolores.* Universidad de Guatemala, 1995.

Scott, Joan W. "Gender: A Useful Category for Historical Analysis." *The American Historical Review,* vol. 91, issue 5, Dec. 1986, pp. 1053–1075. http://xroads.virgi nia.edu/~DRBR2/jscott.pdf. Accessed 1 April 2017.

Dolby, Nadine. "Research in Youth Culture and Policy: Current Conditions and Future Directions." *Social Work and Society: The International Online-Only Journal,* vol. 6, no. 2, 2008, www.socwork.net/sws/article/view/60/362. Accessed 20 May 2009.

Sinisi, Liliana. "La relación nosotros – otros en espacios escolares multiculturales" *Buenas Tareas,* http://www.buenastareas.com/ensayos/Liliana-Sinisi-La-Relaci%C3%B3n-Nosotros-Otros-En/2117167.html 10/05/2011. Accessed 23 Jan 2012.

.

Katja Böhme

Reflection and Attention: Considerations on The Importance of Perception in the Contexts of Pedagogical Reflection in Art Education

Abstract: The *reflection on pedagogical situations* is currently an important part of teacher education. With the implementation of the so-called "practical semester" (in Germany), the question of reflection is attracting more and more interest. During their six months of practical observation in a school, prospective teachers are required to approach pedagogical practice with a scientific attitude. The current debate about specific forms of reflection is thereby characterized by an understanding of reflection based primarily on terms such as measurability, overview knowledge, identification, and classification. By mainly following the paradigms of natural sciences and social research, one can observe a systematic marginalization of the reflective potential of individual and aesthetic perception. The unexpected, the non-visible, and the unavailable dimensions of pedagogical practice do not come into focus. From the perspective of educational philosophy and art education, the current understanding of reflection does not correspond with the main parameters of pedagogical practice, nor to particular aesthetic experiences. Pedagogical situations in art education seem to be an especially fruitful research field for posing the question of how students can reflect on unpredictability and singularity as constitutive dimensions of pedagogical practice. After giving an outline of the current understanding of reflection, in this article I will discuss attention and perception from a phenomenological point of view, viewing these concepts not only as methodical questions for reflective practices, but also as fundamental issues for a reflective approach to pedagogical situations. The following considerations are based on my Ph.D. project, in which I investigate the potential of photographic images for reflective processes in art education. Throughout the text I primarily explore two questions: Why is it relevant and fruitful, especially in art teacher education, to focus on attention as an explicit aspect of reflection? Also, how could it become possible to approach one's own attention? Though both questions are raised in the context of art education, the following considerations provide links to other fields of science and practice.

The View *on* the Other and the View *of* the Other – Reflecting on Art Pedagogical Practice

117 photographs are lying on a table. A university student[1] sitting next to me looks at them. The photographs were taken in an art lesson by the abovementioned student and by a pupil in the 10th grade. In my double role as university teacher and researcher, I am especially interested in the question of how students can reflect on questions concerning the pedagogical practice in art education.

The photographs are the result of a task I gave to the two photographers directly before the lesson started. I invited the 10th grade pupil to participate as usual in the class, and to take a photo whenever something attracted his attention. There was no specification of what exactly should be photographed. The pedagogy student was invited to accompany this pupil during the lesson, and to always take a picture whenever he took a picture. The pupil and the student were thus taking photos simultaneously. Both of them knew about the other's instructions and agreed with the format. It was not a secret observation; instead, it provoked interaction and agreement.

Back at the university, the photographs lie in front of us. Our gazes wander back and forth between the pupil's and the student's pictures. What is his point of focus, and what is hers? What is visible from the student's point of view, and what remains hidden from her view? During our conversation, the student assumes that the pupil's photographs show a specific interest in architecture. Step by step, we try to qualify her impression by putting the pictures in relation to one another. Once connected, the photographs begin to comment on each other.

To elucidate this process, I will give a very short example of how we connected the two perspectives:

The student takes a photo while standing behind the younger pupil, who is apparently also taking a photograph.

---

1   The student is studying art pedagogy at the Academy of Fine Arts in Münster, Germany. The situation, which is the subject of her reflection, took place within a cooperation project between the Academy of Fine Arts, the Art Hall, and the City Council in Münster, 09/2013-02/2014. More information under: http://www.bahnhofsv iertel-muenster.de/fileadmin/Dateien/Daten/10_06_Projektgruppe_Schaltschraenke/ Dokumentation_Schaltschraenke.pdf (01.12.16, p.13)

Fig.1: Student's photograph

The pupil is in a big room with white pillars in front of him. He holds the camera at eye level with both hands. What is in his field of view? The pillars in the foreground or the tripod in the background? From the student's point of view, it is not obvious. An enlargement of the pupil's camera display shows that one pillar is prominently and slightly crookedly placed on the left side of the picture.

Fig. 2: Detail of the student's photograph

His index finger is on the zoom regulator: He may be choosing a certain framing. When we look at the photograph the pupil takes 12 seconds later, one could be surprised: His image looks completely different than what could be expected based on the student's photograph and the enlarged display. The spatial depth is gone and has given way to a remarkable flatness. The pillars become abstract forms that are arranged very accurately. The surface quality reminds one of a painting. The texture of the pillars has a nearly material presence.

Fig. 3: Pupil's photograph

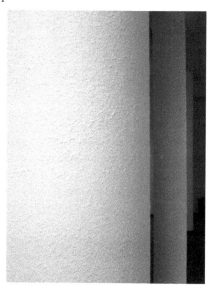

There is a significant difference between the student's and the pupil's photographs. The abstraction, the precise focusing of the camera, the graphic reduction, the visualization of materiality – everything present in the pupil's photograph – could not be guessed by only taking into account the student's perspective. The presumption that the pupil is interested in architecture only becomes perceptible by adding the pupil's photograph. Examining his photograph makes visible that he seems to be attracted by the possibility of designing and transforming the space into an image. The two perspectives (student and pupil) are not completely congruent. The student is attempting to relate her own view on the other to the view of the other. By putting the images side by side, the student can explore new aspects. The difference between the two images becomes the starting point for posing further questions and differentiating one's own presumptions.

(1) Change of Scene – Current Debates about Reflection in Pedagogical Situations

The scene above is part of my research project and directly embedded in current debates in teacher education that focus on developing and investigating possibilities for pedagogical reflection.

Today, "reflection" is a very popular term in German educational discourse. It is becoming a keyword in the debates about pedagogical professionalization, with Sabine Reh formulating in 2004 "professionalization through reflexivity" ("Professionalisierung durch Reflexivität"; my trans.; 358), and Walter Herzog emphasizing that "not technology, but *reflection* is the solution" ("Nicht Technologie, sondern Reflexion lautet das Losungswort"; my trans.; "Welche Wissenschaft für die Lehrerinnen- und Lehrerbildung?" 313). According to Herzog, practitioners need reflection especially in complex situations, in order to act flexibly on the bases of alternative interpretations.

Reflection is also becoming more and more important in teacher education programs, not least due to the implementation of the *Praxissemester* (practical semester). In this practical semester, teacher students spend a complete semester in a school, and are expected to approach pedagogical situations with a research attitude. *Forschendes Lernen* ("inquiry-based learning") has become a guiding concept for university didactics (see Fichten, Wildt). The *Praxissemester* is in this way a new element in German teacher education. In contrast to common internships, the students' stay is extended, which leads to different mentoring needs. University and school teachers cooperate in assisting the students. Seminars before, during and after the practical semester frame their stay in school. Students are required to teach as well as to observe lessons. Whereas specific concepts of coached teaching are already implemented in university didactics (in Berlin e.g. universities work with the concept of co-constructive teaching departing from Anneliese Kreis and Fritz C. Staub), there is still a lack of specific forms of observation and coached reflection (see e.g. Reh "Pädagogische Beobachtung. Pädagogische Beobachtungen machen – Lerngeschichten entwickeln" 65–82). This is an important gap because students spend an enormous amount of lesson time sitting in the background of classrooms and observing pedagogical situations. How students can approach a pedagogical situation with a research attitude is still an open question.

With the introduction of the practical semester, the transfer between institutions – university and school – has become one of the main challenges in teacher education nowadays. How can students be supported in finding fruitful connections between theory and practice (Kraus 28; Hascher 418–440); between teaching and researching; between biographical experiences and pedagogical expectations

(see Peez, Seydel); and – especially concerning art education – between aesthetic
and pedagogical practice (Engel "Gemeinsame und kreative Potenziale in Kunst
und Pädagogik."; Engel and Böhme; Hölscher; Wetzel and Lenk; Dreyer)?

In 1983, Howard B. Altmann came to a conclusion that has still not lost its
validity: "Teachers teach as they were taught, not as they were taught to teach"
(24). Over 30 years later, the mentioned link between university and school is
still a challenge. Reflection thus gains in importance as a meta-dimension of
pedagogical professionalization. Which forms of support are needed and which
specific research methods are practicable for students in practice? I will return to
this question later and outline concrete suggestions in paragraph 5.

The current interpretation of reflection is remarkable, especially from the perspective of art education. In the following paragraphs, I will outline some of the
main parameters of reflection. As Walter Herzog points out, the debate is extremely complex ("Reflexive Praktika in der Lehrerinnen- und Lehrerbildung" 253);
thus, I will focus on a few positions which help to characterize its basic aspects.

In 2012, Wolfgang Fichten published an article about inquiry-based learning
in teacher education. This highly regarded and extensive text gives an overview of
the discussions and presents a certain understanding of reflection within teacher
education:

> It is about a reflection of school practice guided by theory and based on research methods.
> If reflection is not only supposed to move within the horizon of one's own subjective
> assumptions and interpretive patterns, and if it is not just to "confirm" or double them,
> then reflection must rely on scientific knowledge.... Dewe/Radtke (155) have described
> this metaphorically; they suggest that scientific knowledge gives students "eyes which
> determine what the pedagogue sees in her/his field of activity, and what relevances she/
> he places in her/his field of action".
>
> Es geht um eine theoriegeleitete und forschungsmethodisch fundierte Reflexion der
> Schulpraxis (LK 2011, p. 8). Wenn Reflexion sich nicht im Horizont eigener subjektiver
> Annahmen, Deutungsmuster usw. bewegen und diese "bestätigen" bzw. quasi verdoppeln
> soll, ist sie auf wissenschaftliche Wissensbestände als Referenzpunkte angewiesen (vgl.
> Fichten 2005, p. 116). . . . Dewe/Radtke (1991, p. 155) haben dies metaphorisch schön
> umschrieben, indem sie ausführen, dass den Studierenden in der Ausbildung mit der
> Vermittlung wissenschaftlichen Wissens "Augen eingesetzt (werden), die darüber bestim-
> men, was der Pädagoge in seinem Tätigkeitsfeld sieht und welche Relevanzen er in seinem
> Handlungsfeld setzt". (my trans.; 8)

In this short excerpt, Fichten describes the connection between theory and pedagogical practice as the main basis of reflection. A successful and "well-founded"
reflection relies on "scientific knowledge" as an orientation and necessary "point
of reference." To avoid the trap of subjectivity (see also Wyss 74), students need
theory. Fichten refers to a metaphor from Dewe and Radtke in which science is

described as giving us the world to see. Fichten outlines an idea of reflection that is primarily guided by theory.

Another quotation that underlines a certain aspect of the current understanding of reflection can be found in an article by Vetter and Igrisani. A good reflective practice of teachers and students prevails when "on the basis of systematically captured data about pedagogical reality, [teachers and students can initiate] the development of pedagogical processes. Data and information thus become the basis for monitoring processes" ("auf der Basis systematisch erhobener Daten zur Unterrichtsrealität Entwicklungsprozesse für den Unterricht . . . initiieren [können]. Daten bzw. Informationen werden somit zur Grundlage für Steuerungsprozesse"; my trans.; 323).

Reflection is seen as successful when teachers can initiate pedagogical processes on the basis of systematically collected data. The quotation implies a causal relationship between systematically collected data and the arrangement of pedagogical practices. It furthermore suggests that comprehensive information about pedagogical "reality" is transferable to other situations. It is assumed that general knowledge leads to the development and improvement of pedagogical practice. In producing this kind of general knowledge, controlled distance and being able to "step out" of the pedagogical situation are seen as important parameters for valid reflection.

Approaching this interpretation of reflection from a different theoretical background allows us to examine it critically. The perspectives of educational philosophy and theory, for example, shed a completely different light on the current interpretation of reflection: Michael Wimmer, for example, argues that pedagogical practice cannot be understood by generalizing identifications. He says that generalizing identifications necessarily miss the complexity of pedagogical practice (*Pädagogik als Wissenschaft des Unmöglichen* 29). Considering this interpretation of reflection, Wimmer even fears "the exclusion of the different, the other and the alien" ("Exklusion des Differenten, Anderen, Fremden"; my trans.; 29).

Already in the 1960s, Maurice Merleau-Ponty wrote in the text *The Eye and the Mind*: "Science manipulates things and gives up living in them" (159). This is highly relevant in relation to the current interpretation of reflection. A science which gives up its closeness to its field creates an "opposite world," as Gottfried Böhm writes in reference to Merleau-Ponty ("Gegenüberwelt"; my trans.; 295). With more distance, we may be able to get an overview, but we have to pay the price of being excluded.

Closeness, proximity, and involvement are all terms rarely discussed in the current debate about reflection. This is extraordinary, considering that pedagogical practice is based on interaction. The joint presence of different participants is fundamental for pedagogical situations. Thus, the question becomes: *What does general knowledge mean for a practice that is unpredictable, that is based on involvement, and that challenges spontaneous acting?*

Critical positions that consider different notions of reflection are still rare. Werner Helsper, a German educationalist, calls for a reflection that is focused on a single case ("Lehrerprofessionalität"; see also de Boer). The connection between casuistry and pedagogical professionalization is based on the assumption that "a practice which has to deal permanently with the individual understanding of the single case must itself be dealt with by research that also understands the case study as its starting point and object of scientific reconstruction." ("eine Praxis, die es unausgesetzt mit dem individuellen Fallverstehen zu tun hat, [müsste] eine Forschung nahe legen ... die ebenso den Fall als Ausgangspunkt und Gegenstand einer wissenschaftlichen Rekonstruktion begreift."; my trans.; ApaeK).[2]

In art education, similar intentions can be observed. Georg Peez has been investigating the meaning of case studies in the context of art teacher education for more than ten years. Partly in cooperation with his students of pedagogy, he also publishes case studies, for example in the book *Kunstpädagogik und Biografie.* During a seminar in 2003, his students conducted and analyzed narrative interviews with art teachers in school. Peez discusses reflection as a question of scientific research (21). Maria Peters and Ruth Kunz also work on the question of how students can be involved in a scientific approach to pedagogical questions.[3] Peters focuses on *Design-Based Research* as a methodological framing. This is a method to cyclically reflect on one's own acting by repeatedly trying and modifying a certain pedagogical design. Kunz supports students in developing so-called *Forschungsminiaturen* ("research miniatures"; my trans.), which are very small case studies based on empirical material and visualization fitted into the context of Kunz's own research field (134–139).

The reference to the single case is also an important issue for Birgit Engel, a German art educationalist. From a phenomenological perspective, she demonstrates

---

2 ApaeK is the name of an online archive with empirical material based on case studies. The material is freely available and provided by the Goethe University in Frankfurt a.M. The platform addresses university teachers, researchers and students. More information: www.apaek.uni-frankfurt.de/55817517/Idee-und-Konzeption-von-ApaeK (01.12.2016)

3 Their concepts were presented on the conference "Blinde Flecken" in Salzburg, Austria (13.-15.02.2015) under the title: "Fachdidaktische Entwicklungsforschung im Master of Art Education" (13.02.2015).

that sensitive reflection in pedagogical contexts depends on a position in the middle of the situation (see especially *Spürbare Bildung*). Intersubjectivity is a key word in her work and a main way of approaching the aesthetic aspects of pedagogical processes. Instead of focusing on the *empirical reconstruction* of a single case on the bases of qualitative research methods, she discusses the reflective potentials of one's own perception. In her seminars, Engel invites students to participate in experimental and playful situations. Together, they reflect on the experiences they have had and discuss their exemplary meaning for pedagogical situations. Thinking about questions of transfer between university and school are based on one's own experiences and the perception of a joint "presence" ("Gegenwärtigkeit"; my trans.; "Unbestimmtheit als kunstdidaktisches Movens in professionsbezogenen Bildungsprozessen" 81).

Andreas Gruschka, educational theorist, also has the single case in mind when he promotes non-verbal forms of reflection. He especially focuses on the dimensions of pedagogical practice that cannot be translated into language. According to him, pedagogical processes cannot be managed by textual understanding only. Beyond speech, pedagogical situations also have a tremendously important visual component. He proposes searching for specific types of documents that allow the consideration and inquiry of both visible and non-verbal dimensions of pedagogical practice (10).

Despite very different methods and methodologies, the common thread of the above-examined positions is their attention to the single case. Taking up this point of interest from the specific perspective of art teacher education, in this article I will outline some of the basic challenges of art pedagogical practice. What at first glance may look like a detour will deepen the examination of the connection between reflection and specific qualities of art pedagogical practice.

Reflection is a process of reference – to a certain situation, person, question, etc. To think about reflection cannot be decoupled from its subject. Additionally, thinking about reflection requires thinking about specific qualities of pedagogical practice.

My focus lies primarily on open and experimental situations in art education, because they can be especially challenging for novice university students and are often connected with discomfort and insecurity. Art teacher education must deal with this issue, because experimental and open situations are not only dimensions that have to be accepted by art teachers: They are furthermore the motivation and topic of art lessons. More than in other school subjects, uncertainty, unpredictability, and processual openness are especially constitutive for art educational practice (Pazzini 109).

(2) Contexts – Specific Challenges of Open and Experimental Situations

Pedagogical practice in general and open situations in art lessons in particular are characterized by unpredictability. Contrary to current debates in education policy, unpredictability remains a core component of art pedagogical practice (Pazzini).

Every pedagogical situation, no matter how precisely it has been planned in advance, entails the risk and the chance that the situation will develop differently than expected. Pedagogical practice is not a "one-man-show": It is a social situation in which several participants are involved. The process is the product – more or less – of a negotiation.

Michael Wimmer describes how pedagogical practice contains an unavoidable uncertainty ("Zerfall des Allgemeinen – Wiederkehr des Singulären" 425–428; *Pädagogik als Wissenschaft des Unmöglichen* 45–73). When working with pupils, teachers are permanently confronted with the non-visibility, opacity, and unavailability of the other. Teachers cannot know what their pupils think, what they are really interested in, or what they find relevant. This is a question of anticipation, not a question of knowledge. Wimmer creates the term "not-being-able-to-know" ("Nicht-Wissen-Können"; my trans.; 425) to describe a constitutive element of pedagogical practice. This kind of "not-knowing" cannot be solved by certain competencies or data. Quite the contrary: The acceptance of one's own blind spots is fundamental for a conscious contact with the other—beyond appropriation and making the other available. Werner Helsper finds different words for related phenomena: "Antinomies" describe the challenge teachers face when acting within paradoxical structures ("Antinomien des Lehrerhandelns in modernisierten pädagogischen Kulturen" 530–546).

These aspects are also relevant in art pedagogical discourses. In the last 5 years, the interplay between certainty and uncertainty has become subject of increasing debate. Publications such as *Curriculum des Unwägbaren* (Bilstein et al.; Bilstein et al.); *(Un)Vorhersehbares Lernen* (Busse); *Das Unverfügbare – Wunder, Wissen, Bildung* (Pazzini et al.); *Didaktische Logiken des Unbestimmten* (Engel and Böhme); and the research project "Kalkül und Kontingenz" (Schürch and Willenbacher ZHdK, Switzerland, 05/2013 – 10/2015) are representative for this discourse. In the abovementioned publications, art pedagogical practice is discussed in its ambivalence in terms of visibility and non-visibility, saying and showing, predictability and unpredictability, etc.

In open processes, pupils are challenged to explore the world, extend their horizons, and search for new interpretations of the already well-known. "Practices of performing, searching, improvising, experimenting, failing, trying, observing, researching, designing, rejecting, playing, criticising and shifting" ("Praktiken des Performativen, des Suchens, des Improvisierens, des Experimentierens, des Scheiterns, des Erprobens, des Beobachtens, des Forschens, des Konzipierens, des Verwerfens, des Spielens, des Kritisierens und Verschiebens"; my trans.; Engel and Böhme 20) are fundamentally important for the development and initiation of art pedagogical situations.

Didactical concepts in art pedagogy related to this include e.g. aesthetical research (Kämpf-Jansen), displacement (Brohl), mapping (Busse, Heil), artistic field research (Brenne) and so on.

The uncertainty which, in other contexts, is often assessed as a deficit has a different and more positive connotation in art pedagogical situations. Particularly the "gaps" (cf. Brohl) – that is to say, situations in which something is fundamentally unclear and open – bear the potential to shift routines and entrenched forms of perception and thinking. A temporary loss of orientation in an aesthetic process can offer the chance to rediscover the already well-known in an unexpected way (Engel and Böhme 17).

Open and experimental situations appear simultaneously with various forms of work. Depending on the specific assignment, pupils can work on different questions and topics; use different materials; and organise their time by themselves. Thus, the importance of individual coaching by the teacher increases in open situations. Open situations in art lessons contain remarkable dimensions of bodily and practical acting (see Peters). Besides verbal forms of communication, art pedagogical situations are based upon bodily movement, gestures, voice, sounds, touching and dealing with materials, space and so on (see also Engel "Gemeinsame und kreative Potenziale in Kunst und Pädagogik").

In open situations, performativity plays an important role. Sense is created the moment in which something is explored, in which an object is placed on a specific site, in which a view is shifting, or in which a pencil or something else is picked up. Continually new constellations of material, space, and participants emerge. This process is not a by-product or a failure, it is a necessary subject and mode of art pedagogical practice. I borrow the words of Bernhard Waldenfels: "[W]e encounter the ungraspable in the graspable, the unordered in the ordered, the invisible in the visible, the silent in the audible. ..." (*Phenomenology of the Alien* 5).

(3) What Does This Mean for Teachers and Students? Open Art Pedagogical Practice and Professionalization

This kind of practice forces teachers to be open to the specific dynamic of the situation. An article by Eva Sturm carries the wonderful title "With What Appears" ("Mit dem, was sich zeigt"; my trans.). From the perspective of art education,

Sturm focuses on a pedagogical practice which finds its starting point in the dialogue with the other – pedagogical practice that accepts and works with unpredictable and spontaneous twists. Sturm describes pedagogical practice in which a plan cannot be fixed. A plan is an orientation that must be readjusted or, if necessary, completely abandoned.

The aesthetic practices of pupils are partly visible and partly non-visible. Their movements in space, viewing direction, or spatial positioning in front of an artwork or in the context of an art performance are observable by others. These factors may indicate something about the perception, interest, or mood of the observed person. At the same time, however, a pupil's perceptions, experiences, memories, and associations cannot be observed completely. Effects occur that may not be possible to be described with language. According to Maria Peters, an excess of experience remains that cannot be merged with verbal identification and measurement (49–81). It is possible that meanings are hidden in the details; that they cannot be observed directly. At most, meanings might become perceptible in moments where the other is stuttering, in a hesitant gesture, or a lingering view.

What does this mean for reflection? When considering the unpredictability and uncertainty of pedagogical practice, whether or not reflection should target general knowledge is questionable. The mentioned ambiguities raise questions that point to a methodologically different direction: How can those moments be reflected on when they are barely perceptible to the teacher, appear unpredictable, and do not play on the main stage of the pedagogical situation? How can students be encouraged to be open for the emerging situations? How can they become more sensitive to performative aspects of art pedagogical processes?

In my eyes, these questions lead to fundamental shifts in the subjects as well as in the methods of reflection. Following Wimmer, thinking about pedagogical phenomena is not a question of knowing. Against the background of the specific challenges of art pedagogical situations, it seems to be a *question of perception*: Reflection has to enable practitioners to be aware of the present situation. Spoken from the perspective of the students: *Why does a specific aspect attract my attention while another one goes completely unnoticed? Does that mean that this aspect is more important than the other one?*

(4) Attention as an Explicit Topic of Reflection

In phenomenological theory, attention ("Aufmerksamkeit") is a fundamental term in contexts of epistemology and pedagogy. Waldenfels (*Grundmotive einer Phänomenologie des Fremden* 92–108), Meyer-Drawe ("Aufmerken. Eine phänomenolgische Studie") and Blumenberg understand attention as an interplay between "being attracted" and "referring intentionally to something." According to Waldenfels, attention occurs in "the double rhythm of becoming apparent and becoming attentive" (*Phenomenology of the Alien* 6). We notice something, our attention is caught, and we are attracted: What we perceive is not totally under our control (cf. Meyer-Drawe's "Aufmerken. Eine phänomenolgische Studie" 117–126). Especially in phenomenological theory, attention is discussed as a responsive occurrence. We are highly attracted by the unknown and the other because they can inspire curiosity and imagination. We focus on things that – individually – have an appeal ("Aufmerken. Eine phänomenolgische Studie" 125). Whether we like it or not, perception is at least partly directed by the situation itself. As Waldenfels says: It "comes towards us" (*Phenomenology of the Alien* 6).

Thus, the attempt to focus on attention as an explicit topic of reflection faces two basic problems:

I. Perception and attention are ephemeral processes. The moment in which we focus on our perception, our prior perceptions are already gone. There is a temporal rupture between perception and reflected perception (Peters 56). To reflect on one's own perception and attention confronts one with a certain distance. A reflected perception has a different quality. But how can one deal with this distance? How can one "regain" the initial perception (Peters 58)? Working with "memory images" ("Erinnerungsbilder"; my trans.; Engel *Spürbare Bildung* 173–179) is one possibility. Bringing perception to mind by invoking poetic descriptions is another (cf. Peters 145, 158–171; see also Wortelkamp 16–36, 41–42).

II. Another challenge is related to the specific ambivalence of attention: When something attracts our attention, it automatically obscures other parts of the situation (Meyer-Drawe "Aufmerken. Eine phänomenologische Studie" 130; Blumenberg 196). To focus on what has prominently left a trace is comparatively easy. But what about the moments that did not come into focus, or that even could not have been in focus? How can a teacher deal with his/her own blind spots? To make an effort to reflect on both sides of the same coin is important: Especially in art teacher education, an attention through which performative, liminal, and non-verbal aspects of a situation can come to one's mind, ears, and senses (cf. Waldenfels *Phenomenology of the Alien* 6) is needed. Thus, one must deal with both the obvious and the peripheral of perception.

In order to do this, materials are needed in which the processes of attention can leave their traces and inspire a reflection of perception. In light of the aforementioned methodological problems, I work with photography. In the following, I will return to the situation described at the beginning of the text, in which a student reflects on a certain situation in an art lesson on the basis of photographs. In several respects, photographs offer specific possibilities for students to initiate a self-reflective process and to focus on their attention.

(5) Approaching One's Own Perception by the Use of Photographic Images

Studies in the field of teacher education are confronted with the challenge of developing perspectives for basic research as well as for higher education didactics. In my study, reflection is a theoretical as well as a practical question. As a university teacher in art didactics, I work with students who are becoming art teachers. From my point of view, theoretical and practical questions merge. The short example at the beginning of the text exemplarily shows my interest in connecting theoretical research and practical development in the field of didactics. Supporting students in their reflections on certain pedagogical situations on the basis of photographs is the practical side of my research. The reflective potential of photographs revealed itself in 4 main aspects:

I. Photographs are Traces of Perception
According to the theory of Vilém Flusser, photographs are connected to the perspective and perception of the person who has taken the picture (Flusser 100–118). The photographic image shows something and at the same time, it is a trace and link to the photographer's perception/s. Photographs depend on movement in space and frequently on interaction with other people. Thus, looking at photographs confronts the viewer with questions of perception. In performing the described task, the student and the pupil are also the photographers. Photography is not an objective and disembodied eye; it can be interpreted as a trace of spontaneous attention and interaction with the pupil.

II. Photographs Produce a Visual Surplus
Even though Flusser understands photographs as individual gestures and traces, this does not mean that photographs show only those aspects that were intentionally perceived by the photographer. On the contrary, photographs contain a surplus of meaning. Something unexpected can appear suddenly. One can discover a detail in the photograph that was not perceived in the situation itself. Even one's own photograph can show something that was not in focus before. In the example from the beginning, the enlarged display of the pupil's camera became meaningful in comparison with the photograph that had been taken by the pupil himself.

Photographs offer a chance to look into the past in a special way. Their attraction depends on their potential to exceed human perception (cf. Meyer-Drawe "Die Macht des Bildes" 806).

III. Photographs Introduce a Different Temporality

A photograph does not portray the situation itself, which one cannot rewind or fast-forward. Photographs allow a retrospective view of a situation, independent from its original temporality. On the one hand, it is possible to scroll quickly through a broad set of images to get an overview; on the other hand, one can approach the documented situation very slowly. Without the need for action in the situation, looking at photographs offers the chance to discuss details and explore supposed incidental aspects in their pedagogical meaning. A certain situation – as in the example – can be focused on for a much longer time than the situation originally lasted. A situation that originally lasted 12 seconds – the time between the photos of the student and the pupil in the example – can be prolonged as needed.

IV. Photographs Make One's Own View Visible

The juxtaposition of the photographs that were taken at the same time by different persons make different perspectives visible. Every detail that is documented in one's photograph was in the situation itself, at least briefly – even if it did not attract attention. Blumenberg uses the term "Mitwahrnehmung" to describe all the other things *potentially in focus* that can be found in proximity to a certain focus (Blumenberg 194). Reflecting on one's own photographs offers the possibility to refer especially to these aspects.

Photographs taken by others, however, are completely and inevitably outside of one's own perception. Photographs, the self-made but especially the *unknown* ones, bear the "Sting of the Alien" (cf. Waldenfels *Phenomenology of the Alien* 4).

Putting one's own and another's photographs side by side challenges one to think about the situation and about the other in a way that keeps one bound to one's own perspective. The difference between the two perspectives show that one's understanding of the other is always a result of one's own individual and situational perception. Thinking about the other cannot be disconnected from one's own point of view as a (prospective) teacher. Objectifying the other becomes difficult because such a form of reflection critically questions the effects of pedagogical involvement and perceptibility.

(6) Outlook

To return to the situation described at the beginning: The photographs offer the possibility to examine the *micro-processes* of pedagogical practice. They enable a reflection that is related to a very concrete and specific situation. In the case of the example from the beginning, this situation was the pupil's interest in transforming an architectural space into an abstract picture. In my setting, the photographs do not only have the function of refreshing memories. They involve a discussion in which one's own perspective and the other's perspective need to be put in relation to one another. Photographs can help one to reflect on one's own perceptions, which are mostly ephemeral and pre-conscious. They can also help one to discover aspects that were not seen in the situation itself. Shifts in self-expectations and explanations become possible. This can be an interesting starting point for a deeper reflection. The combined perspectives allow a discussion about one's own view, which is never neutral or objective. Every interpretation in the contexts of pedagogical practice is based on assumptions, experiences, and expectations. To reflect on not only a specific phenomenon, but also on one's own view of this phenomenon, as well as on the question of how it attracts attention, can be a fruitful ground for students to develop a responsive understanding of art pedagogical practice. To combine reflection with the attempt to become aware of one's own perception leads to a way of thinking about a certain situation which cannot be decoupled from its singularity. Photographs – especially photographs taken from two perspectives – show, in their ambiguity, that reflection and understanding of pedagogical practice is always a question of awareness. The example from the beginning indicates that what looks like a superficial view at first glance turns out to be an intense examination of space and its abstraction. The use of photographic images offers the possibility to approach the complexity of pedagogical situations as well as their hidden dimensions. Those dimensions, such as performativity, questions of time, the movement of bodies in space, and so on, are especially important for art pedagogy. Image by image, students can be supported in becoming aware of the idea that contingency and ambiguity are constitutive for pedagogical practice. To reflect on the negativity of pedagogical practice and the way it attracts one's own awareness seems to be an important step for pedagogical professionalization.

Bibliography

Altmann, Howard B. "Training Foreign Language Teachers for Learner-Centered Instruction: Deep Structures, Surface Structures, and Transformations." *Applied Linguistics and the Preparation of Second Language Teachers: Toward a Rationale*, edited by James E. Alatis, H.H. Stern and Peter Strevens, Georgetown University Press, 1983, pp. 19–25.

Blumenberg, Hans. *Zu den Sachen und zurück*. Suhrkamp, 2007.

Boehm, Gottfried. "Der stumme Logos." *Leibhaftige Vernunft*, edited by Alexandre Métraux and Bernhard Waldenfels, Fink, 1989, pp. 289–304.

Boer, Heike de. "Pädagogische Beobachtung. Pädagogische Beobachtungen machen – Lerngeschichten entwickeln." *Beobachtungen in der Schule – Beobachten lernen*, edited by Heike de Boer and Sabine Reh, Springer VS, 2012, pp. 65–82.

Brenne, Andreas. *Zarte Empirie: Theorie und Praxis einer künstlerisch-ästhetischen Forschung*. Kassel University Press, 2008.

Brohl, Christiane. "Bewegungen auf unsicherem Terrain und kunstpädagogische Professionalität." *The Missing_LINK: Übergangsformen von Kunst und Pädagogik in der kulturellen Bildung, 2017,* manuscript pp. 1–28 (forthcoming).

Busse, Klaus-Peter. *Vom Bild zum Ort – Mapping lernen*. Dortmund Schriften zur Kunst, 2013.

Dewe, Bernd and Frank-Olaf Radtke. "Was wissen Pädagogen über ihr Können? Professionstheoretische Überlegungen zum Theorie-Praxis-Problem in der Pädagogik." *Zeitschrift für Pädagogik, vol. 27, 1991, pp. 143–162.*

Dreyer, Andrea. *Kunstpädagogische Professionalität und Kunstdidaktik. Eine qualitativ-empirische Studie im kunstpädagogischen Kontext.* kopaed, 2005.

Engel, Birgit. *Spürbare Bildung: Über den Sinn des Ästhetischen im Unterricht.* Waxmann 2003/2011.

Engel, Birgit. "Gemeinsame und kreative Potenziale in Kunst und Pädagogik." *Kunst und Didaktik in Bewegung*, edited by Birgit Engel and Katja Böhme, kopaed, 2014, pp. 106–151.

Engel, Birgit. "Unbestimmtheit als kunstdidaktisches Movens in professionsbezogenen Bildungsprozessen." *Didaktische Logiken des Unbestimmten*, edited by Birgit Engel and Katja Böhme, kopaed, pp. 58–85.

Engel, Birgit and Katja Böhme. "Zur Relevanz des Unbestimmten im Feld der kunstdidaktischen Professionalisierung." *Didaktische Logiken des Unbestimmten*, edited by Birgit Engel and Katja Böhme, kopaed, 2015, pp. 8–33.

Fichten, Wolfgang. "Über die Umsetzung und Gestaltung Forschenden Lernens im Lehramtsstudium. Verschriftlichung eines Vortrags auf der Veranstaltung

'Modelle Forschenden Lernen' in der Bielefeld School of Education 2012."
Lehrerbildung in Wissenschaft, Ausbildung und Praxis, edited by Didaktisches
Zentrum Carl von Ossietzky Universität Oldenburg, diss., pp. 1–29.

Flusser, Vilém. "Die Geste der Fotografie." *Gesten. Versuch einer Phänomenologie*
edited by Vilém Flusser, Fischer Verlag, 1994, pp. 100–118.

Gruschka, Andreas. *Fotografische Erkundungen zur Pädagogik.* Büchse d. Pandora,
1995.

Hascher, Tina. "Forschung zur Wirksamkeit der Lehrerbildung." *Handbuch der
Forschung zum Lehrerberuf*, edited by Ewald Terhart, Edda Bennewirt and Martin Rothland, Waxmann, 2011, pp. 418–440.

Heil, Christine. *Kartierende Auseinandersetzung mit aktueller Kunst: Reflexionsräume und Handlungsfelder zur Erfindung und Erforschung von Vermittlungssituationen.* kopaed, 2006.

Helsper, Werner. "Antinomien des Lehrerhandelns in modernisierten pädagogischen Kulturen." *Pädagogische Professionalität. Untersuchungen zum Typus
pädagogischen Handelns* edited by Arno Combe and Werner Helsper, Suhrkamp,
1996, pp. 521–569.

Helsper, Werner. "Lehrerprofessionalität." *Handbuch der Forschung zum Lehrerberuf*, edited by Ewald Terhart, Edda Bennewirt and Martin Rothland,
Waxmann, 2011, pp. 149–171.

Herzog, Walter. "Reflexive Praktika in der Lehrerinnen- und Lehrerbildung." *Beiträge zur Lehrerinnenbildung*, vol. 13, no. 3, 1995, pp. 253–273, www.bzl-online.
ch/archivdownload/artikel/BZL_1995_3_253-273.pdf. Accessed 10 May 2016.

Herzog, Walter. "Welche Wissenschaft für die Lehrerinnen- und Lehrerbildung?"
Beiträge zur Lehrerinnenbildung, vol. 25, no. 3, 2007, pp. 306–316, https://www.
bzl-online.ch/archiv/heft/2007/. Accessed 15 November 2016.

Hölscher, Stefan. "Unbestimmtheitsrelationen. Impulse zum kunstdidaktischen
Verhältnis von Rahmung und Prozess." *Didaktische Logiken des Unbestimmten*,
edited by Birgit Engel and Katja Böhme, kopaed, 2015, pp. 212–233.

Kämpf-Jansen, Helga. *Ästhetische Forschung: Wege durch Alltag, Kunst und Wissenschaft. Zu einem innovativen Konzept ästhetischer Bildung.* Nomos, 2012.

Kraus, Anja. *Anforderungen an eine Wissenschaft für die Lehrer(innen)bildung.
Wissenstheoretische Überlegungen zur praxisorientierten Lehrer(innen)bildung.*
Waxmann, 2015.

Kunz, Ruth. "Forschen und Lernen in der Berufspraxis." *BUKO Blinde Flecken.
Internationaler Kongress der Kunstpädagogik 2015. 13.-15. Februar 2015 in Salzburg, Dokumentation der Kongressergebnisse*, edited by BÖKWE, 2015, vol. 4,
2015, pp. 134–139.

Merleau-Ponty, Maurice. "The Eye and the Mind." *The Primacy of Perception*, edited by James E., Northwestern UP, 1964, pp. 159–190.

Meyer-Drawe, Käte. "Die Macht des Bildes – eine bildungstheoretische Reflexion." *Zeitschrift für Pädagogik*, vol. 56, no. 6, p. 806–818, 2010, http://www.pedocs.de/volltexte/2013/7170/pdf/ZfPaed_6_2010_MeyerDrawe_Die_Macht_des_Bildes.pdf. Accessed 15 January 2016.

Meyer-Drawe, Käte. "Aufmerken. Eine phänomenolgische Studie." *Aufmerksamkeit. Geschichte – Theorie – Empirie*, edited by Sabine Reh, Kathrin Berdelmann and Jörg Dinkelaker, Springer VS, 2015, pp. 117–126.

Pazzini, Karl-Josef. *Bildung for Bildern: Kunst. Pädagogik. Psychoanalyse.* Transkript, 2015.

Peez, Georg, editor. *Kunstpädagogik und Biografie.* Kopaed, 2009.

Peters, Maria. *Blick – Wort – Berührung: Differenzen als ästhetisches Potential in der Rezeption plastischer Werke von Arp, Maillol und F. E. Walther.* Schöningh, 1996.

Reh, Sabine. "Abschied von der Profession, von Professionalität oder vom Professionellen? Theorien und Forschungen zur Lehrerprofessionalität." *Zeitschrift für Pädagogik,* vol. 50, no. 3, 2004, pp. 358–372, http://www.pedocs.de/volltexte/2011/4815/pdf/ZfPaed_2004_3_Reh_Abschied_von_der_Profession_D_A.pdf. Accessed 1 October 2016.

Seydel, Fritz. *Biografische Entwürfe. Ästhetische Verfahren in der Lehrer/innenbildung.* Salon Verlag, 2005.

Sturm, Eva. "Mit dem was sich zeigt. Über das Unvorhersehbare in Kunstpädagogik und Kunstvermittlung." *Unvorhersehbares Lernen: Kunst – Kultur – Bild,* edited by Klaus-Peter Busse and Karl-Josef Pazzini. Dortmund Schriften zur Kunst, 2007, pp. 71–91.

Vetter, Peter and Daniel Igrisani. "Der Nutzen der forschungsmethodischen Ausbildung für angehende Lehrpersonen." *Beiträge zur Lehrerinnenbildung,* vol. 31, no. 3, 2013, p. 321–332, www.bzl-online.ch/archivdownload/artikel/BZL_2013_3_321-332.pdf. Accessed 15 May 2016.

Waldenfels, Bernhard. *Phänomenologie der Aufmerksamkeit.* Suhrkamp, 2004.

Waldenfels, Bernhard. *Phenomenology of the Alien.* Northwest UP, 2011.

Waldenfels, Bernhard. *Grundmotive einer Phänomenologie des Fremden.* Suhrkamp, 2016.

Wetzel, Tanja and Lenk, Sabine. "Kunstpädagogische Kompetenz braucht eine Haltung." *onlineZeitschrift Kunst Medien Bildung | zkmb,* www.zkmb.de/247. Accessed 15 January 2017.

Wildt, Johannes. "Auf dem Weg zu einer Didaktik der Lehrerbildung?" *Beiträge zur Lehrerinnenbildung*, vol. 23, no. 2, 2005, p. 183–190. www.bzl-online.ch/archiv download/artikel/BZL_2005_2_183-190.pdf. Accessed 15 November 2016.

Wimmer, Michael. "Zerfall des Allgemeinen – Wiederkehr des Singulären. Pädagogische Professionalität und der Wert des Wissens." *Pädagogische Professionalität. Untersuchungen zum Typus pädagogischen Handelns,* edited by Arno Combe and Werner Helsper. Suhrkamp, 1996, pp. 404–447.

Wimmer, Michael. *Pädagogik als Wissenschaft des Unmöglichen. Bildungsphilosophische Interventionen.* Ferdinand Schöningh, 2014.

Wortelkamp, Isa. *Sehen mit dem Stift in der Hand: Die Aufführung im Schriftzug der Aufzeichnung.* Rombach Verlag, 2006.

Wyss, Corinne. *Unterricht und Reflexion. Eine mehrperspektivische Untersuchung der Unterrichts- und Reflexionskompetenz von Lehrkräften.* Waxmann, 2013.

List of Figures

Diversity and Gender
as Learning Scenarios

Anne-Marie Grundmeier and Maud Hietzge

Myth to Reality: Reflexive Body Practices and Textile Art Processes in Education in the Context of (Un-)Doing Gender

Abstract: As mythological characters, mermaids represent seductive women as hybrid personas, whose ambivalent nature often reflects a conflict with their social environment. For thousands of years, these creatures have been enduring symbols of femininity in myth and culture. In contemporary society they play a visible role in children's literature and toys, TV series, movies, and nowadays in youth cultural practice. The question is why "The Little Mermaid" is still such a popular figure in modern life and culture. As a postmodern body practice of predominantly preadolescent girls, a virtual image becomes a provenance for different 'real' practices which acquire and mime sensually mediatized figures of adventurous character, thereby changing the myths again.

After a focused summary of historical investigations, the global and ambivalent figure of the mermaid is described as a phenomenon in relation to modernity and modern receptions. There are several cultural variations such as Mami Wata (Wendl), Jemanya, La Sirène and others (Grundmeier and Hietzge). Aspects of body and costume design are explained in their significance for young girls in the contexts of creativity, self-representation and aesthetic education, all of which are underestimated tremendously in current pedagogy. This leads to the question of whether or not the encounter with the figure of the mermaid can help with diversity and gender issues, and critique the norms that operate in education and society, given that the academic doctrine based on application knowledge underestimates cultural participation, aesthetic experience and appropriation of body knowledge.

Myth, Legend, Fable and Fairy Tale

Underwater creatures have held a fascination for people since the beginning of time. Legends and fables have spread around the globe and have thereby changed gradually. The oldest known depiction is the Semitic goddess Atar'ata, later known as Atargatis, worshipped e.g. in Palmyra. For a long time, the underwater world was foreign, strange and undiscovered for mankind. This might be why numerous stories and tales have been developed around this mysterious underwater world. The curiosity about whether or not these stories contain a grain of truth keeps people interested in them until now. Myths, fairy tales, legends and fables have been extended, modernized and varied all around the world. And all these tales enchant us up to the present time. One character rising from the underwater realm is the mermaid, a mythical figure with uncountable variations. Her character has been changed many times over the centuries and exists in manifold facets and representations (Kraß 14). The unknown and mysterious aspects of a mermaid, in contrast to our otherwise rigidly structured and well-ordered world, are probably what attract people to them. One reason for holding on to myths may be to avoid despairing of the inconsistency and contrariness of our reality (Otto 10–11).

The distinction between the terms myth, fairy tale, fable and legend is vague and therefore cannot always be differentiated accurately. According to Mader (13–18), myths explain nature and the supernatural, as well as reporting on heroes and heroines, gods and demons, the origin of things and the rules of living together in a community. In short: They are a 'living' expression of a certain life and of a specific view of the world. They consist of symbols, related practices and tales of occurrences that are believed to really have happened in the past and are therefore said to be true reports about incidents within an ethnic group. Myths deal with the creation of the world, humanity, culture, death and also with the origin of animals' character traits, the formation of geographic realities and other natural phenomena. Therefore, myths are passed on as stories which have supposedly really happened a long time ago – the "mythical" times – and people are impelled to believe in them through consistency and repetition. The settings of myths are real and precise descriptions of time, place and characters, as it is for example the case with early Greek myths. The plots, however, are fictitious even if they claim to explain life (Reinhardt 148–149). In current mediatized discourses, the old myths are constantly restructured to revive meaning and retain their orienting function. In these web 2.0 times, the roles of virtuality and reality sometimes seem to alternate, and we would like to focus on this phenomenon by investigating the case of the mermaid practice as part of a range of cultural, aesthetic and movement activities.

The infinite realms of the sea have filled early man with horror and fear. The enormous power of these waters trigger great fear of cold, waves that come crashing down, disorientation and an uncertainty of the water's depth. Even early sailors were afraid of drowning in the depths of the sea, of being exposed to the forces of nature or of encountering sea monsters (Heinisch 23). Myths, fables and legends about sea monsters and beasts are therefore present in various cultures. It stands to reason that sea creatures are easily able to scare people due to their enormous sizes, especially if those people have no knowledge about them. Imagine meeting a humpback whale for the first time – a colossus of fifteen meters with warts and bumps that suddenly leaps out of the water. Imagine suffering of hunger and illness after a yearlong sailing trip and then meeting a manatee that mildly resembles a woman. The kind of stories sailors would pass on after such an encounter (e.g. Christopher Columbus and Paracelsus) and the way artists would put these descriptions down on paper in a picturesque way (Ellis 12–14) are thus entirely conceivable. For example, in the center of his famous triptych 'The Garden of Earthly Delights' (~1500) Hieronymus Bosch painted a mermaid next to a figure of a knight with a shark tail, an image that reflects the oral travel reports of the time.

Mermaids are linked to both the element water and human embodiment. The mermaid represents a character with many facets, and affects us in an erotic, inaccessible and mystical way all at the same time. Throughout history, she adopts many figures such as the alluring siren, Melusine, Undine, the sea goddess, the nymph, the water witch, Ophelia, or the mermaid. In contrast to mermen and water spirits, mermaids have been depicted many more times in art and literature. One reason to explain this is that in former times and throughout many religions, women had been described as being soulless, as having humble brain power, and as being much weaker in faith than men, while at the same time leaving a trail of fear because of being the underestimated 'other' gender. The myths around mermaids therefore also developed from these former ideas and relationships between men and women, where men were not necessarily helping women to attain a soul; instead, they were only helping them to have a mere right to exist in society (Kleßmann 10). In the course of time, the role of the mermaid and the way her appearance has been presented has changed many times, especially in the process of Christianization. To this day, mermaids are presented in many different forms in literature, artwork and visual media.

The history of mermaid depiction in the fine arts reflects discursive features of femininity concepts (Hietzge, "From Myth to Reality" 13). Often, mermaids are depicted and described as having a fishtail, the upper part of a human body, and a beautiful face framed by long, golden hair. In some myths and fairy tales, mermaids take on a human form; in others, they have webbed feet. On the one hand, a mermaid is seen as a beautiful, giving seductress; on the other hand, she is presented as a dangerous, life-threatening, elementary force. It was not until Andersen's fairy tale that a mermaid had to put up with severe pains in order to reach the human world (Syfuß 220–221). The late romanticist view silently paid attention to the problems of emancipative womanhood and its cost. If a mermaid wished to go back to her (natural) mermaid world again, there was usually not the difficulty that the Andersen version describes. However, unfaithfulness and betrayal by men are essential characteristics of myths about mermaids. When they actually go to the world outside their realm of the sea, it is usually because of love, and this entails illusionary misjudgments. But before a mermaid is able to live in love with a human man, he must promise eternal fidelity as an indispensable condition. In case this promise is neglected, the human man has to be punished: either the mermaid has to go back to her element or he has to pay for it with his life. Tragedy seems inevitable.

Today, the motif of a mermaid is more than just a figure mentioned in fables and fairy tales (Kleßmann 18). Mermaids already play a major role for young girls between the ages of 6 and 10 due to age-specific literature and visual media. Movies such as Disney's "The Little Mermaid" (1989) or the German adaption "Die kleine Meerjungfrau" (Trites 145–155, 2013) and TV soaps ("H2O: Just Add Water", 2006; "Mako: Island of Secrets", 2013) create an ideal for girls which needs to be discussed from aesthetic, literary and sociological perspectives. This is especially important regarding their gender related, implicit educational impacts (Kraß 17), since different kinds of media have the potential to influence personal background orientations unconsciously and transactionally (Halff 34–44). The existing compositions of mermaid stories look at the transition of the topos which can be found in literature up to the 20th century (e. g. the emancipated version of Ingeborg Bachmann, "Undine geht", 1961). These modern compositions, however, do not include the present perspectives in performances. In current adaptions that are suitable for children, we do not find much about the character's tragedy anymore. Instead, these adaptions are based on *textile metamorphosis* (Scheiper 190) and performance. The way identification is offered by present adaptions is subject to a contemporary change, especially regarding the perception of natural aspects, the self-concept of our own bodies, and aspects of gender. This identification even reaches as far as to an assimilation of nature and a temporary transfer into a fascinating different world that is perceived as an adventurous experience. Various offers of sustainable "sea life education" already make use of these modern facets of how mermaids are presented (Wolbert; Rockefeller). Even in a time where women are no longer conceived as less intelligent than men, they are still taken as genuine in their authority due to their life-giving and protecting nature.

Reception research which investigates media aimed specifically at adolescents and children in relation to mediated body images and practices has only been developed rudimentarily (Schwier, "Neue Medien und jugendliche Bewegungskultur" 375–380). It needs further concretion especially in view of practices and competences that currently arise from the mediated body images and practices. From a methodological perspective, we find links to research that investigates informal learning (Bohnsack et al. 14). Recent discourse research (Bührmann and Schneider 108–141) also involves discursive practices and its considerations. This helps to include and extend the present perspectives of practice and discourse research by examining the interconnection of the patterns of interpretation and practices (Schmidt 13).

The boom of mermaid swimming practice – as of now known as mermaiding – has been triggered during the last decade by the Australian TV soap "H2O: Just Add Water." In contrast to competitive swimming and popular mass sports which are oriented towards a logic of outdoing, mermaiding shows various aesthetic qualities that are less oriented to a judging public but that nevertheless meet more or less the criteria that are adopted by trendy new sports (Schwier, "Was ist Trendsport" 18–31): stylization, spectacularization, action orientation, aestheticization, virtuosity, and a feeling of independence. However, reliable findings about detailed age-specific characteristics and their interpretations do not exist. For the moment, mermaiding can be regarded as a fun variation of the so-called undulation swimming and mono fin diving, which are both based on physical fitness. The idea of mermaiding enables girls to create their space for a youth cultural in-crowd. There are five stages in the trend graph of fashion sports, namely invention, innovation, expression, diffusion, and saturation (Lamprecht and Stamm 107–132). Within this model, mermaiding can be located at the stage of expression.

In our teaching and research project at the University of Education Freiburg (2013–2017) we have been investigating the cultural background and the meaning of current mermaid practices. A survey of pupils participating in a mermaid convention in 2014 (n = 125), showed that those who engaged in intensive mermaiding were usually the ones who had already been active in other swimming practices prior to the mermaid practice. Our finding contrasts with the intentions of educational institutions, although this group was preselected in terms of the participants' high identification with mermaiding. In the daily mermaid practices, even children who were formerly inactive would participate. Unfortunately, these daily activities in numerable German cities could not yet be investigated by a survey. However, the initially marginal offer has been accepted by popular culture and follows the logic of aesthetic self-conceptualization in youth cultures. Within educational research, these juvenile self-conceptualizations are increasingly perceived as forms of cooperative self-organization and as resources to optimize paths to successful learning (Bindel 152). It is important to take into account that researchers need to personally know the practice they examine in order to be able to assess its dimensions (carnal sociology concept, Crossley, "Merleau Ponty, the Elusive Body and Carnal Sociology" 43–63) and enter the spheres of the actors' lives (Honer 75–88). For this reason, the participating university students were trained in mermaiding and apnea diving in order to professionally do training with children.

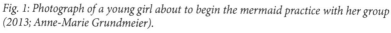

Fig. 1: Photograph of a young girl about to begin the mermaid practice with her group (2013; Anne-Marie Grundmeier).

© Anne-Marie Grundmeier

It is quite a complex setting when practices, media discourses and meta-discourses interact, especially when habitual, stylistic and health-related customs and background orientations are acquired during these processes (Kelle 101–118) and during the research process itself. This interrelation of practices and discourses has not yet been clarified enough. In consequence, the canonical concept of knowledge may end up being revealed as unstable, and thus, more attention has to be put on the processes of performances. Visual methods and physical aspects of how knowledge is constructed increasingly come to the center of attention within educational research (Reh 151–169). Qualitative methods of educational research show that videographic traditions are used as they usually are in interaction analyses and psychology (Knoblauch and Schnettler 9–10; Goodwin 1489–1522). This procedure makes it possible to tightly reconstruct the knowledge and behavioral development that become apparent in body language as well as in performative acts and form the basis of any access to the world (Hirschauer 86). Ultimately, this perspective changes the whole concept of knowledge (Neuweg 12–23; Baumgartner 215–232; Schatzki, "Social Practices" 55–87; Schatzki, "Materiality and Social Life" 35–48). Learning by doing in an aesthetic way plays a crucial role (Bender 73): It creates moments of aesthetic education (Köhnlein 127) and aesthetic ignition

(Kolhoff-Kahl 89–91) that can be judged as surprisingly sustainable despite its temporariness. The keen involvement of the children in our training sessions was made evident during a final project meeting that featured video elicitation interviews that were recorded two months after the mermaid-swimming courses for school children had ended. One of the interviewed girls reported that following YouTube tutorials, she and her friends are currently creating their own mermaid-swimsuits out of fabrics (Interview 24.01.2017, Group 1–2, R09_003).

Another group of girls between 4 to 8 years old was observed by a camera while they dramatically role-played with mermaids that they had painted as alter egos on the pavement. First, they painted the mermaid figures with chalk and then they started role-playing by giving them names, also calling each other by typical mermaid-names. They also collected food for the mermaid figures.

Fig. 2: Photograph of the above-mentioned chalk drawings of mermaids. (2014; Photograph by Susanne Kittel).

However, to this date, the growth of learning by means of aesthetic practices has not been subject to enough research that could legitimize such practices within the mainstream of education. This is why Klepacki and Zirfas (111–139) require clarification on how aesthetic learning is manifested and how it can be improved. First basic reflections and empirical findings regarding cultural education are available for artistic and aesthetic disciplines (Klepacki 49). Cultural education in this respect is now being established as a distinctive academic field (Fink et al. 9–18), but body-related practices are still underrepresented (Lohwasser and Zirfas 271–280).

Education, Body Knowledge and Gender

Questions about the (lived) body are currently and increasingly brought up in the context of thought and knowledge, initiating a break with our concept of knowledge. The physical aspects of knowledge are followed, particularly from the perspectives of the social sciences and cultural studies, with special attention given to the production of knowledge (Klinge). The physicality of the human being has thus been taken more seriously as an important issue of human practice. Body knowledge as a fundamental area of knowledge has so far been rather cautiously accepted within educational sciences. From the perspective of the sociology of the body, based on Bourdieu's Habitus theory (1997), knowledge also includes physical knowledge. His theory provides a basis for a multi-perspective understanding of body knowledge as habitual, incorporated experiential knowledge, which includes action-oriented and sensual experiences as well as their integration into emotional dispositions that may have an effect on cognition (Bourdieu).

The didactics of the aesthetic and cultural disciplines, as well as sport pedagogy, still have difficulties in taking into account the importance of body knowledge in their educational discourse. Thus, a possible approach could be to expand the educational mission of these subjects, by not only focusing on the teaching of theoretical and practical skills but also on the promotion of reflexive perception processing and the general support of personal – heterogeneous – development. Paradoxically, only through this can a serious promotion of competence in its full literal sense be pursued. The dramatic underestimation of the importance of aesthetic education at school may run into the danger that the famous German scientist and philosopher of the Enlightenment, G. Ch. Lichtenberg, foresaw: "I am afraid that the excessively careful education we provide is cultivating dwarf fruit" (Lichtenberg 220). With regard to the current body discourse and the potentials of body knowledge, it is necessary that aesthetic-cultural disciplines such as art, music and textiles, as well as movement science, whose focus is the body, participate in this discourse. The role of body-bound knowledge in the various disciplines, and the way it influences learning and educational processes, must be tested in the classroom, brought into the didactic discourse and ultimately investigated. Examples of aesthetic-cultural projects such as mermaiding can be used to show an access to learning with the body that contributes to the rehabilitation of the body as a dimension of knowledge and education.

In such projects, the expressive dimension of body knowledge is especially stressed, and is deliberately created and staged by practical actions. Learning with the body can be identified as an essential dimension of body knowledge and can be promoted in aesthetic-cultural projects of education. In consequence, the range of possible self-reflectiveness (as a basis for pedagogical professionalism) can be broadened in terms of gender-typical (body) behavior and the analysis of social expectations. On the other hand, an unreflective teaching practice with regard to body knowledge will lead to the strengthening of gender-specific patterns and will thereby inadvertently contribute to the establishment of gender-typical behavior in terms of body and gender ideals.

Pedagogical Aspects

In view of the cultural and educational processes, we find complex relations between media-related influences and the development of physical practices of children and adolescents (Grgic and Züchner 237–247; Schwier, "Jugendliche Körper und virtuelle Welten" 183–196; Schwier, "Neue Medien und jugendliche Bewegungskultur" 375–380; Burrmann 57–74; Hietzge, "Interdisziplinäre Videoanalyse" 14). Looking at the currently still popular example of a mermaid, we can reconstruct interdependencies *in statu nascendi* since a popular practice in the lives of children and adolescents has been created from a virtual impulse and is now being established as an educational learning opportunity. These informal youth groups can be examined with regard to their implications on the alteration of aesthetic processes of self-education. Within that group, we find mainly girls mobilizing themselves in that motion-cultural way. In connection to this, a cooperation model can be developed for swimming or fitness organizations and schools in order to implement aesthetic and cultural practices especially in the 5th and 6th grades. The cooperation model needs to meet requirements of reflexivity (Serwe-Pandrick 25–44), as peer groups usually do not meet the criterion of reflexivity, an often misused notion that is a crucial element of competence acquirement in the prevailing specialized discourse for educational science.

Reflexive body practices are assessed as a defining feature of late modernity (Crossley, "Mapping Reflexive Body Techniques" 1–35). The central element here is the body, which is not taken for granted. Even the aspect of the *living body* is already bound to reflections on its form, health, presentation and social acceptability, all of which interact with spontaneous articulations as in the case of the children's role play mentioned above (Fig. 2), wherein a 4-year old girl commented on her "too fat" mermaid. This phenomenon brings about the necessity to grasp the power of dominating ideal images within processes of subjectivation, especially within adolescence, and to make children able to free themselves from unconsciously adopted norms. But we have to admit that this process starts already within the realm of early education and tends to be a settled cornerstone before entering school: "We are already educated in gender prior to any official education in gender" (Butler 19). We have to ask "what does power do with a body, but also: what does a body do with power? After all, power cannot stay in power without reproducing itself in some way" (Butler 17). And this occurs in a mimetic way at first:

> Mimesis is what I take from another without knowing that I have taken it – it is the way in which the voice, the gesture inhabits me without my knowing it – it is what I take on, appropriate, or what suffuses me, without my having deliberated about it at all. Only later do I come to see that some set of others have taken up residency in me, have inhabited me without quite knowing. Even though I may try to alter this fact, to ask those inhabitants to leave, or try and extricate them from the way in which I speak or move or appear, I can only ever be partially successful, since we are, from the start, social beings. (Butler 20)

Subjectivation on a bodily basis occurs on the basis of tacit involvement. Therefore, aesthetic education is indispensable to come to know these grounds, and the widespread dispense of aesthetic education as a luxury is an index of power structure in its wielding.

Aesthetic education, like action orientation, is a crucial part of school subjects such as art, music, and textile education. It describes a didactic approach which is multi-layered. The word "aesthetic" has its origins in the Greek "aisthesis" and means sensual perception. The basic idea of aesthetic education is to stimulate, motivate, encourage and qualify (Majewski 24). Children and adolescents are supposed to discover, appreciate and extend their aesthetic skills (Kirchner et al. 11), since exploration, comprehension and identification are regarded as essential constituent parts of learning (Dietrich et al. 9). Kirchner and Kirschenmann (81–87) organize aesthetic education in art lessons into the three dimensions: reception, production / expression, and communication, all of which stimulate personal capacities for judgment. The first step is to perceive a topic which merges into a creative and productive activity. The second step takes place in practical working, and the third step presents the communicative dimension with evaluation.

Children and adolescents are stimulated in this last dimension to reflect on the processes they have gone through and they are encouraged to verbalize their impressions. Aesthetic education is therefore an essential part of current learning concepts which put the educated subject into the center of interest instead of predetermined subject-related contents (Dietrich et al. 24). Fantasy, sensitivity, the power of imagination and creativity are to be stimulated and promoted. At the same time, students learn to investigate objects, topics and actual situations critically. Aesthetic education can be described as an opportunity to deal with our personal environments in a creative way by means of our different senses. In the view of Kohlhoff-Kahl (101), textile education as a school subject is especially suitable for aesthetic learning, exploring, planting ideas into students' heads and for critical thinking due to its direct relationship to daily routines and its strong tie to sensual material experiences.

Constructivist subject-related didactics, biographic learning and the promotion of creativity are tightly connected to aesthetic education. All of them put the child as the subject of learning into the center of learning. When students ask questions, verify data and become active in artistic and creative work, they develop problem-solving as well as inquiry-based and exploratory learning strategies. Students learn through their own experiences and through self-organized learning. And in doing so, their level of knowledge increases, and independent thinking and constructing are promoted. The constructivist approach is based on a great diversity of methods, stimuli and ways of learning. It is important to bear in mind that according to the constructivist view, there is not just one correct result; instead, there are many different possible approaches to solving a problem.

Textile art projects demand an extremely high level of responsibility from the students, if the realization of the topic is left solely up to them. However, their creativity can be highly promoted by this challenge. According to Seitz and Seitz (109–110) every child has a creative potential and therefore also has the opportunity to act in creative and constructive ways. Taking all this together, it makes sense to place the mermaid topic within textile education lessons. The more we deal with this topic, the clearer we see that myths are found in the daily reality of students, both in artwork and media and in up to date children's and youth literature. *Pinkification* (Schmiedel) does not only signify a color attribute of Barbie dolls, Lilly Fee or Hasbro Littlest Pet Shop ponies, but a whole imaginary industry unwittingly engaged in a gender attribution that can be found in close context with more or less adventurous mermaid stories such as "The Secret Mermaid" (Mongredien), the Thora series by Gillian Johnson, Liz Kessler's half-mermaid Emily Windsnap, etc.

Final Conclusion and Discussion

The central interest of our investigations is directed at the analysis of practices and discourses *in their interaction* in order to reconstruct the formation of background orientations. The utterances of involved children showed a clear break from traditional tragic concepts of adventurous women, but nevertheless revealed normative orientations concerning the body. Cultural practices in relation to mermaiding need to be gathered by a broad database. In-depth analyses need to be carried out in order to transfer informal and non-formal forms of cultural education into a concept that organizes the cooperation between schools and out-of-school educational organizations. In this respect, it is important to consider what kind of figure this chimera represents in different cultural areas (Melusine, Selkie, Deniz Kisi, Mami Wata, etc.); how it depicts and/or influences the image of women in the cultural and historical course (Dinnerstein 10); and what kind of transformation can be used especially in the context of migration. In relation to this, Butler asks, "Does translation give us some insights into the kinds of agency at work in learning a gender? There is, for instance, a gap between how gender is taught and how gender is learned. And one may well receive conflicting injunctions on how best to do one's gender if one lives between cultures or between languages" (Butler 16–17). Furthermore, she states that "sometimes we have to undo our education, unlearn what we have learned.... And at that point, we have to ask whether the educational projects for which we have fought have lost their critical edge, especially when normalizing standards are imposed by funding sources" (Butler 18–19).

List of References

Bachmann, Ingeborg. "Undine geht." *Das dreißigste Jahr*. Piper, 1961.

Baumgartner, Peter. *Der Hintergrund des Wissens*. Kärtner Verlagsgesellschaft, 1993.

Bender, Saskia. *Ästhetische Erfahrung und ästhetische Bildung in der Schule*. VS, 2009.

Bindel, Tim. *Soziale Regulierung in informellen Sportgruppen: eine Ethnographie*. Czwalina, 2008.

Bohnsack, Ralf et al. *Die dokumentarische Methode und ihre Forschungspraxis*. 3rd ed., VS, 2013.

Bourdieu, Pierre. *Die feinen Unterschiede: Kritik der gesellschaftlichen Urteilskraft*. 25th ed., Suhrkamp, 2016.

Bührmann, Andrea, and Schneider, Werner. "Mehr als nur diskursive Praxis? Konzeptionelle Grundlagen und methodische Aspekte der Dispositivanalyse." *Historische Sozialforschung* 33 (1), 2008, pp. 108–141.

Burrmann, Ulrike. "Betrachtungen zum "Stubenhocker"-Phänomen." *Sport im Kontext von Freizeitengagements Jugendlicher*, edited by Ulrike Burrmann, Sport & Buch Strauss, 2008, pp. 57–74.

Butler, Judith. "Gender and Education." Pädagogische Lektüren, edited by Norbert Ricken and Nicole Balzer, VS, 2012, pp. 15–28.

Crossley, Nick. "Merleau Ponty, the Elusive Body and Carnal Sociology." *Body & Society* 1(1), 1995, pp. 43–63.

Crossley, Nick. "Mapping Reflexive Body Techniques." *Body & Society* 11(1), 2005, pp. 1–35.

Dietrich, Cornelie et al. *Einführung in die Ästhetische Bildung.* 2nd ed., Beltz Juventa, 2012.

Dinnerstein, Dorothy. *The Mermaid and the Minotaur: Sexual Arrangements and Human Malaise.* The Other Press, 1999.

Ellis, Richard. *Seeungeheuer: Mythen, Fabeln und Fakten.* Birkhäuser, 1997.

Fink, Tobias et al. "Zur Kulturellen Bildung forschen: Aktuelle Methodenansätze." *Forsch! Innovative Forschungsmethoden für die Kulturelle Bildung*, edited by Tobias Fink, Burkhard Hill and Vanessa-Isabelle Reinwand-Weiss, kopaed, 2015, pp. 9–18.

Grgic, Mariana and Züchner, Ivo. "Aktivitätsprofile junger Menschen im Bereich Medien, Kunst, Musik und Sport." *Medien, Kultur und Sport*, edited by Mariana Grgic and Ivo Züchner, Beltz Juventa, 2013, pp. 237–247.

Grundmeier, Anne-Marie, and Hietzge, Maud (2016). *Vom Mythos zum Trend.* Presentation at the Museum "Natur und Mensch", 7.6.2016 (unpublished paper).

Goodwin, Charles. "Action and Embodiment within Situated Human Interaction." *Journal of Pragmatics* 32, 2000, pp. 1489–1522.

Halff, Gregor. *Die Malaise der Medienwirkungsforschung: Transklassische Wirkungen und klassische Forschung.* Springer, 1998.

Heinisch, Klaus J. *Der Wassermensch: Entwicklungsgeschichte eines Sagenmotivs.* Klett-Cotta, 1981.

Hietzge, Maud. *Interdisziplinäre Videoanalyse: Rekonstruktionen einer Videosequenz aus unterschiedlichen Blickwinkeln.* Budrich, 2017a.

Hietzge, Maud. "From Myth to Reality – Mermaiding, a Media Induced Movement Culture." *International Journal of the History of Sport*, vol. 34 (Art in Sport History), Taylor & Francis (in review), 2017b.

Hirschauer, Stefan. "Körper macht Wissen." *Geschlechterwissen und soziale Praxis*, edited by Angelika Wetterer, Helmer, 2008, pp. 85–92.

Honer, Anne. *Kleine Leiblichkeiten: Erkundungen in Lebenswelten*. VS, 2011.

Johnson, Gillian. *Thora: A Half-Mermaid Tale*. HarperCollins Children's Books, 2005.

Kelle, Helga. "Die Komplexität der Wirklichkeit als Problem qualitativer Forschung." *Handbuch Qualitative Forschungsmethoden in der Erziehungswissenschaft*, edited by Barbara Friebertshäuser and Annedore Prengel, 2nd ed., Juventa , 2009, pp 101–118.

Kessler, Liz. *The Tale of Emily Windsnap*. Orion Children's Books, 2003.

Kirchner, Constanze et al. *Ästhetische Bildung und Identität: Fächerverbindende Vorschläge für die Sekundarstufe I und II*. kopaed, 2006.

Kirchner, Constanze, and Kirschenmann, Johannes. *Kunst unterrichten*. Kallmeyer, 2015.

Klepacki, Leopold. "Hermeneutik kultureller Bildung." *Forschung zur Kulturellen Bildung: Grundlagenreflexionen und empirische Befunde*, edited by Eckart Liebau, Benjamin Jörissen, and Leopold Klepacki, kopaed, 2014, pp. 45–54.

Klepacki, Leopold, and Zirfas, Jörg. "Ästhetische Bildung: Was man lernt und was man nicht lernt." *Die Kunst der Schule*, edited by Eckart Liebau and Jörg Zirfas, transcript, 2009, pp. 111–139.

Kleßmann, Eckart. "Einleitung." *Undinenzauber*, edited by Frank R. Max, Reclam, 2009, pp. 9–18.

Klinge, Antje. "Körperwahrnehmung: Den Körper wahrnehmen, mit dem Körper wahrnehmen und verstehen." *Inhalte und Themen des Bewegungs- und Sportunterrichts*, edited by Ralf Laging, Schneider, 2009, pp. 96–107.

Knoblauch, Hubert, and Schnettler, Bernt. *Video Analysis. Methodology and Methods*. Lang, 2006.

Köhnlein, Walter. "Ansatzpunkte und Spielräume des Denkens." *Praxis Pädagogik. Ästhetisch bilden*, edited by Joachim Kahlert, Gabriele Lieber, and Sigrid Binder, Westermann, 2006, pp. 122–148.

Kolhoff-Kahl, Iris. *Textildidaktik: Eine Einführung*. 4th ed., Auer, 2013.

Kraß, Andreas. *Meerjungfrauen: Geschichten einer unmöglichen Liebe*. Fischer, 2010.

Lamprecht, Markus, and Stamm, Hanspeter. *Sport zwischen Kultur, Kult und Kommerz*. Seismo, 2002.

Lichtenberg, Georg Christoph. *The Waste Books*, translated and introduced by Reginald John Hollingdale. NYRB Classics, 2000.

Lohwasser, Diana, and Zirfas, Jörg. "Der Körper in Bewegung: Perspektiven auf den Körper und die Künste." *Der Körper des Künstlers: Ereignisse und Prozesse der ästhetischen Bildung*, edited by Diana Lohwasser and Jörg Zirfas, kopaed, 2014, pp. 271–280.

Mader, Elke. *Anthropologie der Mythen*. Facultas Verlags- und Buchhandels AG, 2008.

Majewski, Teresa. *Interkulturelle Projektarbeit in der Kunst-und Kulturvermittlung: Handlungsmöglichkeiten und Entwicklungspotenziale durch ästhetische Bildung und Identitätsarbeit*. Ibidem, 2011.

Mongredien, Sue. *The Secret Mermaid*, vol. 1–12, Usborne Books, 2009–2010.

Neuweg, Georg H. *Könnerschaft und implizites Wissen: Zur lehr-lerntheoretischen Bedeutung der Erkenntnis- und Wissenstheorie Michael Polanyis*. 4th ed., Waxmann, 2006.

Otto, Beate. *Unterwasser-Literatur: Von Wasserfrauen und Wassermännern*. Königshausen & Neumann, 2001.

Reh, Sabine. "Mit der Videokamera beobachten: Möglichkeiten qualitativer Unterrichtsforschung." *Beobachtung in der Schule*, edited by Heike de Boer and Sabine Reh, Springer VS, 2012, pp.151–169.

Reinhardt, Udo. *Mythen – Sagen – Märchen*. Rombach, 2012.

Rockefeller, Susan. *Mission of Mermaid: A Love Letter to the Ocean*, 2012, www.missionofmermaids.com/press. Accessed 31 Jan. 2017.

Schatzki, Theodore R. *Social Practices: a Wittgensteinian Approach to Human Activity and the Social*. University Press, 1996.

Schatzki, Theodore R. "Materiality and Social Life." *Time, Consumption and Everyday Life*, edited by Elizabeth Shove, Frank Trentmann, and Richard Wilk, Berg, 2010, pp. 35–48.

Scheiper, Petra. *Textile Metamorphosen als Ausdruck gesellschaftlichen Wandels*. VS, 2008.

Serwe-Pandrick, Esther. "'The Reflective Turn'? Fachdidaktische Positionen zu einer 'reflektierten Praxis' im Sportunterricht." *Zeitschrift für sportpädagogische Forschung 1*(4), 2013, pp. 25–44.

Schmidt, Robert. *Soziologie der Praktiken. Konzeptionelle Studien und empirische Analysen*. Suhrkamp, 2012.

Schmiedel, Stevie. *Pinkifizierung und Sexismus in den Medien*. 18 May 2013, www.theeuropean.de/stevie-schmiedel/6886-pinkifizierung-und-sexismus-in-den-medien. Accessed 31 Jan. 2017.

Schwier, Jürgen. "Jugendliche Körper und virtuelle Welten." *Der Einfluss der Medien: Vertrauen und soziale Verantwortung*, edited by Martin Schweer, Leske + Budrich, 2001 a, pp. 183–196.

Schwier, Jürgen. "Neue Medien und jugendliche Bewegungskultur." *Im Sport lernen, mit Sport leben*, edited by Zentrum für Interdisziplinäres Erfahrungsorientiertes Lernen. Ziel-Verlag, 2001 b, pp. 375–380.

Schwier, Jürgen. "Was ist Trendsport." *Trendsport: Modelle, Orientierungen, und Konsequenzen*, edited by Christoph Breuer and Harald Michels, Meyer & Meyer, 2002, pp. 18–31.

Seitz, Marielle, and Seitz, Rudolf. *Kreative Kinder: Das Praxisbuch für Eltern und Pädagogen*. Kösel, 2009.

Syfuß, Antje. *Nixenliebe: Wasserfrauen in der Literatur*. Haag + Herchen, 2006.

Trites, Robert. "Disney's Sub/Version of Andersen's The Little Mermaid." *Journal of Popular Film & Television* 18 (4), 1991, pp. 145–155.

Wendl, Tobias. *Mami Wata: Oder ein Kult zwischen den Kulturen*. Lit, 1991.

Wolbert, Linden. *Mermaid Linden Interview on Australia Today Show*. 2010, vimeo.com/15444062. Accessed 31 Jan. 2017.

List of Figures

Hanne Seitz

Things That Matter: Acquiring Knowledge Through Self-Organized Artistic and Cultural Activities

Abstract: The following article[1] presents the *Young Tenants [Junge Pächter]*: a political-activist project that gave youngsters and young adults from Berlin (for a limited period of time) vacant spaces to discover their artistic creativity and craftsmanship, and to practice cultural participation. In contrast to school or out-of-school activities, this project was totally self-organized and strongly based on informal learning. Only when asked did the International Youth, Art and Culture House Schlesische27 [Internationales JugendKunst- und Kulturhaus Schlesische27] – who launched the project – and mentors from various art and cultural institutions, give technical and artistic support.

The project was accompanied by *action research* (Altrichter et al.) and favoured an environmental approach to learning, hereby responding to current discussions about local *educational landscapes* (Mack) and *communities of practice* (Wenger-Trayner). The practice itself was understood as research, to be precise: as *performative research* (Seitz). Young people were regarded as co-researchers – capable of finding creative solutions for the problems that arose while working on their self-determined goals. They not only relied on their explicit knowledge but also gained from their *tacit knowledge* (Polanyi).

We live in a performance-based society. A wide rage of activities are steered by unconcious cultural motifs and affected by the expectations that are conveyed to individuals by people, and especially by the media. The participants of the project were keen and ambitious to perform, but their activities were also led by a complacent attitude and self-centered behavior. Against this background, artistic interventions served to offset these mechanisms in order to deepen the self-reflection and to challenge the practice.

In order to get a deeper look into the practices and the spaces of the project, the following statements are being interrupted by subjective descriptions, 'insights' to the field which illustrate the author's observation in a poetical way.

> "Why is the classroom the main place where lessons take place – who decided that?"
> "More community life on the streets, more participation!"
> "More places where young people can easily showcase their creative work."
> Statements from peer-to-peer interviews (Meyer)

---

1 Parts of this article have been published in German (Seitz and Steinkrauss) and also in English (Seitz "Producing Knowledge").

Berlin Youth Demand Self-Organized Artistic Settings

In a peer-to-peer survey, conducted in 2010, over 300 youngsters and young adults from all over Berlin were asked about their understanding of art, and their interest in creative activities and cultural education programs. They emphasized the shortage of public spaces for young people and complained that (aside from streets, fallow wastelands or shopping malls) the only uncomplicated and easily accessible space was the Internet. Social networks involve no major expenses and offer platforms which give young people visibility; however, they also create a constant pressure to perform and to be up to date at all times. The interviewed youngsters therefore expressed a need for analogue forms of communication that facilitate a deeper and more meaningful face-to-face exchange. Instead of availing themselves of the virtual options provided by the digital media, they wanted to step onto real stages and engage with the physical world of bodies, materials and spaces.

In response to the survey, fifteen Berlin youngsters established a Young Council [Junger Rat] and organized a youth conference aimed at investigating potential forms of active participation for them in the area of art and culture. Most of the conference participants felt that school was not an appropriate place for the sort of creative work they had in mind. Being suspicious of all kinds of educational settings they even hesitated to take up opportunities offered by cultural institutions, e.g. museums, theatres or literature houses. Many of them held prejudices against 'highbrow culture' and associated it with old paintings, dusty museums, long-winded theatre performances, boring concerts, dry lectures and, as they put it, cultural events for "art-zealous middle-class bores." Those who had obviously gained experience in one of the cultural educational programs felt that it had just followed a foreseeable template. They explicitly criticized the fact that the organizing adults who had encouraged the youngsters to participate had in fact strategically 'used' the interaction with them to realize their own project aspirations. Moreover, they felt that such regularly offered programs were not 'artful' enough and often functioned as a 'social repair kit'. The conference participants stated that their own creative endeavor and specific style were not sufficiently acknowledged or even considered to be of artistic value.

The discussions at the conference on basic questions about art and culture were controversial and emotionally guided, but all participants agreed that there was a need for cultural and artistic experiments and a closer engagement with the environment. They asked for a framework that would enable them to become independent and responsible and give them an opportunity to engage in active citizenship. The conference participants finally adopted a kind of manifesto. Their list of demands, addressed to Berlin's City Council, was quite long. It is noteworthy that the first item on the list was their wish to be trusted with the responsibility to run self-organized spaces for artistic and creative activities, i.e. rooms designed by themselves where they would share their skills and creative practices with others and also showcase their cultural achievements for a wider community. After having received broad public attention for being the initiator of the conference, the Young Council started to play an increasingly successful mediating role between young people, cultural institutions, and politicians. And finally, their demand for self-regulated spaces was met. The Berlin-based International Youth, Art and Culture House Schlesische27 which had helped to organize the peer-to-peer survey and provided the space for the youth conference, reacted to the young peoples' formulated needs by facilitating a project called Young Tenants [Junge Pächter].

Insight 1: Village Underground [Dorfplatz unter Tage]: The journey to the tenant room is already an adventure. Small, handwritten signs show the way through the meandering grounds of the former brewery in Neukölln, a district of Berlin center. They lead via a staircase and a dimly lit hall into the catacombs of this old facility. Here, in a little theater space, ten tenants are having a first go at their adaptation of Gertrude Stein's "Dr. Faustus Lights the Lights". Two corridors further, a large room surprisingly features a big window frontage on account of the building's hillside location. In the middle is a self-built kitchen surrounded by sofas. The tenant choir has just been rehearsing for an open-air concert, and now Amando lifts the kitchen crew's spirits by making music on a bass whose strings are made from the type of wire used for bicycle brakes; the vibraphone is made out of plastic tubes and is played with flip-flops. This does not only sound good, but it also looks good. [H. S.]

*Fig. 1: "Inwhitetion" – Neighborhood kids help to renovate the tenant space in Neukoelln. ©
Hanne Seitz.*

Creative Practice Performed by Young Tenants

Being a non-formal and out-of-school education institution in the cultural field,
the Schlesische27 normally offers arts and crafts courses, projects and workshops
for children, youngsters and young adults. In the case of the tenant project, it set
up what might be called a 'program without a program'. This included the handing
over of unoccupied sites to young adults (most of them aged between 17 and 25)
in six city districts. For a limited period of time, they were given the opportunity
to use deserted shops, empty pubs, an old carriage house, etc. in those districts,
to perform their own artistic and cultural endeavors – small events for friends
and youngsters in the immediate neighborhood and possibly from other parts of
the city. The tenants received a small budget and were given full responsibility for
their spaces – on the condition that they would work on a cultural concept, give
themselves house rules, make a financial plan, and invite the public at least once
every three months to certain events.

The project started in 2011 and ended in 2014 and ran for over three cycles (each year from September to June). New members were allowed to join
at the start of a new cycle, which typically began with a so-called project forge

[Projektschmiede] at Schlesische27. Around 80 young people from all over Berlin from different social backgrounds met for a two-day workshop. They were introduced to cultural pilot projects and artistic initiatives (like the architect group Raumlabor, or the members of Prinzessinnengärten that ran the first urban gardening initiative in Berlin).

The author of this article participated in some of their meetings. In her observations, she realized that they offered an inspiring range of ideas as well as a forum for mutual exchange. The young adults also got an insight into organizational and technical issues, such as conflict management, legal issues, budgeting, public relations and the intermediate use of urban spaces.

The participants discussed their ideas at the project forge in randomly formed groups and in creative workshops, developing and designing their so-called hot-forged plans [Heißschmiedepläne] to arrive at initial mutual agreements. They used a wide range of materials to build models and three-dimensional objects which were then displayed on door-sized, black wooden panels to visually express their ideas for the use of their spaces: surreal places like a cinema, an office for social design, a photographic lab, and an outdoor area for urban activities. Witty and creative names for the future spaces were found: Machwerk, Heim(e)lich, Photosphaere, Kreative Köpfe, Dorfplatz Untertage, SpaceShuffle, etc. In the second cycle, the project forge started with a floor plan of six rooms in the so-called Red Hall at Schlesische27, each room representing a tenant space. The former tenants furnished them with one or two items (an armchair, a lamp, a kidney-shaped coffee table from the 1950s, etc.) which attracted the newcomers into the space. Here they began to discuss their visions of a possible usage of this space and again, presented this on a wooden panel.

The young people who got involved in the tenant project were ambitious, courageous, full of energy, and ready to tap into their creativity in order to serve what they perceived as the cultural needs of the wider public. They gradually became promoters and hosts while developing their projects and workshops, also doing the PR-related work. The Schlesische27 engaged professionals dealing with theatre, music, dance, visual arts, or film from various cultural institutions in Berlin to support them, e.g. the Neuköllner Oper, Arsenal Institut für Film- und Videokunst, Tanzwerkstatt DOCK 11, Schlossplatztheater Köpenick, and JugendTheaterWerkstatt Spandau. However, these mentors gave technical, organizational and artistic advice only when the young people explicitly requested this kind of assistance. Working together with the mentors meant that the young tenants could also become more aware of different career profiles in the cultural sector and gradually develop a better understanding of professional working conditions and standards.

Insight 2: Working Manufacture [Machwerk]: A more handicraft-oriented space is located in the residential area of Wedding. In the neighborhood are a Turkish cultural association and a bakery. The tenants invite others to come in. There is a workbench, a rack of bicycle parts, and there is a coffee-stained list of house rules. Tools and wood are scattered everywhere, and there is a table with a self-made silk screen-printing device. A guest pedals away on a jacked up bicycle and uses a nail to spread noise. Numerous generators are connected to a circuit board, an amplifier and self-made speakers from the so-called electro-cave in which, according to the tenants, rickety old bikes are converted into Knight Riders. [H. S.]

Producing and Sharing Knowledge in Tenant Spaces

After getting the keys, the tenants began the renovation and design of their premises. In some cases, this turned out to be very tedious. A bazaar at Schlesische27 provided them with their first items of furniture. Other things they needed were supplied by sponsors or borrowed, free of charge, from supportive individuals, including the mentors. A wide range of activities was developed in the tenant spaces: handicraft-oriented projects, performances, theatre or musical events, workshops, poetry slams and, in one case, the tenants even explored the 'art of living' in the manner of the avant-garde aesthetics wanting to fruitfully merge art and life in order to contribute to artistic and social progress.

Networking between the different groups in the rooms and also among members of the tenant spaces in the other city districts of Berlin generated contact between different communities and youth cultures. Friends and residents in the neighborhood were encouraged to participate in the young tenants' projects. In the beginning, the tenants were not keen at all on asking for help or learning from the expertise of their mentors. The young tenants felt professional enough to work independently and make their own arrangements. In doing so, they definitely sharpened their perception, thus realizing what the ancient Greek called *aisthesis* and *poiesis*. Their learning took place outside of any formal educational services, in environments which posed far greater challenges and were much closer to reality than any school context. The tenants learned to come up with creative solutions and act responsibly in contexts that really mattered to them.

At the general meetings, which were held in the tenant rooms, the young people shared their ideas, their knowledge and, invariably, negotiated personal values and preferences. The discussions were both unsettling and reassuring and, as it seemed to the author, always resulted in the tenants reflecting on and reviewing their own points of view. It was particularly in situations of conflict that they needed to realize that a democratic approach cannot be taken for granted, but that it actually needs to be repeatedly practiced and re-negotiated. There was no prescribed structure or list of functions. The tenants themselves were in charge of formulating the criteria, which were to form the basis for how their project was managed. Nobody controlled them, or checked, for example, if the law on protecting minors was observed, or if the property was used in an appropriate way. And as it seems, they did not abuse this trust. They seized the opportunity to become visible and go public.

This involved a great measure of conflict (e.g. with neighbors). The generally functional orientation of adults contrasted with the young people's desire for a playful and sometimes anarchic rearrangement of their spaces and the use of uncommon and somewhat subversive strategies. Similar to a 'bricolleur', they used the 'inherited' elements, took them apart, and constructed something new. There seemed to be no end to the imagination of the young tenants who, again and again, came up with yet another unconventional use of their spaces.

Having been trusted with responsibility and appreciating the exceptional opportunity to organize themselves, the tenants were soon keen to defy the clichéd image that is often associated with youngsters, i.e. that they are inconsiderate, unproductive, and even destructive. It was quite remarkable (and astonishing to the author) how they started to 'care' for their environment: They talked with neighbors who felt disturbed by the noise levels, helped children to repair their bicycles, and even showed a sense of responsibility for the correct disposal of the chemical liquids they used to develop analogue photographs with. Regarding the wider political context, they shared a deep concern for people who find themselves in life-threatening situations in the Mediterranean and questioned the existing European asylum policies. In their theatre piece "Dr. Faustus Lichterloh", light played an important role. It was understood as a key metaphor for the empowerment of the young people – the 'illumination' of their practices (as one of the tenants said).

Looking back at over three project cycles, it seems that the tenants got what they had asked for: a space to develop and share their own ideas and where they could offer creative workshops, and produce cultural programs and site-specific events. It might not be surprising that the young people were often in the public spotlight. Their projects were met with approval in radio features, newspaper reviews and various other publications. The cultural department of the Berlin Senate even invited them to participate in a discussion on youth and urban culture, and the Federal Government Commissioner for Culture and the Media honored them with an annually awarded prize, the BKM-Preis Kulturelle Bildung 2013. And, last but not least, the tenant project was acknowledged as an example of 'best practice' within a European research network.

Insight 3: Photosphere [Photosphaere]: The old-fashioned stove in a former coach-house in Pankow is as charming as it is ineffective against the cold winter season. It is an experiment conducted under extreme conditions for the six young pioneers from different city districts. They will live and work together for three months and exhibit their self-set goal with photos, videos, texts and paintings, all documenting the ongoing experiment. They avail themselves of the bequests of invited artists as well as those of neighbours and guests during the open-house Sundays. An old Olympia typewriter requires spontaneous writing stimuli, while colours and cameras call for design interventions. In keeping with the Christmas season, 'creative cookies' are baked and a wall is literally filled with small wish lists. [H. S.]

Fig. 2: "Reading" – Exhibition and Poetics in the tenant space in Pankow © Schlesische27.

Performative Research and Artistic Intervention

The research carried out by the University of Applied Sciences Potsdam (FHP) explored the possibilities of self-organization and self-empowerment within the tenant project and introduced it to the European network "Empowering the Future. Youth, Arts & Media" (ETFU). Within this network, the so-called power labs from four European countries (consisting of members of cultural agencies and universities) conducted research on 'best practice'. They developed methodologies and a training program for professionals and organizations with a keen interest in evaluating and improving their work with youngsters and young adults.[22]

The Potsdam-Berlin power lab aimed to focus its research on the practices of self-organization and the further improvement of these practices. While student researchers from FHP conducted participant observation in the tenant spaces, arranged interviews and wrote reports on their findings, the power lab team invited volunteering tenants to the 'Pärflexion-meetings' (a wordplay on Pächter, Perzeption, Reflexion), where they were regarded as co-researchers. They were introduced to how they could plan, observe, and reflect on activities using an action research model, and explore their practice in terms of an interplay between aims, reflection and action. At first, being primarily focused on their activities, the young people were not interested in this kind of research. However, they gradually became engaged and prepared the meetings in cooperation with the facilitators of Schlesische27 and, later, sometimes even called them 'PAC-meeting' (an acronym from Pächter, Aktion and Vitamin C), which sounds like 'pack', a word signifying a cool gang, but (in German) also meaning to grab, to seize or tackle something.

The knowledge gained in qualitative social research usually takes retrospective account of practice and is generated in discursive settings. The tenant project, however, seemed to call for a different logic of enquiry. First and foremost, the research was not understood as a collection and analysis of data gained only by the observation of practice or by interviewing the practitioners. It was meant to highlight the practice itself as research and understood research as the driving force that pervades the practice itself – what Brad Haseman calls a "practice-led" approach (147). The tenants accomplished the goals they had set for themselves on the basis of the knowledge they had – implicit, tacit knowledge and practical ability and, therefore, a knowledge that is embedded in the practice. But, looking at the results, the tenants also gained new knowledge, because their practices, at times, required research at a very basic level: they compared, analyzed, reflected, established preliminary hypotheses, proved their practicability, and solved

---

2   The German research group consisted of Nils Steinkrauss, project manager at Schlesische27, Julia Riedel, research assistant, and myself. The results from all ETFU-power labs and the training modules can be found under <www.etfu.eu>. The research reports written (in German) by students, a flyer and video concerning their view on the tenant project can be retrieved under < https://www.fh-potsdam.de/forschen/projekte/ projekt-detailansicht/project-action/etfu-empowering-the-future-youth-arts-media/>. Further information and videos concerning the tenant project are available under <http://junge-paechter.de>.

problems while they were doing what they were doing. Our research therefore considered both the knowledge embedded in the practice and the reflection that came about while processing, dealing with, and handling practice – so-called "tacit knowing-in-action" and "reflection-in-action" (Altrichter et al. 271 f.). Occasionally, especially in situations of conflict, when complications had arisen and there seemed to be a discrepancy between purported desires and actual effects, activities had to be explained and negotiated. In such cases, neither their practical ability nor their trying out 'in action' was sufficient. The tenants needed to step aside and separate the thinking from the doing and "reflect-on-action" (273). This is an essential prerequisite for any action research or practice-based approach and explicitly for the Pärflexion-meetings, which aimed to undertake inquiry at eye level in order to improve the work. It follows (and repeats) an "action research cycle", which involves observing, reflecting, planning and acting (11 f.).

Against this background, the research that the Berlin power lab conducted in order to gain and conceptualize knowledge about self-organized approaches to good practice called for a distinction between word-based theory about practice and 'practice as it is'. In doing so, we considered what Susanne Langer calls presentational and discursive symbolization (63 ff.). Presentational symbolizations (video, photo, music, theatre, dance, poetry slam, etc.) express implicit and explicit knowledge (that one knows and reflects upon while practicing), whereas discursive symbolizations use language (discussions, interviews, notebooks, questionnaires, etc.) to reflect on and expedite knowledge (that one reflects upon and speaks about through looking at the practice). Therefore, on the one hand, we listened to what the tenants had to say about their activities and, on the other hand, we focused on the products and processes, looking at what the tenants actually did and showed. In the latter case, the work 'speaks for itself' and inscribes understanding and new insights right into the practice, aspiring to be one with it. Here, the knowledge is disseminated and depends upon the act of performed practice and the products deriving from it. It is not expressed in discursive language but in presentational symbolic 'data' which need no textual representation and therefore preserve the complexity of practice, retain its openness, and capture what one may not be able to say, but show. We conceptualized this approach to practice as "performative research".

It goes without saying that our power lab (and particularly the students from FHP) also conducted practice-based research, used traditional social scientific methods, e.g. interviews, group discussions, participant observation, wrote transcripts and minutes, etc. Our observations, inquiries and findings were theorized and put into writing for the final ETFU-Report. Still, the primary aim of the methodology was indeed to focus on practice-led research. Yet, looking at what happened in practice, we observed that the tenants were quite complacent with what they were doing. They hardly ever asked their mentors for professional advice or critique. They were keen to perform and 'knew' how to do it – to stage themselves and to showcase their work. They "appeared to 'have it all' (the correct moves, the correct look, the correct language)" (Herbert 138). At times, our team felt that the tenants should have been more self-critical and should have questioned the substance and content of their activities. We did not want to interfere directly, especially not verbally (knowing, of course, that our mere presence was already an interference). But since the objective of the research process was to push forward existing know-how and impart new knowledge and understanding, our power lab came up with the idea of artistic interventions, in other words, with unexpected presentational symbolizations supplied from the outside. The impulses did not steer the tenants in a certain direction, nor were they directly linked to their activities. They were meant to deepen phases of reflection and aimed at questioning the value of complacent activities, and at making tenants aware of habitual behavior patterns. This was achieved through what we called "reflection-aside-action". Such an intervention could be, e.g. listening to strange music composed by Morton Feldman, holding a Pärflexion-meeting in an unusual spatial setting designed by the architects of Raumlabor, showing photo portraits made by the artist Cindy Sherman, or watching the video of Marina Abramovic's performance "The Artist is Present". The latter, for instance, touched the young people on an emotional level and gave them a sense of what it means to not act and to be oneself in relation to others. They began to understand that artistic practice does not need to be flamboyant, sensational, or loud, but can simply be 'doing nothing': just being attentive and present.

Insight 4: Creative Minds [Kreative Köpfe]: A vacant, long forgotten pub in the so-called New Town of Spandau. Three groups share the space. They do improvisation theatre, set up creative-writing workshops and a photo studio. The activities are being sceptically observed by the neighbours and the district police officer: "Oh, it's a youth project sponsored by the senate, well that's okay then." Whether out of necessity or virtue, here almost everything automatically becomes community work, as all of the programmes are open to the public. Children linger in front of the door before they finally muster up the courage to enter. The son of the district police officer joins the improvisation group – and once, even the officer himself. The photo group (almost

like service providers for friends and occasional passers-by) creates the appropriate
styling for their portraits and works together with a friend who is a make-up artist
for the theatrical staging – experimenting with role models from film history and
making rather unusual photos for a concluding exhibition. [H. S.]

Environmental Approach and Informal Learning

Becoming involved as co-researchers and thus becoming more familiar with an
academic setting was not really the tenants' main concern. They were preoccu-
pied with their projects and it is unlikely that they would ever have organized a
Pärflexion-meeting on their own. But, as it seems, they gradually appreciated the
challenge and potential benefits of reflecting and looking at their actions from a
more distanced point of view. Some of the tenants were even interested in reading
the research reports the students from FHP had written, or an article that had
been published on the project (Seitz and Steinkraus).

Most of the tenants associated 'learning' with school, some even as something
negative. They hardly ever considered their activities in the tenant spaces as a
learning field. But of course, "not all learning is educational." (Whitehead 247)
They did learn – in rather informal arrangements. Additionally, it seems that
both formal institutions (like schools or universities) and non-formal institutions
(out-of-school education) have started to acknowledge these kinds of learning
conditions too: informal learning that takes place in passing, non-arranged, rather
unorganized settings (cf. Rauschenbach, Mack). But, if there are opportunities for
autonomous learning (as in the tenant spaces), young people feel encouraged to
structure and organize such settings and to set up an appropriate framework. The
tenants, as it seems, were guided by individual concerns, but also by their surroundings and the needs of the community. They purposefully worked towards
what might be called key abilities: achieved self-determination (e.g. by engaging
with politics), self-organization (e.g. by structuring their involvement) and self-
regulation (e.g. by getting ethically concerned).

As a result of our investigations on the tenant project in its entirety, our power
lab theorized an *environmental approach* to practice within the culture field.
It aimed to consider "informal learning in urban neighborhoods" (Steffen), to
things that matter to the learner and that are connected to real life situations.
It allowed us to emphasize knowledge as something negotiated in situ, where
people connect via social practices in leisure and working activities and within
"communities of practice" (Lave and Wenger, Wenger-Trayner). Here, the use of

the word environment not only intends to convey the idea of social, economical and ecological benefits for sustainable development, but is understood as a stimulating field in which learning is an evolving, continuously regenerated set of practices. It allows people to take possession of their needs and shape the world by their kinaesthetic and critical thinking abilities, while being involved in their site-specific activities. The tenant project fostered such an environmental approach. Its effectiveness is reflected by the fact that the young tenants mastered their self-generated demands and began to appreciate the importance of other tenants' contributions and those of the community, thus showing an increasing engagement with others. In doing so, they energized their immediate environment and made creative contributions to the use of the urban sphere. Such an approach calls for facilitators who, like agents, build bridges, mediate and connect people who otherwise would not meet. These facilitators only get involved when asked – unless they decide it is necessary to intervene. This may happen when a group reaches a point of complacency or stagnation. The interventions we had in mind take the form of artistic impulses and rely on non-discursive presentational, aesthetic settings. They intended to offset habitual mechanisms, to encourage the young people to become more involved in art making and, ultimately, to contribute to the empowerment of young people.

Insight 5: June Park [Juni-Park]: The closing event takes place in Berlin-Tempelhof. At the start of the tenant project, finding spaces for self-organized artistic and cultural work was not a problem. But by now, gentrification leads to the social marginalization of young people. They are not only in need of cultural space. Their wishes for an urban communal life forms the stone pit for an artistic intervention. The architects of Raumlabor installed a scaffold near the Tempelhofer Feld, a former airport in the heart of Berlin that is now being used as a public park, but whose future use is highly disputed. The construction consists of basic architectural structures, one big enough to serve as a theatre, another one used as a kitchen, and the smaller room-sized ones are for last exhibitions and workshops realized by tenants coming from the different tenant rooms. In their show, the members of the invited youth theatre group suddenly turn into zombies and start to occupy the surrounding field. "They squeeze all the breath out of you, plan luxury apartments on Tempelhofer Feld," says the narrator of the show. "But don't get upset. We've done research and know how to deal with this 'Zombiefication'. We'll dig a giant hole, flood it and drown them. Zombies can't swim." [H. S.]

Fig. 3: "June Park" – The tenant's last domicile and grand finale on Tempelhofer Feld © Hanne Seitz.

Implications and Afterthought

Today's society is a "performance society" (McKenzie). Performance not only extends to the areas of cultural activities, but the term also covers forms of organizational and technical practice as well as the theatricality of our daily lives. There is a constant pressure to perform and, consequently, to evaluate, measure, compare and assess the levels of achievement not only in the economic field, but also concerning individuals and organizations, schools and universities, and even the area of culture (Seitz "Performance-Gesellschaft"). All kinds of data are used in order to improve practices and achieve optimal results and effective management. Therefore, it is not surprising that research in general has also become a key issue in the social, cultural and educational areas. Our research definitely contributed to this development. We did not address the young people as if they were a closed book full of 'data' waiting to be assessed. However, we did locate and examine hidden knowledge and intrinsic motivation, thus running the risk of making this usable and thus exploitable for the neoliberal economy. Already under discussion is the manner in which informal learning achievements can be made creditable within the formal educational system (cf. Werquin). Tenants from Machwerk, for example, who ask "Why is the classroom the main place where lessons take place?", would be delighted to get credit points for their 'knightrider' invention. This feels like a dilemma. But, there is reason to assume, now that the project has come to its end, that they will take further steps, remain critically aware, continue to risk subversive thinking, and maintain the waywardness of art.

The tenants trained their individual awareness and insight through self-education [Selbstbildung] calling upon an essential interplay between feeling, thinking and will, between self, others and the environment. But, the project not only dealt with young people and their self-directed approaches towards learning, it also involved university students that learned, as they did, in-situ. The students worked independently and autonomously on their reports, and learned to challenge concepts and research results critically and with an ethical concern. But perhaps more significantly, they gained an understanding of what it means to master something not yet known. Since no prescribed learning outcome was given, they had to take the risk of diving into practice. Learning did not take place on a conceptual level; rather, it was achieved by participation and performance, by a research approach situated in a culture of practice. As the tenants, they united mindfulness and action and exercised their ability to communicate and interact. These are fundamental competences that any student should aim at developing – not only future social or cultural workers, pedagogues, school teachers or facilitators. The approach does not privilege teaching. It counts on learning as a process and takes into consideration the context, environment and the relationship that connects people to one another and to a certain purpose.

Nowadays, we seem to have forgotten the core principle of humanism: It is not given to us, but needs to be practiced in value-based-social interactions (cf. Nida-Ruemlin). Regardless of whether we are dealing in the educational, social, political, or cultural arena, it is about mindful ways of doing – be it, as here, the social and artistic expertise the tenants gained through their self-organized practices or the skills the students achieved in conducting their research. "The Magic is in Handling" (Bolt).

Bibliography

Altrichter, Herbert, et al. *Teachers Investigate their Work. An Introduction to Action Research Across the Professions.* Routledge, 2008.

Bolt, Barbara. "The Magic is in Handling." *Practice as Research. Approaches to Creative Arts Enquiry,* edited by Estelle Barrett and Barbara Bolt. I. B. Taurus, 2009, pp. 27–34.

Haseman, Bradley C. "Rupture and Recognition: Identifying the Performative Research Paradigm." *Practice as Research. Approaches to Creative Arts Enquiry,* edited by Estelle Barrett and Barbara Bolt, I. B. Tauris, 2009, pp. 147–157.

Herbert, Anna. "Learning Strategies – New Routes for Students to Master University?" *Performativity, Materiality and Time – Modelling the Tacit Dimensions of Pedagogy,* edited by Mie Buhl, Anja Kraus, and Gerd-Bodo von Carlsburg, Waxmann, 2015, pp. 135–148.

Langer, Susanne K. *Philosophy in a New Key: A Study in the Symbolism of Reason, Rite and Art.* Harvard UP, 1957.

Lave, Jean, and Etienne Wenger. "Learning and Pedagogy in Communities of Practice." *Learners and Pedagogy,* edited by Jenny Leach and Bob Moon, Chapman, 1999 pp. 21–33.

Mack, Wolfgang. *Lernen im Lebenslauf – formale, non-formale und informelle Bildung.* Ed. Landtag Nordrhein-Westfalen, Düsseldorf, 2007 <docplayer. org/12308965-Lernen-im-lebenslauf-formale-non-formale-und-informelle-bildung-die-mittlere-jugend-12-bis-16-jahre.html> 25 Feb. 2017.

McKenzie, Jon. *Perform or Else: From Discipline to Performance.* Routledge, 2001.

Meyer, Barbara. *Kunst und Kultur in Berlin – Was geht mich das an? Jugendliche befragen Jugendliche.* Ed. Kulturprojekte GmbH, Berlin, 2010, <http://digital. zlb.de/viewer/resolver?urn=urn:nbn:de:kobv:109-opus-219714> 25 Feb. 2017.

Nida-Ruemelin, Julian. *Humanistische Reflexionen.* Suhrkamp, 2016.

Polanyi, Michael. *The Tacit Dimension.* Anchor, 1987.

Rauschenbach, Thomas, Wiebken Düx, and Erich Sass, eds. *Informelles Lernen im Jugendalter. Vernachlässigte Dimensionen der Bildungsdebatte,* Juventa, 2007.

Rogoff, Barbara. "Observing Sociocultural Activity on Three Planes: Participatory Appropriation, Guided Participation, and Apprenticeship." *Pedagogy and Practice. Culture and Identity,* edited by Kathy Hall, Patricia Murphy, and Janet Soler, Sage, 2008, pp. 58–74. <methodenpool.uni-koeln.de/situierteslernen/ Teaching%20As%20Learning.htm> 25 Feb. 2017.

Seitz, Hanne, and Nils Steinkrauss. "Machwerk, Heim(e)lich & Co. Urbane Spiel-Räume für junge Leute." *Vom Straßenkind zum Medienkind. Raum- und Medienforschung im 21. Jahrhundert,* edited by Benjamin Jörissen and Kristin Westphal, BeltzJuventa, 2013, pp. 81–95.

Seitz, Hanne. "Producing Knowledge in Self-Organized Artistic Settings through Performative Research and Artistic Intervention." *Journal for Drama and Theatre.* XI.1 (2015): pp. 117–133. <research.ucc.ie/scenario/2015/01/Seitz/07/en> 25 Feb. 2017.

Seitz, Hanne. "Performative Research." *Performatives Lehren Lernen Forschen – Performative Teaching Learning Research* (bilingual), edited by Susanne Even and Manfred Schewe, Schibri, 2016, pp. 301–321.

Seitz, Hanne. "Kunst und Bildung in der Performance-Gesellschaft." *Das Geben und das Nehmen. Pädagogisch-anthropologische Zugänge zur Sozialökonomie,* edited by Johannes Bilstein and Jörg Zirfas, BelzJuventa, 2017, pp. 82–99.

Steffen, Gabriele. "Informelle Lerngelegenheiten im Stadtteil." *Informationen zur Raumentwicklung.* 2.3 (2010): 129–141. <www.bbsr.bund.de/BBSR/DE/Veroeffentlichungen/IzR/2010/2_3/Inhalt/inhalt.html> 25 Feb. 2017.

Wenger-Trayner, Etienne, and Beverly Wenger-Trayner. *Communities of Practice – a Brief Introduction.* 2015 <wenger-trayner.com/resources/> 25 Feb. 2017.

Werquin, Patrick. "Recognition of Non-formal and Informal Learning in OECD Countries: an Overview of Some Key Issues." *REPORT Zeitschrift für Weiterbildungsforschung.* 3 (2009): 11–23. <www.die-bonn.de/id/4276/about/html/> 25 Feb. 2017.

Whitehead, Jack. "The Practice of Helping Students to Find Their First Person Voice in Creating Living-Theories for Education." *The SAGE Handbook of Action Research.* Ed. Hilary Bradbury. Sage, 2015, pp. 246–254. <www.actionresearch.net/writings/jack/jwBRADBURY-Chp24.pdf> 25. Feb. 2017.

For further information:

<www.fh-potsdam.de/forschen/projekte/projekt-detailansicht/project-action/etfu-empowering-the-future-youth-arts-media/> 25 Feb. 2017.

<www.junge-paechter.de> 25 Feb. 2017.

<www.etfu.eu> 25 Feb. 2017.

List of Figures

Visual Culture and Media
as Learning Scenarios

Aloisia Moser

Media Abstinence – Why Less Is More: An Essay

Abstract: *In this paper, from the standpoint of a philosopher, different strands of thought are developed to elucidate the human being's relationship to the world and to learning, and the ways in which media enhance or hinder learning. My considerations lead me to recommend a strict media policy for infants and preschool children. The human body and mind develop in tandem and always through being in a larger world. Early childhood education can therefore not focus on the mind alone. When we try to enhance cognitive abilities of children through the use of media, we neglect their capacity to make experiences and to learn through the body. I will put forward the following points, which at the same time constitute the parts of my paper:*

1. Motor Development
2. Learning a First Language
3. Language as a Medium
4. Principles and Methods of Learning: The Ignorant Schoolmaster
5. Conclusion: Media Abstinence – Why Less Can Be More

1. Motor Development

Emmi Pickler, a Hungarian pediatrician who worked with infants at the Lóczy orphanage in Hungary, had one urgent question, namely how to best relate to infants and young children and provide them with the care and education they need to become self-confident and secure adults. From her many years of work experience in the orphanage, she developed several key principles to help caregivers. The most important have to do with the body and its development. Emmi Pickler put *Freedom of Movement* at the top of the list of principles she developed. She argues that infants' natural gross motor development unfolds without the aid of the caretaker. What is most important for the caretaker to understand is that they are not to teach the baby skills and activities that the child can unfold by themselves.[1]

---

1   "As a matter of principle we refrain from teaching skills and activities which, under suitable conditions will evolve through the child's own initiative and independent activity." This is one of the key principles of Pikler's method. See Emmi Pikler and Anna Tardos "Some Contributions to the Study of Infants' Gross Motor Activities" in *Proceedings of the 16th International Congress of Applied Psychology* (ICAP, 1968).

The adult caretaker or educarer's[2] role in the development of the baby is to create a safe space where the baby feels warm and where it cannot hurt itself, and to combine respectful care moments with respect for the child's need to move and unfold at her own pace. It was important for Pikler that the adult does everything 'with' the baby and not to the baby. In an especially poignant example, she describes a mother diapering her baby all the while talking to the dog. For Pikler, the conversation the mother has with the dog would be better lavished on the baby. Yes, the baby does not have language yet, but there is a language of sounds, and there are hands that can communicate, ask and answer. The caretaker can ask the baby, "May I lift up your legs to put the new diaper underneath you?" in so many ways. And it might be good for the caretaker to take the time to wait for the response that the infant's body will give in due time. Babies cannot speak yet, but mothers, fathers, or any caretakers who wait and listen will learn to understand their way of communicating their needs.

A well-meant video[3] found on YouTube shows an infant lying on its back, turning first onto its side and then onto its belly for the first time. The video is subtitled with instructions given to the infant, accompanying the infant while it makes its attempts to move over by itself, in its own time. The irony is that the baby is perfectly capable of "turning around" without the help of the caretaker. The look on the baby's face when it finally manages to make the 180-degree turn is priceless. Pikler's recommendation is to limit the involvement of the adult to caregiving routines and attentive communication with the child as the child is diapered, changed or fed. She also recommends the adult to allow the child periods of time spent first on its back, and later, in a safe environment where it can turn, crawl and sit without interference and help. If a baby cannot get into a certain position by itself, she urges the caretaker not to help her to get into that position. Naturally, Pikler viewed as unnecessary the high chairs, swings, and other devices that aid the child to be at the same level of height as the adult. She especially discourages the use of car seats (outside of the car) or any other aids to put babies in the sitting position before they can sit by themselves. She does not believe that walkers,

---

2   Emmi Pikler's teachings were brought to the United States by Magda Gerber and are best summarized in Gerber's book *Dear Parent: Caring for Infants with Respect* (RIE, 1998). Gerber coined the term "Educarer" for the caretaker who is aware that she or he is also educating, in the specific sense in which Emmi Pikler thought that one should not interfere.

3   "Rolling – Feldenkrais with Baby Liv" (2010) *YouTube*, 22 May 2017, https://www.youtube.com/watch?v=D9Ko7U1pLlg.

or any devices to help the child walk including the helping hands of the parents, are ever needed in the baby's process of learning to walk.

High chairs, baby swings, and even the parents' hands, etc., become crutches or mediating devices that help the children take shortcuts in their natural development. They are aided to sit before they can sit, and walk before they have developed the muscles to walk. Every stage in the process of learning to sit and walk is a development of muscles and thus, shortcuts are not shortcuts in the long run. According to Pikler, who adds a psychological dimension, there is a natural way in which the muscles develop and the movements unfold, and this is why accelerating the process by aiding the child is disrespectful. Therefore, all such devices as well as the helping hand of the caretaker are discouraged by Pikler's method. Babies need no help to reach their milestones.

2. Learning a First Language

When my daughter was an infant and, as many philosophers still believe today, "without language or reason,"[4] I often marveled at fellow parents with their kids strapped in their strollers pointing to trees while exclaiming "tree," and pointing at flowers while exclaiming "flower" or the very flower's name. This led me to think about the theory of language that we inherited, that of ostensive definition. Is that how children learn language? By pointing at something and saying its name?

But what about the learning that took place while the baby was in the womb? Think of the sounds and noises of the mother's body and movements: fast paced, more slowly, still. Listen to the heartbeat. When the baby grows, we say at some point that the baby now has "ears" and can hear. But what did it do before then? There are also sounds that come from the outside. The mother's voice, her practicing the piano, the father's voice. By the time the baby is born, it knows the voices and sentence melodies. It may not be able to understand, but it has been well primed to start guessing. And it already has some language: when something is off, it cries. The adults try to interpret the cries, mainly through trying to stop the crying. Milk – soothing – milk – swaddling – milk. Little by little, these interactions take on the form of words. Shhh – quiet baby – singing. But how does the child transition from the non-verbal to the verbal?

Returning to Pikler once more, she was also adamant about waiting to see what the baby needs instead of shushing it. She was against giving milk at every occasion

---

4   The belief that infants are like animals without a rational soul goes back to Aristotle. *Aristotle's On the Soul*, translated by H.G. Apostle (Peripatetic Press, 1981).

to calm the child down. Her slogan was, "observe and wait."[5] The baby's cries are the first words that try to tell us something. It is not always hungry. It is often tired and overwhelmed by the sensory input from the outside world. Giving the baby milk whenever it cries or rocking it in our arms into a hypnotic state are actions that do not necessarily mean we are treating the baby with respect. We have lost the chance to understand what the baby tries to communicate.

What becomes clear in this discussion is that it does not seem to be the case that there is a teacher of language who has a better or worse method to introduce children to words or grammatical rules that may or may not already exist in them.[6] We say "they soak it up like a sponge." And the rapidity with which they add words to their vocabulary is astounding. It seems, however, that there is no rhyme or reason to this initiation into language. They seem to learn their first turn of phrase in a way similar to how they learn to turn their bodies.

3. Language as a Medium

In this part of the paper I will speak about language as a connection or medium between us and the surrounding world. It seems obvious that language is the way in which we represent the world to ourselves, how we speak or think about the world. It is as if we are on the inside and thought is how we communicate with ourselves, while the world is on the outside and language is the way in which the connection from inside to outside is made. Philosophy is often interested in how the language or thought that connects to the world is true or false.[7] Thought and language are here thought to be media that connect to the world. Is language expressed thought, then? The inside brought to the outside? Do we speak in language to ourselves on the inside? What kind of connection is made here?

There are different strands of philosophy, and some go beyond the idea that there is a world, and then a human being *in* the world that communicates his or

---

5   Magda Gerber, ed. B. J. Weaver, *Dear Parent: Caring for Infants with Respect* (Los Angeles: RIE, 1998), p. 20.
6   In the world of first language development, we speak of inside-out theories and outside-in theories, depending on whether nature or nurture comes first. Pikler's account leans toward the nurture side, despite the core importance of the body.
7   I am referring to the analytic tradition of philosophy and its correspondence theory of truth. For example B. Russell asserts that a statement, to be true, must have a structural isomorphism with the state of affairs in the world that makes it true. For example, "A cat is on a mat" is true if, and only if, there is in the world a cat and a mat and the cat is related to the mat by virtue of being on it. See Russell, B. 1903. *The Principles of Mathematics*. Cambridge University Press.

her relation *to* the world. Phenomenological thinkers like Martin Heidegger[8] start with the idea that we are already thrown into the world ('Geworfenheit') and that in this thrownness we endeavor to figure out the different ways we relate to the world. In this process, we cannot think of language as media, or as something that mediates between the world and us, but instead must recognize that they themselves are the fabric of the world.

Here is the thought that interests me: If we think of language as a medium, as a shortcut that helps us refer to a tree with the word tree, e.g., picking out the brown branch with leaves from a tree and calling it a tree later helps us to point to a host of different branches with different leaves and apply the term tree to those as well, then we can certainly say that language is a fabulous tool to make our lives easier. The question, then, is how we learn language or concepts so that we can use them as tools.

On account of the language learning that we discussed earlier, we cannot say that there are concepts ready to be picked up by us. Rather, it seems that our experience ought to be described more like a growing of language muscles, a repeated attempt at expressing something, a guessing game that eventually leads us to use the right terms. Language as a medium is not something that we learn bit by bit, but something that we grow (into). Language is not a tool that we use, but is more genuinely a part of us.

4. Principles and Methods of (Language) Learning: The Ignorant Schoolmaster

In *The Ignorant School Master: Five Lessons in Intellectual Emancipation*,[9] Jacques Rancière argues that "what all human children learn best is what no master can explain: the mother tongue." Rancière writes: "We speak to them and we speak around them. They hear and retain, imitate and repeat, make mistakes and correct themselves, succeed by chance and begin again methodically, and, at too young an age for explicators to begin instructing them, they are almost all—regardless of gender, social condition, and skin color—able to understand and speak the language of their parents" (ibid.).

But Rancière also recounts a story about second language learning, of a teacher who, having emigrated from France to the Netherlands, does not speak the

---

8   See for example Martin Heidegger's *Being and Time*, translated by John Macquarrie and Edward Robinson, (Blackwell, 1962).

9   Jacques Rancière, *The Ignorant School Master: Five Lessons in Intellectual Emancipation.* (Stanford University Press, 1991, p. 5).

language of his students but nevertheless manages to teach them French by giving them a French book—*Telemaque* by Fenelon[10] in a Dutch translation and letting them learn French the same way they had learned their mother tongue: "by observing and retaining, repeating and verifying, by relating what they were trying to know to what they already knew, by doing and reflecting about what they had done. They moved along in a manner one shouldn't move along—the way children move, blindly, figuring out riddles" (10). They started with the first sentence and chapter by chapter they had to write short essays in French until in no time they had learned French, with no master to teach them.

The Ignorant School Master: Five Lessons in Intellectual Emancipation tries to debunk two myths about intelligence. On the one hand, there is the intelligence of the small child or of the common folk, who perceive only by chance and interpret the world in a circle of habits. On the other hand, there is the methodological intelligence of the schoolmaster who can easily move from the simple to the complex, from the part to the whole, and who can reason and explicate. What Rancière criticizes is that in the former, the intelligence of the pupil is usually disregarded while the one of the schoolmaster is held highly as the right example. Pupils have to cope with the fact that the master explicates and thus forces them to understand that they do not understand unless someone explicates. Their intelligence is disregarded by a principle of explication that according to Rancière is a principle of stultification. Knowledge is not something that the schoolmaster has and then explicates to the student; instead, knowledge constitutes itself during understanding. Explications hinder and thus stultify understanding. We can think of the schoolmaster's explication in the same way we have thought about the caretaker's help when the child learns to sit or walk. By doing something for them that they are capable of doing themselves and that they must do themselves to learn, we hinder the child's development. In the same way in which we do not start with an empty slate and then introduce concepts, principles to learn our first language, we are capable to learn anything without needing a master who gives us explications and principles to go by.

5. Conclusion: Media Abstinence – Why Less Can be More

I have developed different strands of thought to elucidate our relationship to the world and to learning. The question about whether media enhance or hinder learning is not directly tackled; however, in the parts of my paper I show that

---

10 Fenelon, Francois de. *Telemachus* (Texts in the History of Political Thought, 1994).

our ideas of what a medium is and what learning is need to be put to the test. If language is a way to represent the world correctly or incorrectly, then knowledge can be taught as a matter of truth and falsehood. However, if language is our way of being in the world and if learning language is not accomplished through learning the right concepts or having the right deep structures in place but by developing language through habit and trial and error, then it is paramount that we are given the space to develop not just our first language, but all our knowledge through ourselves.

The idea of language as a medium is akin to the idea of media as crutches that help us learn and understand the world. But like the idea that a cushion that helps a child sit might hinder the muscle development that would come with learning to sit by oneself, the idea that media help children learn must be scrutinized to the point where we see that media may actually hinder the intellectual development of the child.

While my considerations lead me to recommend a strict media policy for infants and preschool children, I am not saying that media are bad in themselves and that we cannot learn through them. My recommendation has to do with the stultification that Rancière addresses in his book. If young children can turn to media for everything and get a quick explanation through videos and games, they will not need to grow their own thinking muscles. As a matter of fact, they will not grow their own language or medium that is the connection to their world; instead, they will be dependent on ready-made explications by others. Early childhood education cannot focus on feeding the mind tutorials and videos. When we try to enhance the cognitive abilities of very young children with the use of media, we neglect the children's capacity to make experiences and to learn through their own bodies and [developing] minds.

Bibliography

Aristotle. *Aristotle's On the Soul*. Translated by H.G. Apostle, Peripatetic Press, 1981.

Fenelon, Francois. *Telemachus*. Texts in the History of Political Thought, 1994.

Gerber, Magda. *Dear Parent: Caring for Infants with Respect* (ed. B. J. Weaver). RIE, 1998.

Heidegger, Martin. *Being and Time*. Translated by John Macquarrie, and Edward Robinson, Blackwell, 1962.

Lyon, Irene. "Rolling – Feldenkrais with Baby Liv." Online video clip. *YouTube*. YouTube, 24 July 2010, https://www.youtube.com/watch?v=D9Ko7U1pLlg.

Pikler, Emmi and Anna Tardos. "Some Contributions to the Study of Infants' Gross Motor Activities." *Proceedings of the 16th International Congress of Applied Psychology.* ICAP, 1968.

Rancière, Jacques. *The Ignorant School Master. Five Lessons in Intellectual Emancipation.* Stanford University Press, 1991.

Russell, Bertrand. *The Principles of Mathematics.* Cambridge University Press, 1903.

Wittgenstein, Ludwig. "Philosophische Untersuchungen." *Werkausgabe Bd. 1 Wittgenstein.* Frankfurt am Main: Suhrkamp, 1995. [*Philosophical Investigations* (trans. G.E.M. Anscombe, ed. G.E.M. Anscombe, R. Rhees). Prentice-Hall, Inc, 1958.

Michael Waltinger

Media and Cultural Education – A Means to Social Cohesion in a Multicultural (Media)World

Abstract: In an increasingly mediatized world (Lundby; Hepp and Krotz), media usage is as much entangled in everyday life as everyday life is mediated (Röser 7; Paus-Hasebrink). The media are important agents of socialization (Hoffmann and Mikos) and are involved in the social construction of the world, as they carry social meaning and reproduce dominant social norms and ideologies (Devereux 19ff.). In doing so, the media contribute to the audiences' forms of knowledge, not only about their immediate social surroundings but also about more distant contexts, places and cultures (Devereux 20).

As the world becomes an increasingly globalized place, the flow of media images generally follows this trend. It does so, however, in a quite unequal fashion, creating what might be called a divided global village, where uneven flows of media images in their re-presentation (Devereux ch. 3 and 7) often reproduce the inequalities of the social world (Waltinger; Hall et al.). Additionally, both the current refugee situation and the immigration countries in which good parts of the population are foreign-born, testify that it is also the flow of people that tends to become more global, making the world a smaller and denser place.

When globalized media worlds increasingly become intercultural life worlds, media education has to become part of essential education, because it is desirable that people are able to competently navigate through and participate in those media-life-worlds (Süss et al. 122). Cultural education needs to become integral, since the concepts of cultural relativism and cultural sensitivity (Jandt 427) allow to appreciate different cultures without measuring them against own standards. The university as a place for social development could and should be a forum in which such knowledge is actively formed.

1. Introduction

Being born and raised in Nigeria, Novelist Chimamanda Adichie gave a talk at "TEDglobal 2009" in Oxford, where she shared with the audience a taste of what it meant for her to move to the Unites States for university studies as a teenager. She says:

> I left Nigeria to go to university in the United States. I was 19. My American roommate was shocked by me. She asked where I had learned to speak English so well, and was confused when I said that Nigeria happened to have English as its official language. She asked if she could listen to what she called my "tribal music," and was consequently very disappointed when I produced my tape of Mariah Carey. She assumed that I did not know how to use a stove.

Now, this idea or projection that Adichie's roommate had of her – or of Africa respectively – is what the novelist then called a "single story". This was also the title of the address that she gave at Oxford: "The danger of a single story." But what does Adichie mean by a "single story"? She indeed refers to a story about someone or something – but the "single story" is defined by being (a) a random, decontextualized and often uninformed snippet of a whole, and, even worse, (b) often the only story available. And this is exactly what renders the "single story" problematic. Adichie puts it like this: "The single story creates stereotypes, and the problem with stereotypes is not that they are untrue, but that they are incomplete. They make one story become the only story."

While stereotypes certainly are somewhat helpful in reducing complexity in everyday life, making social environments easier to comprehend and navigate, they become delicate if people get discriminated against or appear in a distorted light because of such classifications (Öztürk 2). It is exactly this problematic character of the "single story" that Adichie's roommate got entangled in.

Regardless of whether or not Adichie's account is anecdotal in character, we may well imagine her roommate as the incarnation of all those members of society that also – due to a lack of an appropriate frame of reference – carry with them rather undifferentiated and essentialized images of what is often called "the other".

The reason for this surely may be understandable: If we follow Wa'Njogu on the example of Africa in his article "Representation of Africa in the Western Media", "most Westerners have never visited and may never visit Africa, yet they hold an image of Africa in their minds" (76). "Africa in the Western media", he goes on, "is constructed through metaphor. The metaphors selected for the communication of Africa's stories, however, do not come from Africa, but from stereotypes of Africa that have permeated Western culture" (76). Similar things may be true for other places such as China, Syria, Afghanistan or India. If we now add to the equation Niklas Luhmann's famous formula of "Whatever we know about our society, or indeed about the world in which we live, we know through the mass media" (1), it may not seem all too surprising that a differentiated idea about faraway places and cultures may be difficult to obtain.

While the intention is not to invoke long discarded hypodermic-needle or stimulus-response-models of unidirectional and monocausal media effects – of course there is the agency of the subject, media appropriation, and all that – it is still necessary to recognize that in an increasingly mediatized world (Lundby; Hepp and Krotz), media usage is as much entangled in everyday life as everyday life is mediated, to an extent that is symbiotic and almost inseparable (Röser; Paus-Hasebrink). Due to that, the media are important agents of socialization

(Hoffmann and Mikos) and are involved in the social construction of the world, as they do not only occupy a lot of people's time, but also carry social meaning and scripts while they reproduce dominant social norms, belief systems, discourses and ideologies (Devereux 19ff.). In doing so, the media contribute to people's forms of knowledge, not only about their immediate social surroundings but also about more distant contexts, places and cultures (20). At the same time, the "media draw upon a wide range of taken-for-granted assumptions about the social world: assumptions that, more often than not, go unquestioned by media professionals and audiences alike" (20).

Now, in today's world, it is not only the media as institutions and image flows that are by and large increasingly globalized (while there of course are exceptions and inequalities; see e.g. Devereux; Asante et al. or Thussu), but also the flow of people around the world that intensifies. Both the current refugee situation and the immigration countries where good parts of the population are foreign-born, testify that the world is becoming a denser and more interconnected place. Sweden has been spearheading Europe by far for many years, being the country with most asylum applications and refugee intake per capita (Ritzi 5 and 9). Also, about every fifth person that is living in Germany has their roots elsewhere (Zandonella 5).

This is why it is essential, through media and cultural education, to proactively foster social cohesion by for example, reflecting on the mixing of people and cultures, the images that those people and cultures have of one another and where those are coming from, in situations that cover a mélange of host cultures, guest cultures, and anything in between.

This outline of ideas certainly needs some more unfolding. Hence, in the following, the focus shall first of all lie on the question of 'global media' and the alleged 'global flow of media images'. In combination with that, it can be helpful to give some thoughts to the representation of the abovementioned faraway places, cultures and people in those image flows. Building on this discussion, media and cultural education will be suggested as an integral part of public higher education, because in an increasingly interconnected world, it might lead to improved social cohesion and is therefore deemed desirable.

2. How 'Global' are 'Global Media Flows'?

As the world becomes an increasingly globalized place, the flow of media images generally follows this trend. It does so, however, in a quite unequal fashion, creating what might be called a divided global village, where uneven flows of media images in their "re-presentation" (Devereux 3 and 7) often reproduce the inequalities of the social world (Thussu pt. 3). This matters, because in as much as economic institutions have economic power through material resources and political institutions have political power through authority, cultural institutions such as religion, but also the media, have symbolic power through means of information and communication (Thompson 17 – quoted from Flew 5).

Kai Hafez in his book "The Myth of Media Globalization", which analyzes several media systems like international reporting, film, TV, internet, or media policy, brings forward the idea that there is most likely no structurally equal world media system in the sense of balanced media flows and media power. Global media flows are predominantly uneven and hegemonic, offering little to no considerable alternatives to the dominant images of others. Daya Kishan Thussu, in an article titled "Mapping Global Media Flow and Contra-Flow", by and large, reaches similar conclusions. While he identifies the 'dominant flows' that largely emanate from the global north, he also points out an increase in what he calls 'subaltern flows' (Thussu 221) that "create new transnational configurations" (229), from peripheral southern urban creative hubs such as Cairo, Hong Kong, or Mumbai (230). While those flows are relevant and important, they are still very disparate in comparison to the dominant flows in terms of volume and economic value, which is why caution is required when talking about a potential rise of non-Western media (221ff.). With regard to the Hollywood dependency, for instance, a 2005 report of the UNESCO states that "more than one-third of the countries in the world do not produce any films at all, while Africa as a whole (constituting [by then; M.W.] 53 countries) has only produced just over 600 films in its history" (quoted from Thussu 227).

Others are no less cautious about the potential of the subaltern to create correctives or contra-flows to the depictions and narratives of the hegemony. While 'Nollywood' (the Nigerian film industry) and 'Bollywood' in India are the major producers of motion pictures besides Hollywood (Acland and UNESCO Institute for Statistics 8), the often less formal character of these film industries makes it difficult to plug into the dominant networks of global media flows (Miller 117). On top of that, the mere availability of such media content does not help, if it is not systematically embedded into the programming of local media stations (Orgeret 51ff.).

At times, the new, participatory media such as YouTube and the Web 2.0 are emphasized as media that could potentially empower people because they allow for easy 'talking back' and creative ways of self-presentation (Wall 393). In the context of Africa, Wall advanced a study that sought to trace possibilities of alternative representations of stereotypes about Africa on YouTube, but the results in that regard were rather disappointing. Videos that were tagged with 'Kenia' or

'Ghana', for instance, received little attention; however, most of the videos uploaded came from accounts that were registered in Europe or North America (398ff.). Wall sums up the findings of her study as follows:

> More broadly, the findings here suggest that YouTube enables the average westerner in particular to become a chronicler of other peoples in faraway lands just as travelers and missionaries 'discovered' Africa in previous centuries. . . . Indeed, many of their contributions to YouTube reinforce and naturalize stereotypes. . . . [A]ge-old inequities still exist and still allow westerners to dominate. (405)

3. The (Logics of) the Representation of 'the Other' in the Media

When it comes to the representation of others in the media, where the word 'representation' may be defined as "using language [or symbols; M.W.] to say something meaningful about, or to represent, the world meaningfully, to other people" (Hall 1), language and symbols obviously play an important role, i.e. if we accept a constructionist take on language and symbols, meaning that we agree on the view that "meaning is constructed in and through language" (1).

Now language is based on making distinctions. A 'chair' for example refers to a class of objects that you can sit on and that, on top of that, have an armrest – as opposed to a stool. With this concept in mind, anything that we can see in the world can be categorized as to whether it is a chair or not, according to the agreed definition of what a chair is. While this might be pretty straightforward, it is easy to overlook the fact that such contrasts or categories as expressed by a language are not a 'reality', but only a more or less random construction that often incurs meaning only culturally. 'Reality' does not even force us to have a name for things that allow us to sit on them – it just makes practical sense to name those objects, because they have a meaning in everyday life (Stefanowitsch 28). When it comes to categorizing color, for instance, human beings are capable of physiologically distinguishing an almost unimaginable amount of several million colors or shades of colors. This wealth of perceptual information is organized into the meaningful categories that different languages and cultures provide. While the English language distinguishes colors such as red, orange, yellow, green, blue, or purple, speakers of Shona in Zimbabwe would use only four different terms to distinguish the same spectrum. It would be dangerous, however, to infer that speakers of Shona are not aware of the differences that are perceived by speakers of English, just because they use different labels to organize them (Jandt 57f.). Those differences might well just not matter to them; therefore, perhaps there is no need to construct them linguistically. Hence, while appearing to be a 'reality' to the users of each language, none of those colors are less or more real. And while it may be perfectly fine to label dogs or horses as food in one culture, this may be beyond the imaginable in another culture; however, labelling them as a pet does not make one version of 'reality' universally more true than the other (59f.).

Most of the distinctions above are pretty innocent and it does not really matter if they have any objectively true equivalent. If we treat sitting accommodation unequally (by placing armchairs in the living room and stools in the bathroom, for instance) or degrade them (by finding the former more comfortable than the latter), not much harm is done. The same cannot be said for human beings. While some perceived differences might, at first glance, also have correspondence in 'reality' – such as "black" or "white" – a closer look will reveal that there are different 'shades of black' that move along a continuous spectrum (Stefanowitsch 28). It gets truly problematic when such blurry distinctions that are 'based on reality', become charged with negative properties.

The representation of the other in the West often invokes binaries such as the 'primitive other' vs. the 'modern us'. Communities in Africa, for instance, in Euro-American thought, are often referred to as 'tribal', invoking pre-modern associations, while the very same type of categorization in the northern hemisphere would more neutrally be called an 'ethnic group' (Wa'Njogu 77). The descriptive language used plays an important role in constructing perceptions, for instance: when people are said to live in 'huts' and not homes; when people reportedly have a 'traditional belief' and not religion; or when they have a 'kinship system' and not relatives (Arndt sec. 9). Thus, it may indeed be hard to appreciate anything to do with this 'other' as equal, on eye-level, or at least as a valid and possible alternative to what is taken for granted. One of the problems related to that is the invisibility of some of these underlying operational logics. Peggy McIntosh, in her insightful Essay "White Privilege – Unpacking the Invisible Knapsack" reflects that "whites are taught to think of their lives as morally neutral, normative, and average, and also ideal, so that when we work to benefit others, this is seen as work which will allow 'them' to be more like 'us'" (33). This is also evident in the many people who do not even reflect on 'Whiteness' as a racial identity – this is how strong the normativity is (35).

When we watch movies, we can for instance see Bruce Willis as a professional U.S. soldier in the 2003 film "Tears of the Sun", kindly trying to save a warn-torn Nigeria, as he argues that "God has already left Africa" (Orgeret 53). Beautiful sundowns, acacia trees, Africa's depiction as a romantic scenery and pristine Garden Eden, and not to forget the infamous "struggling but smiling African", are of course, the other extreme (47). Another issue is an often quite undifferentiated and de-contextualized news coverage about larger places such as Africa, where more than a billion people, 54 countries and over 2000 different languages apparently often share little more than the experiences of resistance and domination within the 'big black continent' (Wasserman 7) – a place that always seems to become but never belong (Uimonen 35). The website "AfricaIsACountry.com" – the name says it all – is an excellent source for media criticism in those directions.

While much of what has been said so far may well be "only naive and unreflecting projections" (Hoffers sec. 4), the structurally problematic patterns of dualisms, essentialism and ethnification are rather apparent: As dualism differentiates between 'us' (inclusion: 'the modern west') and 'them' (exclusion: 'the primitive other') (Wa'Njogu 77) and essentialism ascribes exclusive properties to this other (Eide 66), we can understand (media-) ethnification as a "one-sided, dominant media focus on a person or group as an ethnic other, an emphasis on her difference (from a presumed 'us'), based on her being (more or less) visibly different or on a tacitly presumed background that differs from the mainstream" (66). Particularly problematic is a pattern that Andreasson has called "reductive repetition": "Reductive repetition [repeatedly] reduces the diversity of ... historical experiences and trajectories, sociocultural contexts and political situations into a set of core deficiencies" (971).

This is, then, pretty close to what Adichie has brought forth when talking about the "single story". In this process, one category is often defined in a hegemonic manner as the 'norm' while the 'other' (i.e. anything that the 'norm' does not comprise) is imagined as the 'deviation' from this norm (Sturken and Cartwright 111). So while it appears 'normal' to some to be white, secular, to think that a romantic relationship is an affair between two individuals, that the proper way to eat is with silverware and to believe that "life is what you make it", it must necessarily feel strange to be of color, to be muslim or polytheistic, to interpret marriage as an affair between two extended families, to consider the hands as a suitable eating utensil and to leave one's "fate in gods hands".

This logic has been thoroughly described as "Orientalism" by Edward Said. By opposing the Orient to the Occident, the focus is much less on a particular place or people, but much more on the Orient as a western cultural construct of the strange, peculiar, and odd. Let us consider a final example on this logic, and have a look at what Horace Miner in his essay "Body Ritual among the Nacirema" has to say:

> The daily body ritual performed by everyone includes a mouthrite. Despite the fact that these people are so punctilious about care of the mouth, this rite involves a practice which strikes the uninitiated stranger as revolting. It was reported to me that the ritual consists of inserting a small bundle of hog hairs into the mouth, along with certain magical powders, and then moving the bundle in a highly formalized series of gestures. (quoted from Yep 341)

In this account, the Nacirema become an exotic and 'primitive' Other. The point of this narrative then becomes apparent, when Miner reveals that this paragraph is a parody only, using a certain type of language to describe the Americans (which is Nacirema spelled backwards) brushing their teeth (341).

While all of the above has included many examples from Africa, since this is the author's research background, much of what has been said so far can also be observed in current everyday developments, such as those events that have been coined, in pre-determinist fashion, a refugee 'crisis'. Devereux in his book "Understanding the Media" writes that the fact that "media coverage tends to problematize minorities is confirmed by a large number of studies" (191). He then goes on to describe several examples, in which the media for instance construct connections between race and crime (191). This is something that I have noted myself by observing, in a rather unstructured manner, people's everyday discussions of the refugee situation. "Some of them are criminals" or "I read they bother people in the streets" are rather common remarks that I have witnessed. Resentments can be strong, and it was not long ago that a group of masked men in Stockholm's city center chased and beat up what the media in their coverage referred to as "Non-Swedes" – an incident obviously connected to fear and disorientation. I have commented, about a year ago, on such misconceptions and misconstructions like "the criminal immigrant" on my blog thinkbeyondborders.org. In this piece, I have attempted to develop the point that while criminal statistics may at times show that the variables "migration background" and "deviant behavior" may correlate, there is no causality. And this is a very important fact that the media often blur or omit. The short explanation to this correlation is: Crime is mostly caused by social and not cultural factors. The slightly longer explanation is that crime often has to do with social inequality, disempowerment, tough conditions of socialization, and so on. This is exactly what many immigrants went through – and continue to go through – while being in the asylum procedure: not being able to choose where to live, difficulties in moving around freely, difficult access to education and finance, having no family around, and never knowing what the asylum decision might bring – all this causing a tremendous amount of stress that can be extremely hard to cope with. This is an unfortunate, but very important context that mainstream media, more often than not, rather obscure than illuminate.[1]

---

1 See http://thinkbeyondborders.org/gefangen-in-empathiemangel-und-unverstaend-nis-ein-kommentar-zum-grassierenden-fluechtlingshass.

4. Conclusion: Media and Cultural Education as a Means to Social Cohesion in a Multicultural (Media) World

We, then, need media and cultural education to (a) understand said media flows and constructions in order to reflect and de-construct and also to (b) understand how to approach belief systems, values or cultures that are distinct from our own.

What could help here would be an increased engagement with questions of mutual (cultural) understanding in order to allow for and facilitate social cohesion. This involves questions such as:

- What are the (media) images that 'we' have of 'others'?
- What are the (media) images that 'others' have of 'us'?[2]
- How do these imaginations come into existence? What mechanisms of representation are at work?

Gust Yep in his essay on "Encounters with the Other – Personal Notes for a Reconceptualization of Intercultural Communication Competence" writes that

> [t]he citizens of the twenty-first century must learn to see through the eyes, hearts, and minds of people from cultures other than their own. Several important trends of the late twentieth century have transformed the world into a global village: technology development, globalization of the economy, widespread population migration, the development of multiculturalism, and the demise of the nation-state in favor of sub- and supranational identifications. In order to live meaningfully and productively in this world, individuals must develop their intercultural communication competence. (339)

Having that said, Yep also reminds us that when conceptualizing such intercultural communication competence, we need to question the assumption of white, middle-class culture as being the center or 'ideal-order' against which other cultures are then compared (339): "Competence and acceptance from whom? Who decides the criteria? Who doesn't? Competent or acceptable on the basis of what social and historical context? To assume that ... [communicators] negotiate mutual rules of appropriate conduct is to deny the power of ideology, historical structures, and limitations on the file of choices" (339).

Departing from what Tu Weiming calls "an old world of divisions and walls to a brave new world of connections and webs" (497), we need "genuine dialogue as mutual learning that we will be able to achieve unity in diversity and build an integrated global community" (496). While the world has never before been so interconnected and interdependent (however far away it is from being a

---

2   See e.g. Said or Hall for the concept of the 'other' and 'otherization'. For a coverage of the topic of 'other' and race in the media, see e.g. the edition of Rodman.

monolithic global village), this is especially important, because even as this process encourages and is characterized by diversity, there is also a tendency towards asserting one's own culture, because globalization also accentuates local awareness, consciousness, sensitivity, sentiment and passion (499).

So when (globalized) media worlds increasingly become (intercultural) life worlds, media education has to become part of essential education, because it is desirable for people to be able to competently assess, navigate through and participate in those media-life-worlds (Süss et al. 122). In the context of Africa, for instance, Orgeret calls for a "media literacy about Africa" (59) that will not only allow for critically and reflectively interrogating one-sided and stereotypical representations of the continent and its peoples, but also for a questioning of those aspects that are completely left out (59). Furthermore, cultural education needs to become integral, since the concepts of cultural relativism and cultural sensitivity allow to appreciate different cultures from within their very own logics, history and contexts, without measuring them against own standards (Jandt 427). While cultural sensitivity refers to not making any "value judgements based on one's own cultural values about other cultures' practices or artifacts" (i.e., better or worse, right or wrong) (427), cultural relativism means the appreciation of the fact that "the differences in peoples are the results of historical, social, and geographic conditions and that all populations have complete and equally developed cultures" (427). This is also to say that while two systems A and B may be perfectly functional within their own system's logic, the application of system A's rules for an explanation or understanding of system B's workings may be a forlorn undertaking – not because one of the two systems is superior to the other or on a different state of so-called 'development', but simply because the rulebooks are different. Playing chess on the rules of backgammon will just end up somewhat messy. Fuglesang advances this powerful idea on the very first page of his early book "About Understanding – Ideas and Observations on Cross-Cultural Communication". He writes: "It is my belief that a culture cannot be justly described in the concepts of another culture. It can truly be rendered only through its own means of expression" (13).

The university as a place for social and personal development could and should be a forum in which such knowledge is actively formed and fostered. In an educational context, it is especially intercultural pedagogics that can contribute to this mission, if this sub-discipline is understood as one that aims to pedagogically intervene in xenophobic, racist, or ethnocentric world views by challenging the norms and stereotypes of the dominant systems (Niesyto "Interkulturelle Medienpädagogik" 5; "Interkulturelle Medienbildung" 864).

References

Acland, Charles R., and UNESCO Institute for Statistics. "From International Blockbusters to National Hits. Analysis of the 2012 UIS Survey on Feature Film Statistics." *UIS Information Bulletin No. 8*, http://www.uis.unesco.org/culture/Documents/ib8-analysis-cinema-production-2012-en2.pdf, 2012. Accessed 1 March 2017.

Adichie, Chimamanda. "The Danger of a Single Story." *TEDglobal 2009*, 2009, http://www.ted.com/talks/chimamanda_adichie_the_danger_of_a_single_story.html. Accessed 1 March 2017.

Andreasson, Stefan. "Orientalism and African Development Studies: The 'Reductive Repetition' Motif in Theories of African Underdevelopment." *Third World Quarterly*, vol. 26, no. 6, 2005, pp. 971–986.

Arndt, Susan. "Kolonialismus, Rassismus und Sprache. Kritische Betrachtungen der deutschen Afrikaterminologie." 2004, http://www.bpb.de/gesellschaft/migration/afrikanische-diaspora/59407/afrikaterminologie?p=all. Accessed 1 March 2017.

Asante, Molefi Kete, Yoshitake Miike, and Jing Yin, editors. *The Global Intercultural Communication Reader*. Routledge, 2014.

Devereux, Eoin. *Understanding the Media*. 3rd ed., Sage, 2014.

Eide, Elisabeth. "Strategic Essentialism and Ethnification. Hand in Glove?" *Nordicom Review*, vol. 31, no. 2, 2010, pp. 63–78.

Flew, Terry. *Understanding Global Media*. Palgrave MacMillan, 2007.

Fuglesang, Andreas. *About Understanding – Ideas and Observations on Cross-Cultural Communication*. Dag Hammarskjöld Foundation, 1982.

Hafez, Kai. *The Myth of Media Globalization*. Polity Press, 2007.

Hepp, Andreas, and Friedrich Krotz, editors. *Mediatized Worlds. Culture and Society in a Media Age*. Palgrave MacMillan, 2014.

Hall, Stuart, Jessica Evans, and Sean Nixon, editors. *Representation*. 2nd ed., The Open University; Sage, 2013.

Hall, Stuart. "The Spectacle of the 'Other.'" *Representation* 2nd edition, edited by Stuart Hall, Jessica Evans, and Sean Nixon, The Open University; Sage, 2013, pp. 215–287.

Hoffers, Ellen. "Afrika in unseren Köpfen." 2010, hhttp://afrikabilder.blogsport.de/2010/04/12/afrika-in-unseren-koepfen/. Accessed 1 March 2017.

Hoffmann, Dagmar; and Lothar Mikos, editors. *Mediensozialisationstheorien. Modelle und Ansätze in der Diskussion*. 2nd ed., VS Verlag für Sozialwissenschaften, 2010.

Jandt, Fred E. *An Introduction to Intercultural Communication. Identities in a Global Community*. Sage, 2007.

Luhmann, Niklas. *The Reality of the Mass Media*. Stanford University Press, 2000.

Lundby, Knut, editor. *Mediatization of Communication*. DeGruyter/Mouton, 2014.

McIntosh, Peggy. "White Privilege. Unpacking the Invisible Knapsack." *The Race and Media Reader*, edited by Gilbert B. Rodman, Routledge, 2014, pp. 33–36.

Miller, Jade. "Global Nollywood: The Nigerian Movie Industry and Alternative Global Networks in Production and Distribution." *Global Media and Communication*, vol. 8, no. 2, 2012, pp. 117–133.

Niesyto, Horst. "Chancen und Perspektiven interkultureller Medienpädagogik." 2005, Speech at the 22.GMK-Forum in Bielefeld: www.gmk-net.de/fileadmin/pdf/Niesyto.pdf. Accessed 1 March 2017.

Niesyto, Horst. "Interkulturelle Medienbildung." *Handbuch der Erziehungswissenschaft* (vol. III/2,), edited by Gerhard Mertens et al., Schöningh, 2009, pp. 863–870.

Öztürk, Asiye. "Editorial." *APuZ (Aus Politik und Zeitgeschichte) – Schwerpunktthema Ungleichheit, Ungleichwertigkeit*, vol. 62, no. 16–17, 2012, p. 2.

Orgeret, Kristin Skare. "Mediated Culture and the Well-informed Global Citizen. Images of Africa in the Global North." *Nordicom Review*, vol. 31, no. 2, 2010, pp. 47–61.

Paus-Hasebrink, Ingrid (2013): "Medienwelten, Medienhandeln, Medienaneignung, Medienkompetenz. Medienpädagogische Theoriebausteine überdacht." *Medienbildung in einer sich wandelnden Gesellschaft. Festschrift für Horst Niesyto*, edited by Bjoern Maurer et al., kopaed, 2013, pp. 25–40.

Ritzi, Nadine. "Flüchtlinge. Themenblätter im Unterricht, Nr. 109." *Bundeszentrale für politische Bildung (BpB)*. 2015, www.bpb.de/themenblaetter. Accessed 1 March 2017.

Rodman, Gilbert B., editor. *The Race and Media Reader*. Routledge, 2014.

Röser, Jutta. "Einleitung: Zu diesem Buch." *MedienAlltag. Domestizierungsprozesse alter und neuer Medien*, edited by Jutta Röser, VS Verlag für Sozialwissenschaften, 2007, pp. 7–14.

Said, Edward W. *Orientalism*. Penguin Classics, 1978.

Stefanowitsch, Anatol. "Sprache und Ungleichheit." *Ungleichheit, Ungleichwertigkeit. APuZ (Aus Politik und Zeitgeschichte)*, vol. 62, no. 16–17, 2012, pp. 27–33.

Sturken, Marita and Lisa Cartwright. *Practices of Looking: An Introduction to Visual Culture*. 2nd ed., Oxford University Press, 2009.

Süss, Daniel, Claudia Lampert, and Christine W. Wijnen. *Medienpädagogik. Ein Studienbuch zur Einführung*. 2nd ed., Springer VS, 2013.

Thussu, Daya Kishan, editor. *Internationalizing Media Studies*. Routledge, 2009.

Thussu, Daya Kishan. "Mapping Global Media Flow and Contra-Flow." *International communication. A Reader*, edited by Daya Kishan Thussu, Routledge, 2010, pp. 221–238.

Uimonen, Paula. "'Number Not Reachable': Mobile Infrastructure and Global Racial Hierarchy in Africa." *Journal des anthropologues*, 2015, pp. 142–143.

Wall, Melissa. "Africa on Youtube. Musicians, Tourists, Missionaries and Aid Workers." *International Communication Gazette*, vol. 71, no. 5, 2009, pp. 393–407.

Waltinger, Michael. "Afrika(ner)bilder in westlichen Medien. Ungleichheit und die Repräsentation des Anderen im Zuge globaler Kommunikationsflüsse." *Medienbildung in einer sich wandelnden Gesellschaft. Festschrift für Horst Niesyto*, edited by Bjoern Maurer et al., kopaed, 2013, pp. 279–290.

Wa'Njogu, John Kiarie (2009): "Representation of Africa in the Western Media: Challenges and Opportunities." *Media and Identity in Africa*, edited by John Middleton and Kimani Njogu, Edinburgh University Press for the International Africa Insitute, 2009, pp. 76–83.

Wasserman, Herman. "Introduction: Taking It to the Streets." *Popular Media, Democracy and Development in Africa*, edited by Herman Wasserman, Routledge, 2010, pp. 1–16.

Weiming, Tu. "The Context of Dialogue. Globalization and Diversity." *The Global Intercultural Communication Reader*, edited by Molefi Kete Asante, Yoshitake Miike, and Jing Yin, Routledge, 2014, pp. 496–514.

Yep, Gust A. "Encounters with the 'Other'. Personal Notes for a Reconceptualization of Intercultural Communication Competence". *The Global Intercultural Communication Reader*, edited by Molefi Kete Asante, Yoshitake Miike, and Jing Yin, Routledge, 2014, pp. 339–356.

Zandonella, Bruno. "Migration und Integration. Themenblätter im Unterricht, Nr. 111." *Bundeszentrale für politische Bildung (BpB)*. 2015, www.bpb.de/themen blaetter. Accessed 1 March 2017.

Barbara Vollmer, Dietrich Dörner and Sibylle Rahm

Individual Creativity and Its Impact on the Co-Construction of Ideas

Abstract: Collective interpretations of life in cultures need to be seen as vibrant frameworks with flowing transmissions between one another (Rahm). Being confronted with innovation, individuals as well as groups need to shape change. In order to do so, they need to release familiar orientations, overcome uncertainty and be creative.

Artists overcome well-known orientations, e.g. by forming hypotheses or adapting perceptions and ideas to each other ("Emotion und Flow-Erleben"). Carefully observing people as they work creatively could show us more explicitly how new ideas emerge.

In our case study, 21 participants deal with randomly generated meaningless sentences and a picture that induces cryptic meaning. Also, they arrange items in an aesthetic way and finish one drawing. The participants are video recorded while they think aloud. The first results showed that their acting regulation varied a lot. In a second part, based on the first one, two individuals who had differed in their ways of dealing with the previous situation are placed in the same room. They are then observed as they co-construct ideas with each other.

The study is an important contribution to the understanding of the tacit processes accompanying innovation and to explaining group creativity more precisely. The results are a first step towards sustaining creative learning in the classroom.

Keywords: creativity, visual perception, tacit knowledge, innovation, inspiration

1. Introduction

In a rapidly changing world, everybody has to cope with the challenges that come from change in each and every sector of our lives. Changes concern the environment (e.g. global warming), employment (loss of life-long workplaces), relationships (changing family structures), health (e.g. pandemics), wealth (increasing poverty), demographic change (changes in the age pyramid), heterogeneity in cultures, and changing values in our societies (Townsend). We understand cultures as common orientations concerning values and beliefs that give direction to people's actions. Universities, which are traditional places for research and development, assist in finding answers to the abovementioned complex problems. They have to offer opportunities for lateral thinking.

Creativity is considered a problem-solving strategy (Dörner) that is strongly associated with personal growth and cultural evolution. Personal growth and team learning depend on opportunities to discover one's own potential (Senge; Kruse;

Rahm). Accordingly, educational facilities should feel responsible for sustaining adequate problem-solving strategies. Universities already offer such opportunities as they can be seen as places where different knowledge forms exist simultaneously. Collective interpretations of life in cultures need to be seen as vibrant frameworks with fluid transmissions between one another (Rahm). Universities have – in their capacity as places of culture – an important impact on their students taking on new roles. Thus, university students studying to become teachers need to responsibly assume their new roles as teachers. In the changeover from student to teacher, a major aspect for further participative and democratic orientations is the process of dealing with problems. As Kraus points out, "context sensitivity and continuous multimodal-knowledge-based, and highly context-related convincing activities are especially crucial for pedagogical action." (Kraus 56). Creativity as a knowledge form that promotes multi-perspectivity, multi-modal, diverse thinking and sensitivity to ambiguities helps develop intelligent knowledge and critical thinking, and serves as the basis for democratic participation. Similar to creative processes, the process of classroom teaching involves uncertainty and is full of potential for new experiences. As Senge explains, teachers need to be able to handle ambiguities and differences between vision and reality in order to meet change (174). The comprehension of over-inclusive thinking will be easier if it is based on own experiences (Cropley). Therefore, creativity as a main tool for instructional leadership needs to be made central (Guilford; Vygotsky; Beghetto; Wiater) in universities as well as in schools.

2. The Need for Creativity in the 21st Century

Life in the 21st century is characterised by great uncertainty (Beghetto 447) and schools have to find answers to social change (Beghetto; Dalin). Therefore, many researchers identify and develop creativity as a key educational goal (Guilford; Vygotsky; Plucker, Beghetto & Dow). As a result of the increasing complexity of life in the 21st century, Plucker, Beghetto & Dow claim that students need to be better equipped. Furthermore, Patry states that teachers need to be creative in order to cope with uncertainty.

We know that artists relinquish well-known orientations during the creative process, but why or how they cope with this remains an open question. Which mechanisms foster the emergence of ideas, and which do not?

Multiple investigations give evidence to show that schools inhibit rather than foster creativity (Robinson). For instance, investigations show that teachers tend to see creativity as a disruption rather than as a tool that embraces challenges, even though they claim to want to foster creativity (Cropley; Post et. al.). However, there is considerable uncertainty with regard to the possible reasons for this contradiction. Several authors believe that functional goals are the cause (Cropley; Hentig), while Beghetto considers 'teaching to the test' and sublime mechanisms to be likely causes.

Furthermore, there are currently no proven methods of fostering creativity in schools. Smith and Smith asked teachers how they would define creativity. They identified four types of responses: Some teachers mention specific programs such as the 'Thinking Hats Approach' of Edward de Bono or Csikszentmihaly's concept of flow; others focus on specific techniques they use, such as brainstorming or mind mapping; a third group tries to be open to students' ideas; and the fourth type of response is concerned with new ideas for teaching. Similarly, the creative personality is open to new ideas and situations. Being highly sensitive to problems, creative personalities are tolerant of ambiguities and have special endurance (Schuler & Görlich).

Urban believes that an anxiety-free learning environment is essential and accordingly offers advice on achieving this goal. According to Amabile, creativity is associated with intrinsic motivation and may thus be hindered by competition, social measurement and fear of criticism. This has led Beghetto to argue for caution with regard to the encouragement of competition and social comparisons. He suggests that teachers inform students in advance whenever their work will not be graded. Meanwhile, learning-centered approaches argue that teachers need to accept that there are different solutions to problems; they should also encourage students to ask questions. Hentig and other researchers believe that the time allotted for the encouragement of an open learning environment; the contribution of students' own ideas; their exploration and contemplation; as well as for critical thinking is essential. Similarly, Cropley claims that the power of endurance needs to be trained by presenting students with authentic problems. Cognitive and aesthetic approaches underline the complexity of creative processes According to Vollmer ("Emotion und Flow-Erleben") and Urban, the alternation between activity and tranquility needs to be recognised and utilised on the grounds that creative work consists of an ebb and flow in the level of activity; Hentig and others support the recognition of basic sensual experiences and emotions as crucial elements in learning experiences; Vygotsky as well as Parthey promote the use of imaginative power in order to find new research; consistently, Dörner ("Problemlösen als Informationsverarbeitung") suggests that students be confronted with situated and complex problems. This places the focus once more on the role of teacher competences. In the settings mentioned above, teachers need to trust their pupils to be able to find adequate solutions and invest in their commitment, autonomy and responsibility. In order to enhance students' and teachers' dealing with complexity and uncertainty, Combe & Paseka introduce the idea of situated creativity as a relevant competence for teachers. Since implicit theories influence the way in which teachers respond to pupils, they have also been claimed to play an important role in the teaching of creativity (see *inter alia* Chan & Chan, 185).

3. Field of Research and Definitions of Creativity

The task of producing a coherent definition of creativity has proved demanding. Despite differing on many points, all definitions of creativity stipulate three conditions for the product of a creative process: the product must be new; the product must be original; and the product must be relevant, either on a social or individual level. Whether a product is new or original depends either on its relevance for society – in which case its newness and originality are judged by outside parties – or on the recognition of an individual – in which case newness and originality are determined by the individual, for whom the product may have been hitherto unknown. (This argument is most often used in pedagogical contexts.) Nowadays, researchers have given up on the idea of creative genius and assume instead that creativity is a human ability available to everybody.

Historically, research on creativity has involved three fields: the arts, psychology and philosophy. Whereas philosophers have focused on questions of aesthetics and beauty, psychologists have been more interested in the way that people solve problems. During the period of industrialisation, there arose a fascination for genius ideas and those who conceived them. Thus, researchers investigated biographies of high-achievers, such as artists, architects and researchers. Field-theoretical approaches by *Gestalt* psychologists interpreted creativity in a manner that included the field in which creativity took place. Furthermore, they focused on emotion, motivation, sensuality and the senses. The underlying foundation here was the theory of behaviour in accordance with Lewin: $V=f(P;U)$. Following Lewin's theory, it is assumed that behaviour can be described as a function that includes the person as well as the field. Thus, behaviour should be seen as an integrated process that consists of complementary thinking and imagination as well as analytical thinking, instead of an addition of a series of single elements. The approach of *Gestalt* psychology sparked further research into field theory (Lück), eventually resulting in problem-solving research, including research on creativity. With the upcoming interest in the advancement of industries came the development of the measurement of intelligence. Eventually, the question arose as to the role that creativity should play in these models. Aesthetics has now developed into a sector of research in its own right. Like fine arts and philosophy, scholars in this field have an aesthetic approach to creativity. Thus, nowadays there are four fields involved in the research on creativity: the arts, philosophy, psychology and aesthetics. In the current study, we aim to combine psychological and aesthetic approaches.

Since each of these four fields has its own perspective, they also differ in their definitions of creativity. Within the field of aesthetics, researchers such as Starker show that dealing with uncertainty is an essential part of aesthetic work; Arnheim claims that dealing with the arts constitutes a way of achieving order (Arnheim); and Donne proposes in her dissertation on lyrics that so-called "unity among diversity" allows the reader to perceive and appreciate inherent patterns and beauty. The interplay between desire and aesthetics has already been mentioned by Fechner. Although this may be accurate, the enigmatic character of aesthetics is an essential component in its beauty (Voigt). This may explain why aesthetics resists all attempts to define it (Trebeß), and why this debate is shaped by plurality (Barck).

Psychological researchers focus on creativity as a problem-solving mechanism. Rhodes breaks creativity down into these 4 components: the problem, the person, the process and the press. The resulting combination of these parts demonstrates what is creative and what is not. In addition, some authors stress originality: In order to be socially accepted as being creative, a product needs to be different, new and innovative (Sternberg). Furthermore, in order to be inventive, products need to be exceptional, of high quality, and suitable to the particular task (Smith & Smith).

With regard to creative processes, there are evident connections between personality traits of creative individuals and creative processes ("Emotion und Flow-Erleben"). One prominent model for such creative processes is the model of Wallas. In retracing diaries of creative people, Wallas found four phases of creativity, namely Preparation, Incubation, Illumination and Verification. These phases are still used today, although often in slightly altered forms. They will be outlined in the following chapter in more detail.

Whether the need to be creative helps or hinders creative thinking depends on the amount of pressure placed on the individual. There is some evidence that ideas evolve under high pressure. On the other hand, this contradicts the idea of the arts as being free of any strictly defined purpose. This idea does not lead its practitioners towards any clearly-set goal but instead results in practising trial and error, and in using principles of chance and playful experiments (Voigt; Cropley).

4. Current State of Research on Creative Processes

Research into creative processes began at the turn of the 20th century. Catherine Cox closely examined 300 biographies of 'creative geniuses' and in the same year, Wallas published his theory of the four phases of the creative process. Current models of creative processes are still based on his theory.

The first phase observed by Wallas is that of Preparation, where impressions, facts, tasks or problems are collected. This phase is characterised by hard work and the involvement of the being. The problem is investigated intensely, using all the senses. In the second phase, known as Incubation, the artist or researcher does not find a way or solution to the problem, thus becoming more and more eager and involved in attempts at problem solving, but also more and more frustrated and restless. It is in this phase that many give up. In the third phase of Illumination, a solution is found. The solution or idea evolves suddenly and in an unpredictable way, e.g. while resting. Wallas describes such sudden ideas as follows: "They [the ideas] came particularly during the slow ascent of wooden hills on a sunny day" (Wallas 54). Wallas concludes three remarkable effects of sudden ideas: They come as a sudden "flash of success" (Wallas 95f.); they consist of vague irritations, a feeling that something is wrong and must be changed; and they involve the emotions. As Poincaré puts it, these emotions play a role "as a frequent directing force of the association process, and, as a still more frequent accompaniment of that process" (Wallas 75). In the fourth phase, known as Verification, the product is tested in regard to its viability, compatibility and quality.

Wallas introduces three new concepts regarding his theory: The first is "intimidation": "It was a vague impression of mental activity" (Wallas 97). Secondly, he introduces the concept of a "sudden idea", which had been previously noted by Poincaré. Finally, the concept of the "flash" is described by Wallas as follows: "But when the association had risen to the surface, it expanded into an expression of joy" (97).

As mentioned, Wallas' research, particularly his four phases, has been extremely influential. Many researchers have continued to work on his foundation, expanding or altering his phases of the creative processes. Especially noteworthy is Haseloff, who further divides the creative process into six phases. Between the phases of Preparation – described by him as a phase of Problematising – and Incubation, he adds a phase of Exploration. Haseloff regards the phase of Incubation as a phase of oblivion, in which a non-verbal, symbolic reorganisation of experiences takes place. He furthermore adds a phase of Regression (i.e. in singular) that includes relieved ambitions, as well as uncommitted and playful operations. The phases of Illumination and Verification occur as described by Wallas (Haseloff 89f.).

Similarly, Torrance, another influential researcher in this area, in "Rewarding Creative Behavior" asserts that creative thinking takes place in the course of realizing problems and difficulties, finding gaps in information and discovering missing elements. This is followed by attempting to fill in the blanks, formulating and re-formulating hypotheses on what could fill those gaps, and finally, conveying the results.

Correspondingly, Dörner ("Problemlösen als Informationsverarbeitung" 92ff) sees the phase of Incubation and sudden ideas as coherent. He assumes that sudden ideas correspond with a phase of forgetting during which less important aspects are lost. This gives more relevance to important aspects and promotes the emergence of sudden ideas. He suspects that cognitive structures are linked to one another and that these links differ in strength. Thus, "the sensibility of the sublime self for harmony and elegance" (Wallas) could help in assessing the importance of ideas. Over-inclusive thinking in relaxed situations might bring forth a solution. Accordingly, an external stimulus, such as a simple visual inspiration, could lead to a change in the cognitive imaginative structures of a creative individual.

Hertlein believes that creative processes vary from individual to individual. In his dissertation, he interviewed twenty-seven artists about their artistic output. The results of his study show that 21% of the artists had sudden ideas, of which 2% conceived a sudden idea even before beginning their work. For 35% of the artists, the ideas were vague in the beginning. Vollmer ("Emotion und Flow-Erleben") even found different kinds of artistic creation within just one artist. By examining diaries detailing their artistic work, she not only found sudden ideas but also gradual approaches to creativity. Emotions of happiness as well as frustration played an important role. The artists were deeply involved, drawing from personal experiences and trying to give meaning to their work. In some cases, the artwork would 'talk back' to them, thus generating answers for problems they were going through. The artists were experiencing flow, caught up in time and space, unable to accurately detail the length of the creative process. Upon close examination of their descriptions of their work flows, it was found that the artists compared differing cognitive schemes and improved them accordingly. Different types of cognitive schemes, emotions and perceptions interacted, influencing each other and adapting accordingly. These results should be tested in terms of their application, not only for artists, but also for a wider range of people.

In Vollmer's dissertation (in progress) possible ranges of such behaviour in creative processes are investigated. This article focuses on the question of how people and organisations conceive new ideas.

The question of how to define creativity therefore remains unclear, as there are different fields involved and few definitions offer an interdisciplinary approach, as shown above. We hope that our interdisciplinary and holistic study, which includes both aesthetics and psychology, will help improve current discussions and encourage more interdisciplinary work. Whether inventions are unconsciously generated as sudden ideas or whether they arise step by step is an open question. While Wallas describes the creative process in terms of sudden inspiration, Weisberg finds many examples of a more gradual process. The foundation of this discussion is the idea that unconscious processes are involved in the emergence of new ideas. The careful observation of creative subjects at work could more explicitly show how new ideas emerge and whether or not differences between individuals exist. This may lead to the answer to the question of how to encourage creativity. In order to foster creativity, it is necessary to know which strategies help students, and which phases of motivation they may go through. Research in this area could shed light on which strategies teachers should use to foster creativity.

5. Methods and Research Design

Adopting a phenomenological approach enables us to take implicit knowledge forms into account as we look at behaviour in creative processes. The goal of Vollmer's study is to gather further information about how people deal with creative situations and possible conclusions that can be drawn. Twenty-one participants (a mix of pupils between the ages of 13 to 18 and adults older than 18) were asked to take part in a simulation during which a Think Aloud Protocol (Konrad) was implemented. Such simulations provide an authentic environment for investigating behaviour in complex situations. Other research involving simulation methods have been conducted, for instance, by Frederiksen and Dörner's group (Amelang).

The participants' behaviour was recorded on video. During the simulation, the participants were confronted with three tasks. First, they were presented with a text comprising of randomly generated and thus meaningless sentences and a picture that required cryptic interpretation (Fig. 1). The participants were required to give their first interpretation of the sentence, and the image combinations that came to mind. The caption under the photograph may be translated as "Tyranny has always focused a product into its sights. The politburo's sweatshirt made the provinces appealing to people. Rock music gives up tough mutually shared qualities to accompany for years the legacy of the units of operation, to define the opening for one hundred million people." In the second situation, they were given a tray with items that may have appeared to be irrelevant to one another.

The participants were required to arrange them in an aesthetically pleasing way (Fig. 2). Thirdly, they had to finish an incomplete drawing comprising only of fragmental lines (Fig. 3).

In a second simulation, based on the first, two individuals whose approaches to solving the first situation had differed greatly were placed in the same room. They were then observed as they worked together to co-construct ideas. After both simulations, the participants were interviewed using the method described in the Think Aloud Protocol. This involved the participants' watching the videos of themselves and commenting on them. Thus, their cognition and motivation could be reproduced. The participants could not use familiar cognitive schemes or procedures to find ideas; consequently, they had to find innovative and creative ways to deal with each task and find a solution that could represent "unity among diversity" (Kant). The solution to such dialectic problems is challenging, as the enigmatic character results in a high level of uncertainty, which we believe to be an essential part of aesthetic work.

In an attempt to examine the dynamics of cognition and motivation, the Think Aloud Protocols were analysed with Qualitative Content Analyses (Mayring) and the Psi-Theory of Dörner ("Bauplan einer Seele").

Our study can hence reconstruct different approaches to challenges and may help to identify different processes in aesthetic behaviour, in an attempt to find theoretical implications. It is hoped that the results of this study will promote creativity in the education system.

6. Results

The task was undoubtedly difficult to handle. Only seven of the twenty-one participants in the case study could be investigated closely. (The remaining fourteen could not be accepted as several only described the text and picture combinations but did not solve the creative task; others did not talk aloud; and some dropped out because of technical difficulties.)

We found huge variations in activity regulation. A short overview of these variations will be given in the following explanations. Some participants gave up halfway through the simulation while others were determined to follow through and were open to unknown situations. Hans[1] was upset and did not want to spend any more time on the task: "This does not make any sense for me, therefore, this is the

---

1   The real names of the participants have been changed for this article.

point where I don't want to keep on doing this ..." (Sim.1).[2] Creative participants who came up with ideas were shown to have more strategies in their repertoire than those who gave up. Comparing the performances of Herbert and Hannah, the difference in the use of strategies is convincing: While Herbert stuck to patterns of performance at school, Hannah used her imagination by recalling personal memories, describing the picture in an integrative manner as she "blurred" her words while talking aloud about the indistinct scene, and used different speech rhythms and facial expressions as she read and modified the text over and over again. She rearranged words, reversed them, asked questions, drew and wrote in order to come up with a coherent solution.

Even when unable to suggest a solution to a task, some participants showed great perseverance. Hubert acted strategically: "I have tried to work in a rather strategic way" (Sim. 3). However, he did not find a solution until he began following vague instincts. This applied to both the first and second simulations. While he was arranging the tray, we could observe his changes in strategy (see Fig. 2): In the beginning, he arranged everything according to their length. Then, he reflected on why he had done so: "First the BEAUTY then the FUNCTION (.)[3] not the other way around (.) first the function then the beauty (.) well (0.3) but this doesn't fit somehow (.) even if it is wrong in the order of length (.) [I like] the BALL (.) [I like] it to be here" (Sim. 2).[4] In his process of reflection, he realized that this strategy had not lead to a coherent solution. Also Hedwig was ready to give up, when she suddenly had a flash of an idea that changed her perspective. Hannah was driven by various emotions (anger, a creative longing, humor, and disappointment) and a vivid imagination fuelled by her interpretations of the stimuli. Her emotional, personal and pleasure-orientated behaviour recurred again and again, and can perhaps be made clear in the following notes from the Think Aloud Protocol: "In my opinion, this picture ... in combination with the text ... is (.) uhmm (.) pretty disturbing (-) but yet in some way there is (.) some meaning, some artistic meaning because in a certain way emotions arise ..." (Sim. 1). This participant was heavily invested in the tasks and conceived many new ideas – as she showed in the Think Aloud Protocols – by imitating feelings or situations. There were also participants who tried a variety of options. Horst, for instance, made use of the recourse of making up a story: "And HE or SHE ... realizes (.) that (a person) is following him or her in the DARK (-) and he or she is trying (-) to escape (.) from (.)

---

2   All the translations of the transcriptions from the study have been made by the author of this article.
3   We use (.) to refer to a short break or pause in the speech, and (-) to mean a longer break.

this person (1.5) OR to be able to get to his or her home or hotel (.) depending on whether he or she (.) is visiting (.) or living there" (Sim. 1). By being open to situations that were previously unknown to them, they were able to undergo "productive uncertainty", allowing personal involvement in the given situations. Participants who had many ideas did not only use strategies; other procedures were observed that were by no means cognitively controlled. Likewise, Hannah, who was motivated and eager, expressed her displeasure at having to function within a system. She was interested in her own imaginations and invented an idea on the text (Sim. 1). Harald's imaginations were rather humorous. He even tried out needless actions, like setting a heavy figure on top of a light ball.

Dealing with uncertainty meant an engagement of willpower, and offered the participants the chance to shape their ideas, as well as inciting both tension and interest in the task. The high level of uncertainty involved in the study offered the participants the chance to produce ideas, and gain knowledge and self-efficacy. In several cases, we identified a link between finding underlying structures and letting go of reasoning. Two participants let go of reasoning and instead followed their instincts, thereby finding underlying structures and new ideas or views. Additionally, another participant even opened up emotionally, coming up with themes of great significance and immersing herself with all of her senses in the new situation at hand.

In the second and third situations, which involved more visual tasks, almost all the participants started to imagine something. Thus, Hans drew "his apple tree beside his house" and "a dog that does not exist" (Sim. 3). We propose that the limited use of the senses in aesthetic tasks may cause a prelingual use of schemes that brings forth the construction of personal meaning as well as helping to shape identity. This might be linked to the fact that artists recall past personal experiences, perhaps enabling them to cope with the ambiguities in the task at hand (see also "Der kreative Prozess als Bewältigungsstrategie"). Embodied knowledge forms can thus be retrieved by following vague feelings, imagination and imitation. As Haseloff had discovered, relieved ambitions and playful elements as seen in phases of regression seem to sustain these processes. Furthermore, creative processes seem to offer unexpected experiences that give shape and meaning to the personality.

In the second simulation, there were contradictory results: In the first co-construction, the participants were reluctant and hesitant to work together, despite being instructed to on two occasions. Eventually, after 52 minutes of intense work and a third request, they started to pool their ideas. The second co-construction, on the other hand, lasted only 6.09 minutes in which the participants barely co-constructed. We do not have all the results yet (especially with regard to the second co-construction), but we propose the following reasons for their reluctance in the first co-construction: First, each expected their partner to be an uninteresting co-worker; secondly, each participant wanted to shape a vague idea into a clear idea first, before working with a partner. The participants were required to be open to one another on a personal level, since co-creation depends on the mutual acceptance of the partners' views and a willingness to share one's own ideas. It is perhaps understandable that the participants were as a whole unwilling to share their ideas as part of a team without having had the opportunity to clarify their ideas as individuals first.

All the creative participants used distinct strategies in order to deal with uncertainty and be self-efficacious: Some recalled acoustic schemes; others visual ones. Often, the participants used the same strategic patterns across the situations, even though each situation addressed different senses and fields of knowledge. As was made clear in their Think Aloud Protocols, participants used reflection on what they did in order to cope with the situation.

Personal involvement seems to be inherent to creativity. The more cognition, emotion and action-schemes are involved, the better problems seem to be understood in their complexity, leading to a more adequate implementation of new solutions. This corroborates the results of Lewin and his colleagues, who found out that exposure to situations that are subject to change fosters changes in behaviour.

Fear of being emotionally hurt may hinder successful co-construction. Therefore, in order for co-construction to be successful, it is necessary for co-workers to be open not only to the sharing of ideas but also to being honest with their partner despite the risk of receiving potentially hurtful comments.

7. Conclusion

The study uncovers a wide range of behavioural patterns that may encourage creativity in students. The differences in behaviour range from logical thinking with an end result to behaviour that seemingly has no end goal. There seem to be several main motives that lead to patterns that either foster creative thinking or reduce it. We can comprehend more accurately and systematically how people handle uncertainty as they motivate themselves to deal with creative tasks.

Summarizing the results, we would like to discuss the following four theses. First: Aesthetic experiences are an elementary part of human life. They offer the chance to cope with difficulties, to inspire, to discover and solve problems, multiply and encourage new ideas. Interestingly, participants who came up with many ideas enjoyed playing with possibilities, dealing with uncertainty, and pushing themselves to the limits of their capabilities. These participants seemed to find strategies that could help them to fully utilise their imaginations. In doing so, they may also be able to cope with challenging situations in their everyday life.

Second: Many subjects do not know how to deal with aesthetics or how to come up with ideas. Participants who found it challenging to deal with uncertainty also found it hard to conceive new ideas. Instead, they would attempt to find a reason for their lack of success. Therefore, we identified the ability to deal with uncertainty as essential for aesthetic experiences.

Third: Aesthetics needs to be seen as a central part of learning. Creating empathy, being imaginative, dealing with emotions as well as having a good sense of humour may help in finding multi-perspective views on problems. Creative tasks can hereby enable students to dismantle, to invert and join, and to reflect on and be open to new tasks. In order to conceive new ideas, individuals should relinquish familiar orientations, overcome uncertainty and be creative. The ability to gain self-efficacy is essential for sustaining endurance. Students who feel sufficient continue searching, even if they do not find solutions. The results explicitly show that an accepting environment is crucial in order to face uncertainty in creativity and innovation.

Fourth: We still do not know enough about the effects and outcomes of the co-construction of creativity. As we have already seen, these patterns differed from participant to participant. Embodied knowledge forms could be retrieved by following vague instincts or imaginations as participants imitated views or processes etc. As far as we could see, emotions and mimesis seemed to be crucial for implicit knowledge forms and for conceiving new ideas. There is furthermore some evidence that aesthetic experiences enable people to feel empathy. Further investigations should be made on this subject. With regard to further research, we recommend that sufficient time for extensive creative experiences be provided.

Following this argumentation, universities should provide spaces for further studies and experiments on aesthetics and its co-construction. They should enable individuals to pursue their own interests, to come up with new ideas, as well as to share and debate ideas.

Our results prove the current study to be an important contribution to the understanding of the tacit processes that accompany innovation. It is a first step in the attempt to explain, more precisely, group creativity and the co-construction of ideas in the classroom. However, it also shows that further research in this area is needed. In particular, more research into the connection between aesthetics and education is needed in order to sustain creative learning in the classroom. Moreover, further research into co-construction involving different types of creative workers would no doubt prove interesting.

Figure 1. The photograph to be interpreted.

Tyrannei hat sich ein Produkt immer ins Blickfeld gerückt. Den Provinzen sprach das Sweatshirt des Politbüros Leute zu. Rockmusik gibt zähen gemeinsamen Sachen um das Erbe seit Jahren mehr politisch einhergehende Arbeitseinheiten, um für hundert Millionen Menschen die Öffnung zu bestimmen.

Figure 2. The tray with seemingly unrelated items.

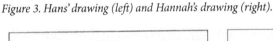

Figure 3. Hans' drawing (left) and Hannah's drawing (right).

8. Bibliography

Bildungskommission NRW. *Zukunft der Bildung – Schule der Zukunft. Denkschrift der Kommission "Zukunft der Bildung – Schule der Zukunft" Beim Ministerpräsidenten des Landes Nordrhein-Westfalen.* Hermann Luchterhand Verlag, 1995.

Amabile, Teresa M. *Creativity in Context.* Westview Press, 1996

Arnheim, Rudolf. *Kunst und Sehen.* Walter de Gruyter, 1965.

Baader, Meike Sofia. "Weitreichende Hoffnungen der ästhetischen Erziehung- eine Überfrachtung der Künste?" *Curriculum des Unwägbaren,* edited by Bilstein, Johannes et al., 2007, pp. 113–131.

Barck, Karlheinz, editor. *Ästhetische Grundbegriffe. Historisches Wörterbuch in sieben Bänden.* Metzler, 2000.

Beghetto, Ronald, A. "Creativity in the Classroom." *Handbook of Creativity,* Cambridge University Press, edited by James Kaufmann, 2010, pp. 447–466.

Bohnsack, Ralf. *Qualitative Bild- und Videointerpretation.* Verlag Barbara Budrich, 2011.

de Bono, Edward. *Serious Creativity. Using Lateral Thinking to Create New Ideas.* Harper Collins, 1992.

Brandstätter, Ursula. *Erkenntnis durch Kunst. Theorie und Praxis der ästhetischen Transformation.* Beltz, 2013.

Chan, D.W. & Chan, L. "Implicit Theories of Creativity: Teachers' Perceptions of Student Characteristics in Hong Kong." *Creativity Research Journal* 12. 3 (1999) pp. 185–195.

Combe, Arno and Paseka, Angelika. "Und sie bewegt sich doch? Gedanken zu Brückenschlägen in der aktuellen Professions- und Kompetenzdebatte." *Zeitschrift für Bildungsforschung:* zbf, 2(2), 2012, pp. 91–107.

Csikszentmihalyi, Mihalyi. *Flow. Das Geheimnis des Glücks.* Klett Coda, 1997.

Dalin, Per. *Theorie und Praxis der Schulentwicklung.* Luchterhand, 1999.

Donne, Verena Delle. *Die Schönheit der Lyrik psychologisch erklärt.* Neumann, 2012.

Dörner, Dietrich. *Problemlösen als Informationsverarbeitung.* Kohlhammer, 1976.

Dörner, Dietrich. *Bauplan für eine Seele.* 2nd ed. Rowohlt, 2008.

Guilford, Joy Paul. "Creativity." *American Psychologist.* 5. 9 (1950), pp. 444–454.

Haseloff, O. "Fünf Stufen der Kreativität." *Manager-Magazin,* 1971, Nr. 2, pp. 83–90.

Hentig, Hartmut. *Kreativität. Hohe Erwartungen an einen schwachen Begriff.* Beltz, 2000.

Hertlein, Joachim. *Persönlichkeit, Motivation und der Schaffensprozess bildender Künstler.* Dissertation, Universität Bamberg, 1990.

Konrad, Klaus. "Die Methode des lauten Denkens." *Forschungsmethoden der Psychologie,* edited by E. Bamberg et al., Hogrefe Verlag, 2014.

Kraus, Anja. *Perspectives on Performativity. Pedagogical Knowledge in Teacher Education.* Waxmann, 2016.

Kruse, Peter. *Next Practice. Erfolgreiches Management von Instabilität.* Gabal, 2011.

Lück, Helmuth. E. *Lewin und die Feldtheorie.* Beltz, 1996.

Mayring, Philipp. *Qualitative Inhaltsanalyse.* Beltz, 2015.

Mey, Günther, and Katja Mruck, editors. *Grounded Theory Reader,* VS Verlag für Sozialwissenschaften, 2011.

Meyer-Drawe, Käte. "Spiegelbilder. Ein Beitrag zur Bilder-Skepsis." *Der skeptische Blick,* edited by M. Erhardt, et al. VS Verlag für Sozialwissenschaften (2011) pp. 157–169.

Parthey, Heinrich. "Phantasie in der Forschung und Kriterien der Wissenschaftlichkeit. Kreativität in der Forschung." *Wissenschaftsforschung Jahrbuch 2012,* Wissenschaftlicher Verlag, 2013.

Patry, Jean-Luc. "Schulunterricht ist komplex – Kann da Theorie noch praktisch sein?" *Salzburger Beiträge zur Erziehungswissenschaft,* Jg.4 (1), 2000, pp. 44–59.

Patry, Jean-Luc. "Methological Consequences of Situation Specifity: Biases in Assessments." *Frontiers in Psychology* vol 2, 17.2.2011, *http://journal.frontiersin. org/article/10.3389/fpsyg.2011.00018/full*. Accessed 27.3.2017.

Patry, Jean-Luc. "Antinomien in der Erziehung." *Professionalität im Umgang mit Spannungsfeldern der Pädagogik*, edited by Christian Nerowski, et al., Julius Klinkhardt, 2012, pp. 177–187.

Plucker, Jonathan A. et al. "Why Isn't Creativity More Important to Educational Psychologists? Potentials, Pitfalls, and Future Directions in Creativity Research." *Educational Psychologist* 39, 2009.

Post, Swantje et al. "Professionelle Handlungskompetenz von Lehrpersonen an den BIP Kreativitätsgrundschulen und an den staatlichen Grundschulen." *Persönlichkeits- und Lernentwicklung an staatlichen und privaten Grundschulen. Ergebnisse der PERLE-Studie zu den ersten beiden Schuljahren*, Waxmann, 2013.

Rahm, Sibylle. *Einführung in die Theorie der Schulentwicklung*. Beltz, 2005.

Robinson, Ken. *Out of our Minds. Learning to be Creative*. Capstone Publishing Inc., 2011.

Selting, M. et al. (2009). "Gesprächsanalytisches Transkriptionssystem 2 (GAT 2)." *Gesprächsforschung – Online-Zeitschrift zur verbalen Interaktion*. 2009, pp. 353–402. *www.gespraechsforschung-ozs.de*, Accessed 14.2.2017, Senge, Peter. *The Fifth Discipline*. Currency, 2006. Schuler, Heinz, and Yvonne Görlich. *Kreativität*. Hogrefe Verlag, 2007.

Starker, Ulrike. *Allerliebst und Rätselhaft*. Peter Lang, 1998.

Smith, Jeffrey. K., & Lisa. F. Smith. "Educational Creativity." *The Cambridge Handbook of Creativity*, edited by James C. Kaufman and Robert J. Sternberg, University Press, 2010, pp. 250–264.

Torrance, Ellis Paul. *Rewarding Creative Behavior. Experiments in Classroom Creativity*. Prentice Hall, 1965.

Townsend, Tom. "School Improvement and School Leadership. Key Factors for Sustaining Learning. The Impact of Change on Education." *Schulentwicklung und Schulwirksamkeit. als Forschungsfeld. Theorieansätze und Forschungserkenntnisse zum schulischen Wandel*, edited by Heinz Gunter Holtappels, Waxmann, 2014, pp. 99–122.

Trebeß, A, editor. *Metzler Lexikon Ästhetik. Kunst, Medien, Design und Alltag*. Metzler, 2006.

Urban, Klaus. *Kreativität – Herausfordeung für Schule, Wissenschaft und Gesellschaft*. Lit-Verlag, 2004.

Vygotsky, Lev Semyonovich. "Imagination and Creativity in Childhood." *Journal of Russian and East European Psychology*, 42 1- 2, Nr. 1, orig. 1967, 2004, pp. 7 97.

Voigt, Sabine. *Das Geheimnis des Schönen*. Waxmann, 2005.

Vollmer, Barbara. *Emotion und Flow-Erleben als Determinanten für Motivation und Handlungsregulation im kreativen Prozess*. MA thesis, Universität Bamberg, 2010.

Vollmer, Barbara. "Der kreative Prozess als Bewältigungsstrategie." *Musik-, Tanz- und Kunsttherapie* no 3, edited by Klaus Hörman et al., 2012, Hogrefe, pp. 167–173.

Wallas, Graham. *The Art of Thought*. Butler and Tanner LTD, 1927.

Wiater, Werner. "Theorie der Schule." *Studienbuch Schulpädagogik,* edited by Hans Jürgen Apel and Werner Sacher, Klinkhardt, 2009.

9. List of Figures

Anja Kraus

Sensitive Threshold – Awakening Aspects of the Corporeal-Auditive Reflexivity of Teenagers in the Classroom

Abstract: This article refers to humanistic European pedagogy and didactics as an explicit normative framework for the modeling of classroom education. Departing from this approach while at the same time criticizing its normative frame, it will be argued that many relevant aspects of knowledge – that are decisive in our acting, intuitions, preferences, and decisions – defy articulation. As tacit dimensions, they influence the questions we ask; successful or failed learning processes; and precarious or promising personality development. Bodily phenomenological research explores these dimensions.

Making use of an example of art-based didactics, which follows the idea of phenomenological research in education, the question is raised as to how corporeality forms an integral moment of learning processes. Especially of interest is the reflexivity created in a specific art-based project space in terms of distinct learning effects. The project space in question is constituted by the interactive sound installation, *Sensitive Threshold*, which the author developed as a means of learning, didactics, and art-based research in order to explore the corporeal, auditive, and artistic modes of learning and reflexivity. The concept of *Sensitive Threshold* was influenced by the work of the author as a teacher at the *Free Comenius School Darmstadt* (grades 1–9) in 2003. This free school applies humanist pedagogy and didactics in the tradition of John Amos Comenius.

Keywords: Tacit knowledge, corporeal reflexivity, media, art-based research, art-based learning, intercultural education

The concepts of the early theoreticians of European humanist pedagogy and didactics, such as John Amos Comenius (1592–1670), Jean-Jacques Rousseau (1712–1778), and Johann Heinrich Pestalozzi (1747–1827), merged into the movement of reform pedagogy in the 20th Century and influenced the concepts of the so-called "free schools" that are now situated all over Europe. One of these schools is the *Free Comenius School Darmstadt/Germany*. The main precepts of humanist pedagogy and didactics are described in the first paragraph of its official website:

"Omnia sponte fluant absit violentia rebus"
Everything flows on its own impulse; violence shall be apart from the things.
This quote from the namesake of our school, Jan Amos Comenius (1692–1679), defines the main philosophy of our school.

> The conceptual approach of our school refers to progressive educational approaches that start from the learner as the most active in his/her own learning processes, interpreting learning as both active and social. The basis for our work is thus formed by the young person, his/her willingness to learn and to work, as well as by the everyday world of experience. The curiosity and creativity of children are not reined in, but given space and a framework for development. (my trans.; see FCS in progress)

The theologist, philosopher, and pedagogue Comenius lived in the 16th Century and worked in several nations of the Holy Roman Empire (today Germany, the Czech Republic, Poland, and other countries). He regarded spontaneous, freely chosen, and self-determined creativity and curiosity to be the starting points of general learning. The aim of pedagogy and didactics, according to him, was the liberation of the Christian individual: Through learning, the eyes would open to all of creation and the individual would use the communicatory functions of speech, images, and printing to appreciate the Divine Cosmos. The didactics that served this aim had to combine 'autopsia' (eyewitness observation) with 'autopragmasia' (doing something by oneself).

According to the trailblazer of humanistic European pedagogy, Wilhelm Dilthey (1833–1911), Comenius created the first European theory of educational methodology in terms of didactics. Following Comenius' line of thinking, although mostly without explicitly referring to Christian belief, several progressive educational approaches (cp. John Dewey and many others) at the turn of the 20th Century advocated self-determined learning by foregrounding experiential learning as the most effective learning method. While general learning goals are outlined in governmental papers and by teachers, the specific goals of learning are set and worked out by the learners themselves. Learning results are communally reflected on and assessed in the classroom. By means of these common reflections, a sense of democratic community amongst the pupils is supposed to be developed. A large amount of independent schools function according to these precepts, including those founded by Maria Montessori, Célestin Freinet, Peter Petersen, and also by parent initiatives.

The *Free Comenius School Darmstadt* (serving the grades 1–10) was founded by parents in the year 1982 and is a steadily growing and successful public school. According to its concept (see: FCS in progress), the exploration of learning and citizenship stands in the foreground of school education. Therefore, the pupils gather by grade at the beginning of the week to commonly reflect on the results of their learning. On the basis of the official county curriculum, they decide what topics should be treated in the week to come, and what didactic approaches might best fit the challenges they foresee. Teachers give them advice but do not make the decisions.

One can say that today, progressive education is being threatened by political calls for an evidence-based governance of schooling and pedagogy, usually reducing didactics in the classroom-to-classroom management. To fulfill today's quality requirements, the fundamental ideas of progressive education must undergo scientific examination. This contribution serves this aim by examining didactic practices from a phenomenological perspective.

The Body as the First Means of Learning and Didactics

Tracing back education to 'autopsia' and 'autopragmasia' means looking at the Christian God's creation as the first means of learning and didactics. Hereby, Comenius referred to 'causa formalis' as a sense inherent to sensuality. Humanistic European pedagogy and the anthropological or phenomenological approaches to education of today stress the body as the primary means of learning (cf. Anderson-Levitt 2015).

In the following, pedagogical learning theory that refers to bodily phenomenology constitutes the main focus, by which one is ultimately thrown back to oneself as a human being and bodily existence. We do not only perceive the objects given to us with our senses; we also relate ourselves to our environment by means of the body. On the one hand, systematic learning, learning strategies and disciplines primarily aim at seeing the body as a kind of vessel for our thoughts, and as an object that is available for us. We then refer to the body we *have*. On the other hand, in social learning, in the education of emotions, or in poetics or the arts, learning appears to our body in terms of a sensitive, responsive, and attentive center that is the body we *are* (cp. Plessner 1982). The body we *are* is social and (more or less) sociable, influenced by socially and culturally framed previous experiences of which we are (to a large extent) only pre-consciously and pre-predicatively aware. However, a separation of discursive-conceptual mediation and authentic immediacy is not possible. We develop our sociality via our physical being in the interplay of spontaneity and reflexivity.

A central statement on bodily phenomenology with regard to learning is that "the how of learning retreats into darkness" (Meyer-Drawe; 2008; 90, my trans.). *How* we learn something is for the most part neither visible to us nor to others. That is to say, the dispositions, spontaneous reactions, habitus, and normative patterns that substantiate the judgments and actions of learners cannot be fully grasped. Learning can thus be understood only by the idea of corporeality not only as a device, but also as an agile and living interface between the self, others, and the world. Maurice Merleau-Ponty (1968) provides the framework for this understanding of the body by pointing out that rational thinking is founded in corporeality, that is to say, we judge reality pre-consciously and pre-predicatively, and our learning is spontaneously shaped. Merleau-Ponty thus regards corporeality and our pre-reflexive knowledge as not contrary to rationality. Instead, the body foregrounds rationality as complex, subjectively highly important, and action-relevant knowledge. This implies that our access to the world and to ourselves is always already interwoven with assessments, concepts, and ideas. Thus, learning is not regarded as the taking of distinct steps that are built on one another so that the desired learning goal and a certain stock of knowledge are acquired, directed by the strong will of the autonomous subject; instead, success in learning is seen as an ephemeral part of directed and materially framed seeking and exploring processes. Jean Lave (1998) and Martin Weingardt (2004) point out that 'testing' is a primary characteristic of learning: Because a learner does *not* know what s/he will know when s/he has reached a certain learning goal, learning is characterized by openness and a plurivalent nature. The fact that neither the paths nor the results of one's own learning can be precisely known right from the beginning makes it possible to be open to learning processes.

Progressive educational approaches that start from the idea of the learner being the most active in his/her own learning processes can be expanded by drawing on the bodily phenomenological approach. Applying this perspective to didactics turns away from an interpretation of didactics as methods of instruction only following a rational agenda to engage pupils' minds. Moreover, within body-phenomenological didactics, a dominant concept of rationality is replaced by the endeavor to draw on corporeal processes that will empower a pupil to be active in, and even master his/her own learning processes. Self-determination and self-responsibility is then not only understood in terms of control, but as responsiveness to socially and culturally framed previous experiences. Within the said progressive educational approaches, many possible paths and learning objectives are pre-structured in settings of open learning.

In this contribution, the question of how corporeality forms learning will be followed up by exploring the reflexivity and distinct learning effects created in an art-based project space. Reference to art has specific implications that we will examine in the following chapter.

Reflexivity in Art

Nelson Goodman (1968) describes the 'languages of art' as the specific expressions of art that tie experiences of pre-consciousness to rational thinking. Processes of making art nearly always integrate both aspects: spontaneous and intuitive actions are incited, while at the same time distance is taken, e.g. in order to reflect on these actions. In this regard, art has innovative and vanguard functions. These functions are often connected to a certain refusal to make sense. Artistic strategies are to a large extent characterized by forms of modifying, questioning, or disrupting normative value judgments, e.g. those made on the basis of common-sense obligatory values. Moreover, art addresses its viewers and participants with a particular semantic gap, and, as subjective and queer as an impulse of an artwork might be, it has a social dimension since it requires the recipient to develop his/her own concepts of the world by referring to his/her own personal experiences as a social being. Thus, art does not merely delimit systems of meaning; it can, like all human behavior, also be characterized by its provision of existential orientation. Art is a specific form of world and meaning-making. It always includes corporeal judgments. Reflexivity in art is therefore marked by emotions, subjective experience, memories, and personal values. By actively dealing with images of socially relevant concepts, features, rules, etc. *in art*, one's own ability to accomplish a task or to deal with certain challenges can be experienced.

The range of possibilities for providing meaning through artistic undertakings is broad. This becomes clear especially when an artistic work is understood as an argument in the sense of the 'linguistic turn'.[1] According to this paradigm, an artwork is not seen as a representation of a reality behind it, but as a text that includes its own social connotations, and creates reality in a not entirely rational and predictable way. The complex expression of art can be perceived in terms of an "obtuse meaning" (Barthes 1970), which, compared to rational judgment, creates a surplus of sense. In terms of the reception of art as ruled by the task of gaining orientation, one can also speak of art as participating in 'world-making.' This may become most clear in educational settings.

It is beyond doubt that, first and foremost, our body in its immediacy and authenticity opens up to the fields of the social, of history, nature, art, culture, in short, to all phenomena of the world in which we live. Corporeally transmitted experiences are interpreted by Martin Seel in 1991 (51; my trans.) as distinct orientation knowledge in the form of a sensitive self-presence: "In aesthetic perception we are aware of ourselves as percipients, not merely as self-conscious beings but as beings who let their corporeal sensorium become explicitly active.

---

1   The linguistic turn is a major development in Western philosophy. It describes the point in the early 20th Century where philosophy and the other humanities started to focus primarily on the relationship between philosophy and language. The term was mainly popularized by Richard Rorty. However, the widespread and interdisciplinary movement referred to many different definitions of 'linguistic'.

Accordingly, categorization begins with the demarcations and contrasts inherent to subjective aesthetical impressions."

One can win a certain agency over pre-conscious and pre-predicative aesthetic value judgments by reflecting on them, e.g. in terms of "justified purposes and aims" (Marotzki 2003; 4; referring to Mittelstraß 2002; my trans.). Specific aspects of pictures are aesthetically put into an order, or into imaginaries that are related and subordinated to one another. Such arrangements are somewhat socially decreed, or at least appear to be. In a pedagogical situation, such orders can be revealed by means of artworks. Art can create space for linking a perceived reality to associations other than the familiar ones, leading to justifying said reality in a new, different way. It can therefore also help to promote reflexivity in a culturally non- or at least less-exclusive way than conventional imaginaries propose.

However, Christina Thürmer-Rohr (1994) confronts all our perception with the ethical directive to not construct for oneself a carved image of the concrete other. She argues that the laws of seeing are the predominant models for understanding in Western cultures, and that they imply modes of organizing things into a hierarchy, of ordering them, of allocating them to one another, of regulating and subordinating them. She concludes:

> The priority of seeing as a metaphor for the sensible and 'right' has far-reaching consequences for interpersonal orders. Attempts at understanding are taken out of the dialogical and perishable context and become ascertaining, categorizing, judging acts.... Sight is assertive because it aims at making pictures. To make oneself an image, to create images means building constraints, making limitations, becoming distant. The picture barges into the place of the still open reality.... He who visualizes the other ... denies the foreign, unexpected, still-undecided in the other. (116; my trans.)

Wilfried Lippitz (1999) continues Thürmer-Rohr's argumentation by stating that we extract what is familiar to us from the imaginary. The mere perception of artworks is thus no guarantee for getting a more differentiated view of a subject. However, there is the possibility to inhibit this process of assimilating diverse phenomena through reflexivity: in our case, through aesthetically based reflexivity developed by *making* art.

As stereotypical orientation knowledge derives from corporeal categorization and evaluation as well as the creation of an image of a (supposedly) different other, and as this knowledge is connected to pre-conscious and pre-predicative aesthetic value judgments, they can only be changed on this level. To avoid a problematically biased kind of seeing and categorizing, the process of a reflected transformation of images into sounds can be helpful.

Phenomenological Methodology

The perspective of bodily phenomenology provides not only a theory of learning but also a long tradition of phenomenological research in education as a differentiated sub-discipline of the educational sciences. All the different approaches are based on the understanding that the matter of study and the approach to it are inseparable, and that one cannot abstract from pre- and non-scientific forms of meaning (cp. Brinkmann 2010). Besides, there is a shared mistrust towards scientific methodization and objectivation of psychological nature. The preferred scientific method within phenomenology is the 'exemplary description.' Lippitz (1984; 32f; my trans.) writes: "By giving examples, one can show reflection best. Examples are of the structure of reflexivity as they refer to a signified thing. They also aim at the subjectivity of the comprehending person that is best communicable in a context of instruction."

This art-based study is regarded as an 'exemplary description' for evoking aspects of the corporeal-auditive reflexivity of teenagers in the classroom according to the bodily phenomenological approach. In the following section, the research setting will be described first. Then, some of the specific features that came up during the school project on the topic *Sounds of Love* will be outlined and analyzed in terms of their implications regarding an artistic corporeal and auditive treatment of ethnic and cultural stereotypes.

Art-Based Didactics by Means of a Sound Installation

The author developed the sound installation *Sensitive Threshold* during her employment at the FCS Darmstadt as a teacher of liberal arts and ethics in the year 2003. The idea came from her observation of the weekly students' meetings: their general ideas about school sometimes caused trouble but at the same time held great emancipatory potential. Some ideas could be utopian, such as "What if the school were a swimming hall, a pub, a greenhouse, or a zoo?", or consist of serious questions, problems, or suggestions. Originally, *Sensitive Threshold* was developed to enable the students to make their hidden ideas heard. Since 2008, the sound installation has been installed at a secondary school in Berlin (2008–2010), at a primary school in Pattonville (in 2010), and (from 2010 onwards) at a school in Berlin that teaches all grades of public schooling (1–13) and is where *Sensitive Threshold* is currently installed. A cooperating teacher conducted a series of projects.

The interactive sound installation consists of cameras that assess six areas in the entrance hall of a school. When a person steps into one of these areas a sound file is activated, and by stepping into another area a different sound is heard. By the combination of various sounds at the same time, activated by different persons, a sound-collage is generated.

The installation auditively intervenes into a space in the school. At the same time, it intensifies the already existing transitional character of the corridor. Thus, it creates a specific arena for learning. The educationally motivated concept of *Sensitive Threshold* is especially led by the following consideration: Social community is ruled by a responsivity based on corporeal and auditive experiences. Before a child learns to speak, s/he is already sonically and physically addressed by others and responds to this, at the beginning of her/his life without words. Integration into a community takes place through these responses. In general, the aural and corporeal transmission of information can serve as a means of forming or creating knowledge about a social community, as well as putting it at stake. One may think of the various sounds of the city, which communicate aspects of its structure and atmosphere, which may perhaps motivate a specific form of moving around in the city. In a radio-play, ambient sounds are artistically produced. Another example is an audio-guide intentionally used in a museum in order to make topics in the fields of history, politics, culture etc. audible by means of texts and sounds. Through recorded ambient sounds, music, verbal explanations, etc., a broad and distinct knowledge about a culturally significant situation or concern can be mediated. The retrieval of the auditive information is related to a way of moving through the museum.

Other forms of auditive and corporeal appropriation of social structures are artistically framed body movements, promoted especially through the inclusion of media technology into our daily lives. Increasingly, we not only move in the real world but also in virtual realities, causing all kind of effects on walking or moving our hands and heads.

The *Sensitive Threshold* functions as an 'open artwork' (cp. Eco 1989); that is to say, the artistic statement is completed by the recipients in a corporeal and interactive way. Eco describes this interaction as an interplay between the artwork and the recipient during the process of perceiving, thinking and – in some cases – while engaging with the artwork.

In general, there are different possibilities of working with the installation as an 'open' or 'floating artwork' in school. The following proceeding was preferred in our case:

1ˢᵗ phase (1ˢᵗ lesson): The first challenge is the search for a topic with which learning contents can be translated into sounds. Here, educational contents are connected with sensual experiences, activating very individual funds of knowledge.

2nd phase (1st lesson): Once found, the topic[2] (such as *Life in the Middle Ages* etc.) is translated into imaginary scenes that are as near to real life as possible: in this case, to historical as well as present realities.

3rd step (1st lesson): Then, subtopics (like *Market in the Middle Ages, Conferring a Knighthood,* etc.) are formulated. By doing research in books, on the Internet, etc., the students analyze these subtopics in terms of different environments and agencies. They look for and collect sounds that fit the sceneries and situations according to their own understandings.

4th step (2nd – 3rd lesson): They find the sounds (e.g. on the Internet) or they produce them by different means. While experimenting with different forms of creating sounds and combining them, they let their divergent thinking come into play.

5th step (workshop): Meanwhile, external helpers teach some pupils sound editing. Then, the pupils arrange the sounds in the installation, according to instructions that they themselves formulated. The young experts test various sound constellations by walking through the foyer and discussing different combinations with their peers.

The human-physical characteristics of sounds such as pitch, timbre, onset, temporal envelope, formant-glide, dynamic compression, signal-to-noise-logic, sound spectrum, blending ambient sounds or music with verbalizations and micro-intonation appear here as narrative qualities, as do the spatial characteristics of sounds such as echoes, localization of the acoustic source, acoustic frequency, and sound pressure.

6th step (follow-up): The sound experts discuss the different effects and options with their classmates. In general, it becomes apparent that distinct musical themes (leitmotifs) or sounds allow narratives to be recognized, whereas information deficits and ambiguities evoke challenging emotional reactions, like fear or lack of control. However, meaning usually turns out to not only be directed by the strongest association connected to a sound, but also by the different room acoustics or the microphone type and placement. The pupils create their own artwork as they mutually develop a final sound installation that is then used by other students who move their bodies through the foyer, picking up the auditively presented situations in emotional, imaginative, or cognitive ways. The impressions, experiences, and

---

2   Other topics developed during projects with the interactive possibilities of *Sensitive Threshold* include: *Sounds of Everyday Life, Dying and Death, Atmospheres of a Metropolis, Love, Temperate Zones of Africa, Footsteps, Amber,* etc.

thoughts of the creators and the audience, as well as common notions and special-ist terms, serve as further impulses for informal and formal learning.

The study focuses on a project that took place in the spring of 2008 at a sec-ondary school in Berlin in an 8th grade class. The project was developed by the teacher and the students over a period of four weeks, for about two hours a week. From the 5th phase onwards, the head teacher was assisted by two IT specialists. The project was interdisciplinary and covered the school subjects of ethics, liberal arts, and language (German).

In order to phenomenologically investigate the impact of *Sensitive Threshold* on learning in its phenomenological understanding, participatory observations by the author as action research took place in the classroom and during all the project phases, as well as in the foyer during a school break. The teacher also gave some information to the researcher about her didactical intentions after each lesson. The following description consists thus of three perspectives: a 1st order perspective of the researcher describing her observations; the presentation of the reconstructions of the teacher's intentions from a 2nd order perspective; and a 3rd order perspec-tive using said description as an example for the development of aspects of the corporeal-auditive reflexivity of teenagers in the classroom.

A group of girls (13–14 years old) with Arabic, Turkish, German, and Bosnian cultural backgrounds had freely chosen the topic *Sounds of Love*. The cooperating teacher told me that she had immediately connected two main learning goals to their choice: First, to elaborate some aspects of the students' plans for their lives. Second, to motivate and enable them to grasp their own cultural backgrounds in flexible, descriptive, imaginative, experience-oriented, appreciative, and controver-sial ways. Thus, in her didactical considerations, the teacher focused mainly on the different cultural backgrounds of the pupils. At first, she invited the pupils to ex-press, with their bodies, the different characters that they connected to a wedding party, a subject associated with specific cultural expressions and experiences. They were then asked to "freeze" in their poses. The pupils spontaneously formed four mostly mono-cultural teams: an Arab-Muslim, Turkish-Muslim, Bosnian-Muslim, and a German-Christian working group. While practicing the various scenes again and again, the pupils, according to their teacher, were allowed to discover the complexity of the topic in an experience-related, dialogical, and progressively value-neutral manner. In the sense of Gilles Deleuze (1968) they were involved in a process of 'difference and repetition', which allowed a change of meaning by repeating one and the same action during a creative and not pre-determined process. A space was created to depart from the stereotypical meaning-making implied by the initial ethnic approach.

A consensus on the joint topic of *Love* was soon reached: Love should be the reason for marriage. Then, controversies arose on questions like the arrangement of a marriage, marital age, the basic conditions of love, the quality of love, etc. In the next lesson, the teacher motivated the pupils to find subheadings such as *Being in Love, Daily Sounds of Love*, etc. The teacher's aim was to transform the complex controversies into distinct concepts, which included essential cultural as well as practical meanings, in an attempt to avoid cultural stereotypes. Here, the pupils associated more concrete situations to make them audible, while also concentrating on the essential questions inherent to these situations. For example, the sound of television and the noise of domestic appliances were associated with the subtopic *Daily Sounds of Love*. The pupils decided to record these sounds at home. While transforming ideas into sounds, the question arose on whether the noise of a vacuum cleaner is a *Sound of Love* or not: What is the connection? A discussion, which departed from the ethnic approach of the teacher, developed between the pupils. Michelle,[33] for example, remarked that in her future marriage, boredom and indifference would never arise and that she would prevent it by any means. In response, Sosda pointed out that this was every doting couple's wish, but that hardly anyone ever succeeded. Then, Nese interjected that quarrels are a part of a relationship: "Because only those who argue can get along again. And this refreshes love!" In a group work, eight sounds were assigned to each of the discussed topics, which related to essential biographical aspects and visions about the girls' current and future lives. The topic *Argument* was thus set to sound through weeping, begging, slamming doors, yelling at someone, etc. Some of the listed sounds turned out to be too vague: For example, when discussing *Yelling at Each Other* as part of an argument, the question arose of how exactly a quarrel takes place, and which typical statements are made. This offered a learning cause for a further lesson on the topic *Culture of Criticism*, in which the researcher was not present. Another topic was *Dancing Steps in Arabic Weddings*. For this, the dances had to be made and the footsteps recorded. Quickly, girls from another class of the same year who were regarded as the best dancers were asked to come. The music was played through the girls' mobile phones as they danced. Two sound artists, who educated two pupils to edit audio material, attended the workshop. In testing out various sound combinations, several problems arose. For example, the section *Argument* was situated at the place that drew the most visitors, but

---

3   The names of the pupils have been changed for this article.

the pupils wanted the wedding sounds to be the most frequently heard. Another challenge was to position the sounds with different cultural references smoothly next to each other. For this, the physical characteristics of sounds had to be connected to the narrative and spatial qualities of the different sounds. Thus, the order of sounds was created by coordinating the different topics and the corporeal and spatial adequacy of their representation. The result of this coordination of the opinions or meanings brought in by individuals was shared by the whole group, even though not everybody agreed with every opinion. At the end of this project, the group of girls proudly led some fellow students through the foyer, the visitors honing in on peculiarities like a specific student's voice on an audio file. As they moved through the installation, the pupils constantly made new discoveries: "Isn't this Sosda's voice saying that she doesn't want to get married? Is this sound about sadness and love? Why does love sound like a vacuum cleaner?"

Results: Corporeal and Auditive Dimensions of Reflexivity

With the aid of *Sensitive Threshold,* the pupils staged sounds that are present in their everyday lives within their inner social and cultural spheres – within their families. They chose sounds that they felt represented the given topic best. As they applied their everyday and acquired knowledge to the school topic in an empathetic, corporeal, and auditive way, the topic became vivid, relevant, and detailed. The often anonymous school space became a personal space that could present and reveal intimate messages. This represents the main idea of progressive education, of setting one's own learning goals by combining 'autopsia' (eyewitness observation) with 'autopragmasia' (doing something by oneself), in this case, in terms of developing the corporeal-auditive reflexivity of the pupils in the following ways:

- By creating insight into various everyday cultures and creating their own 'didactics', the pupils also formed a new, heterogeneous, culture together.
- Another impact of the work with the sound installation was a response effect: Listening to their own recorded sounds offered the pupils the possibility to reflect on the expressions of their own life-worlds.
- At the same time, one could see that the pupils grasped the topic in a multifaceted and highly refined way. The final sound installation was used by other pupils who moved their bodies through the foyer, picking up the auditively presented situations in emotional, imaginative, or cognitive ways. The impressions, experiences, and thoughts of the creators as well as of the perceivers served as a basis for further learning processes. Knowledge then turned out to be bound to interpretation and to different layers of significance, such as

emotions, imaginations, and cognitions ruled by experiences, impressions, and concepts.

– By working with the *Sensitive Threshold,* body-based learning was also expressed by the insight of the pupils that certain subject knowledge corresponds to concrete sceneries and that rational thinking is founded in corporeality.

– The pupils came to understand that the narrative qualities of sound are dependent on diverse factual conditions. During their experiments with different sounds and sound combinations, they discovered the complex characteristics of sounds in their dependency on spatial and physical circumstances, thus putting aside their original intention of transforming a real situation into sounds in a naturalistic way.

– Furthermore, there is little doubt that the *Sensitive Threshold* blazes the trail in the handling of pre-predicative and pre-reflexive value judgments in a reflexive mode. In this case, the confrontation of a group of teenagers with individual, social, and cultural aspects of their lives was made productive in terms of education. In this example, the ethnic working groups were abandoned in the discussions. In a continuing discursive process, stocks of knowledge were moreover presented, attained, put to the test, and reworked. In this instance, the image of the other was not fixed; (working with) sounds made it flow. One cannot see learning; however, there are certain indications that the very audible scenery was found in a dialogical process based on corporeal demarcations, values, preferences, and measurements, which at the same time were put at stake.

More generally spoken, out of the bodily phenomenological perspective, fundamental ideas of progressive education such as self-determined learning and self-responsibility can be scrutinized. Modes of aesthetical and performative reflexivity can be created through the interdependence of materiality and sensation in the experience of corporeality. Such a development of reflexivity by corporeal-performative and aesthetic – especially auditive – experiences can be encouraged by the 'open artwork' *Sensitive Threshold.* The spaces for interpretation that are opened up here can serve as a path to literacy and *Bildung* in its broadest sense, of embracing knowledge also in its social and aesthetical dimensions. To more soundly investigate these rather general and rough aspects of art-based, open or floating learning, a more scientific research setting should be applied. This article proposes a scientific means, via the learning setting *Sensitive Threshold,* of gaining insights into the corporeal-auditive reflexivity of teenagers in the classroom. Certainly, one can find many more examples and pathways for this kind of art-based learning.

References

Anderson-Levitt, Kathryn. "Educational Anthropology and Allied Approaches in Global Perspective." *Zeitschrift für Erziehungswissenschaft* 18/1, 2015, pp. 89–100.

Barthes, Roland. *Elements of Semiology*. Hill and Wang, 1986.

Brinkmann, Malte. "Phänomenologische Forschungen in der Erziehungswissenschaft." *Erziehung. Phänomenologische Perspektiven*, edited by M. Brinkmann, Königshausen & Neumann, 2010, pp. 7–19.

Deleuze, Gilles. (1968) *Difference and Repetition*. University Press, 1994.

Eco, Umberto. *The Open Work*. University Press, 1989.

FCS (in progress), School Concept. Available at: http://www.fcs-da.de/174-0-Konzept.html [last access: 2016–02–13]

Goodman, Nelson. *Languages of Art: An Approach to a Theory of Symbols*. Oxford University Press, 1968.

Lippitz, Wilfried. "Exemplarische Deskription – die Bedeutung der Phänomenologie für die Erziehungswissenschaftliche Forschung." *Pädagogische Rundschau*, 38/1, 1984, pp. 3–22.

Lippitz, Wilfried. "Differenz-Konstruktionen. Grundsätzliche Überlegungen zu Differenzerfahrungen im Verhältnis von Kindern und Erwachsenen." *Behinderte in Familie, Schule und Gesellschaft. Themenheft: Zumutungen im pädagogischen Feld*, 3/1999, pp. 42–49.

Marotzki, Winfried. "Online Ethnographie.Wege und Ergebnisse zur Forschung im Kulturraum Internet." *Jahrbuch Medienpädagogik 3*, Opladen: Leske + Budrich, edited by B. Bachmair, L. Diepold and C. Witt, 2003, pp. 149–165.

Merleau-Ponty, Maurice. "Eye and Mind." Merleau-Ponty, M.: *The Primacy of Perception and Other Essays*, Northwestern University Press, 1964, pp. 159–190.

Mittelstrass, Jürgen. "Bildung und ethische Masse." *Die Zukunft der Bildung*, edited by N. Killius, J. Kluge and L. Reisch, Suhrkamp, 2002, pp. 151–170.

Plessner, Helmuth. "Anthropologie der Sinne." *Gesammelte Schriften III*, edited by G. Dux, O. Marquard and E. Ströker, Suhrkamp, 1980.

Seel, Martin. (1991), "Kunst, Wahrheit, Welterschließung." *Perspektiven der Kunstphilosophie. Texte und Diskussionen*, edited by F. Koppe, Suhrkamp, 1991, pp. 36–80.

Thuermer-Rohr, Christina. *Verlorene Narrenfreiheit: Essays*. Orlanda-Frauenverlag, 1994.

Index of Authors

Peter Baumgartner is Professor of Technology-Supported Learning and Multimedia and Head of the Department of Interactive Media and Educational Technologies at the Danube University Krems. His research interests are: theory of teaching and learning with special focus on eLearning / eEducation, (higher education) didactics, and informal learning.

Katja Böhme is a scientific assistant in the department of Art Education at the Berlin University of the Arts and the Academy of Fine Arts Münster, Germany. She is writing a Ph.D. in Art Education, and her research focuses on the potentials of photography to reflect the relationship between contingency and *Bildung*. Since 2014, she has been co-editing, together with Birgit Engel, the book series "Didaktische Logiken des Unbestimmten" (Didactical Logics of the Uncertain), published in the Kopaed Verlag.

Prof. em. Dr. Dr. Dietrich Dörner is Chair of Theoretical Psychology at the University of Bamberg, Germany, and winner of the Leibniz Prize in 1986. His research interests are thinking and acting in complex realities, and theory formation in the field of interplay between acting and behavior.

Stela Maris Ferrarese Capettini is a Ph.D. Candidate in Social and Human Sciences in the National University of Luján, Argentina. She is a graduate of Physical Education specializing in Interculturality and has a master's degree in Communication Sciences, specializing in Communicational Problems in Intercultural Contexts, from the University of the Frontier, Chile. She is the founder of *Allel Kuzen Museo del Juguete Étnico* (Museum of Ethnic Toys) in Neuquén, Argentina. Her fields of research include: ethnic games, intercultural pedagogy, and gender.

Katarina Elam has a Ph.D. in Aesthetics and is an Associate Professor of Educational Science with a specialization in Aesthetics in the Department of Social and Behavioral Studies at University West. Her research interests include: aesthetic philosophy, embodied knowledge, emotions, aesthetic experience, and teacher training.

Isabell Grundschober is a researcher in the Department of Interactive Media and Educational Technologies at the Danube University Krems. Her research interests include the validation of informal and non-formal learning, eLearning, and (higher education) didactics.

Anne-Marie Grundmeier is a Professor of Fashion, Textile Sciences and their Didactics at the University of Education, Freiburg. She is Head of the Department of Fashion and Textile and Head of the Institute for Everyday Life, Culture, Sports and Health. Her research interests include: fashion and textile sciences with an emphasis on aesthetic and cultural education, education for sustainable development, and vocational education.

Dr. Maud Hietzge is a Senior Lecturer (*Akademischer Oberrätin*) at the Institute for Everyday Life, Culture, Sports and Health in the University of Education in Freiburg, Germany. Her special fields of research include video and multimodal discourse analysis, body sociology, tacit dimensions of interaction and learning arrangements, and teacher education.

Tarja Karlsson Häikiö, has a Ph.D. in Art History and Visual Studies, and is an Associate Professor in Visual and Material Culture in the Department of Visual and Material Culture, Academy of Design and Crafts at the University of Gothenburg. Her research interests are aesthetic and transformative learning, early childhood education, teacher training, visual arts education, and visual culture studies.

Anja Kraus is an Associate Professor in Educational Sciences at Linnaeus University, Sweden. Among her research interests are pedagogical theories of learning, tacit knowledge, corporality and heterogeneity in school, the integration of certain approaches in liberal arts into didactical concepts and into empirical classroom research, and anthropological questions.

Christina Inthoff (*1985) has been working since May 2015 as a researcher and teacher at the Institute for Art – Film Studies – Art Education at the University of Bremen. There, she is writing her dissertation in the field of art education on the topic "visual knowledge productions in the artistic-experimental process portfolio- KEPP" while working as a research assistant in the Creative Unit FaBit.

Ellen Kobe is an artist and curator based in Berlin. She studied Fashion, Painting and Graphics at the Academy of Art Berlin-Weissensee. She was invited for a residency in Villa Arson, Nizza, after she finished her studies 1992 at the École des Beaux Arts in Marseille (DAAD) France, with a Diploma in Art. Her main interests are interventions in public areas; performances; curating contemporary art exhibitions in historic locations based on the space and the present bearing of specific locations; and gender-identities. She became a fellow of the Academy of Arts, Berlin, Villa Serpentara in Olevano Romano, Italy, in 2015. www.ellenkobe.de

Feiwel Kupferberg has a Ph.D. in Sociology, and is Professor Emeritus in Pedagogics in the Department of Culture, Languages and Media (KSM) at Malmö University. His research interests include: art and aesthetics, creativity, entrepreneurship, European history, migration, and social sciences.

Rasoul Nejadmehr has a Ph.D. in Philosophy of Education. His research interests are: Critical Theory, Critical Race Theory, cultural and educational policies, decolonial and postcolonial studies, studies in cultural hegemony and dialogic knowledge processes.

Aloisia Moser is an Assistant Professor of Philosophy in the Department of the History of Philosophy at the Catholic Private University in Linz, Austria. Her research interests include: philosophy of language and philosophy of mind from both the analytic and continental points of view, Kant and 19th-century philosophy, Wittgenstein and 20th-century philosophy, pragmatism, and feminism.

Maria Peters is a Professor in Art Education at the university of Bremen, Institute for Art – Film Studies – Art Education. Her research interests include: different research projects in the areas of contemporary art theory, art education, art works, digital media and diversity, art and cultural mediation in the museum (such as: performativity and art; aesthetic-biographic aspects in art mediation; the relationship between art images and language; and educational media in cultural facilities). https://www.forex.uni-bremen.de

Prof. Dr. Sibylle Rahm is Chair of the School of Pedagogy at the University of Bamberg. Her research interests include teacher education research, school leadership and school improvement.

Lara Rodríguez Sieweke is an assistant researcher at Linnaeus University, Sweden. She has a master's degree in English Philology from the Complutense University of Madrid, Spain, a master's degree in Teaching Spanish as a Foreign Language from the University of Alcalá, Madrid, and a Master of Arts (Literature-Culture-Media) from Lund University, Sweden. Her research interests include: intermedial studies, English literature, and art mediation.

Margareta Wallin Wictorin has a Ph.D. in Art History and Visual Studies, and is a Senior Lecturer in Cultural Studies at the Faculty of Arts and Humanities, Karlstad University. Her research interests are: aesthetics, art education, cultural studies, and comics research from intercultural and postcolonial perspectives.

Michael Waltinger (M.A.) is a Doctoral Candidate at the Department of Media Pedagogy at the University of Education (Ludwigsburg, Germany). His research interests are: media and communications research with an emphasis on developing countries; qualitative and ethnographic research methods.

Hanne Seitz is Professor of Theory and Practice of Aesthetic Education at the Potsdam University of Applied Sciences. She received her doctoral degree at the University in Frankfurt a.M. and gained her practical expertise in the area of dance-theatre practices and performance art. Her research interests include historical anthropology, contemporary art and theatre practices, artistic intermedial studies, English literature, and art mediation.

Band 63   Airi Liimets: Bestimmung des lernenden Menschen auf dem Wege der Reflexion über den Lernstil. 2005.

Band 64   Cornelia Matz: Vorbilder in den Medien. Ihre Wirkungen und Folgen für Heranwachsende. 2005.

Band 65   Birgitta Hamann: Grundfragen der Literaturdidaktik und zentrale Aspekte des Deutschunterrichts. 2005.

Band 66   Ralph Olsen / Hans-Bernhard Petermann / Jutta Rymarczyk (Hrsg.): Intertextualität und Bildung – didaktische und fachliche Perspektiven. 2006.

Band 67   Bruno Hamann: Bildungssystem und Lehrerbildung im Fokus aktueller Diskussionen. Bestandsaufnahme und Perspektiven. 2006.

Band 68   Ingeborg Seitz: Heterogenität als Chance. Lehrerprofessionalität im Wandel. 2007.

Band 69   Margret Ruep / Gustav Keller: Schulevaluation. Grundlagen, Methoden, Wirksamkeit. 2007.

Band 70   Harald Schweizer: Krach oder Grammatik? Streitschrift für einen revidierten Sprachunterricht. Kritik und Vorschläge. 2008.

Band 71   Martina Becker / Gerd-Bodo von Carlsburg / Helmut Wehr (Hrsg.): Seelische Gesundheit und gelungenes Leben. Perspektiven der Humanistischen Psychologie und Humanistischen Pädagogik. Ein Handbuch. 2008.

Band 72   Sigvard Clasen: Bildung im Licht von Beschäftigung und Wachstum. Wohin bewegt sich Deutschland? 2009.

Band 73   Gerd-Bodo von Carlsburg: Enkulturation und Bildung. Fundament sozialer Kompetenz. 2009.

Band 74   Hermann-Josef Wilbert: Musikunterricht im Rückblick. Eine alternative Musikdidaktik. 2009.

Band 75   Britta Klopsch: Fremdevaluation im Rahmen der Qualitätsentwicklung und -sicherung. Eine Evaluation der Qualifizierung baden württembergischer Fremdevaluatorinnen und Fremdevaluatoren. 2009.

Band 76   Leonard Wehr: Partizipatorisches Marketing privater Hochschulen. Corporate Identity als Ziel von Bildungsmarketing. 2011.

Band 77   Konstantinos D. Chatzidimou: Microteaching als erlebnis- und handlungsorientierte Methode im Rahmen der Lehrerausbildung und der Didaktik. Eine theoretische und empirische Untersuchung. 2012.

Band 78   Miriam Lange: Befähigen, befähigt werden, sich befähigen – Eine Auseinandersetzung mit dem Capability Approach. 2014.

Band 79   Eva Rass (Hrsg.): Comenius: Seiner Zeit weit voraus...! Die Entdeckung der Kindheit als grundlegende Entwicklungsphase. 2014.

Band 80   Cornelia Frech-Becker: Disziplin durch Bildung – ein vergessener Zusammenhang. Eine historisch-systematische Untersuchung aus antinomischer Perspektive als Grundlage für ein bildungstheoretisches Verständnis des Disziplinproblems. 2015.

Band 81   Rüdiger Funiok / Harald Schöndorf (Hrsg.): Ignatius von Loyola und die Pädagogik der Jesuiten. Ein Modell für Schule und Persönlichkeitsbildung. 2017.

Band 82   Lara Rodríguez Sieweke (ed.): Learning Scenarios for Social and Cultural Change. *Bildung* through Academic Teaching. 2017.

www.peterlang.com